Reason and Religion

Religion is relevant to all of us, whether we are believers or not. This book concerns two interrelated topics. First, how probable is God's existence? Should we not conclude that all divinities are human inventions? Second, what are the mental and social functions of endorsing religious beliefs? The answers to these questions are interdependent. If a religious belief were true, the fact that humans hold it might be explained by describing how its truth was discovered. If all religious beliefs are false, a different explanation is required.

In this provocative book Herman Philipse combines philosophical investigations concerning the truth of religious convictions with empirical research on the origins and functions of religious beliefs. Numerous topics are discussed, such as the historical genesis of monotheisms out of polytheisms, how to explain Saul's conversion to Jesus, and whether any apologetic strategy of Christian philosophers is convincing. Universal atheism is the final conclusion.

Herman Philipse is Distinguished Professor Emeritus at the University of Utrecht, the Netherlands. He is the author of *God in the Age of Science? A Critique of Religious Reason* and of numerous publications on many philosophical topics.

CAMBRIDGE STUDIES IN RELIGION, PHILOSOPHY, AND SOCIETY

Series Editors

Paul K. Moser, *Loyola University, Chicago*
Chad Meister, *Bethel College, Indiana*

This is a series of interdisciplinary texts devoted to major-level courses in religion, philosophy, and related fields. It includes original, current, and wide-spanning contributions by leading scholars from various disciplines that (a) focus on the central academic topics in religion and philosophy, (b) are seminal and up-to-date regarding recent developments in scholarship on the various key topics, and (c) incorporate, with needed precision and depth, the major differing perspectives and backgrounds – the central voices on the major religions and the religious, philosophical, and sociological viewpoints that cover the intellectual landscape today. Cambridge Studies in Religion, Philosophy, and Society is a direct response to this recent and widespread interest and need.

Recent Books in the Series

Roger Trigg
Religious Diversity: Philosophical and Political Dimensions

John Cottingham
Philosophy of Religion: Towards a More Humane Approach

William J. Wainwright
Reason, Revelation, and Devotion: Inference and Argument in Religion

Harry J. Gensler
Ethics and Religion

Fraser Watts
Psychology, Religion, and Spirituality: Concepts and Applications

Gordon Graham
Philosophy, Art, and Religion: Understanding Faith and Creativity

Keith Ward
The Christian Idea of God: A Philosophical Foundation for Faith

Timothy Samuel Shah and Jack Friedman
Homo Religiosus? Exploring the Roots of Religion and Religious Freedom in Human Experience

Sylvia Walsh
Kierkegaard and Religion: Personality, Character, and Virtue

Roger S. Gottlieb
Morality and the Environmental Crisis

J. L. Schellenberg
Religion after Science: The Cultural Consequences of Religious Immaturity

Clifford Williams
Religion and the Meaning of Life: An Existential Approach

Allen W. Wood
Kant and Religion

Michael McGhee
Spirituality for the Godless: Buddhism, Humanism, and Religion

William B. Parsons
Freud and Religion

Charles Taliaferro and Jil Evans
Is God Invisible?: An Essay on Religion and Aesthetics

David Wenham
Jesus in Context: Making Sense of the Historical Figure

Paul W. Gooch
Paul and Religion: Unfinished Conversations

Reason and Religion

Evaluating and Explaining Belief in Gods

HERMAN PHILIPSE
University of Utrecht

CAMBRIDGE
UNIVERSITY PRESS

University Printing House, Cambridge CB2 8BS, United Kingdom

One Liberty Plaza, 20th Floor, New York, NY 10006, USA

477 Williamstown Road, Port Melbourne, VIC 3207, Australia

314–321, 3rd Floor, Plot 3, Splendor Forum, Jasola District Centre, New Delhi – 110025, India

103 Penang Road, #05–06/07, Visioncrest Commercial, Singapore 238467

Cambridge University Press is part of the University of Cambridge.

It furthers the University's mission by disseminating knowledge in the pursuit of education, learning, and research at the highest international levels of excellence.

www.cambridge.org
Information on this title: www.cambridge.org/9781107161733
DOI: 10.1017/9781316676615

© Herman Philipse 2022

This publication is in copyright. Subject to statutory exception and to the provisions of relevant collective licensing agreements, no reproduction of any part may take place without the written permission of Cambridge University Press.

First published 2022

A catalogue record for this publication is available from the British Library.

Library of Congress Cataloging-in-Publication Data
NAMES: Philipse, Herman, author.
TITLE: Reason and religion : evaluating and explaining belief in gods / Herman Philipse, University of Utrecht.
DESCRIPTION: Cambridge, United Kingdom ; New York, NY, USA : Cambridge University Press, 2022. | Series: Cambridge studies in religion, philosophy, and society | Includes bibliographical references and index.
IDENTIFIERS: LCCN 2021057972 (print) | LCCN 2021057973 (ebook) | ISBN 9781107161733 (hardback) | ISBN 9781316614068 (paperback) | ISBN 9781316676615 (epub)
SUBJECTS: LCSH: Faith and reason. | God–Proof.
CLASSIFICATION: LCC BL51 .P51475 2022 (print) | LCC BL51 (ebook) | DDC 210–dc23/eng/20220106
LC record available at https://lccn.loc.gov/2021057972
LC ebook record available at https://lccn.loc.gov/2021057973

ISBN 978-1-107-16173-3 Hardback
ISBN 978-1-316-61406-8 Paperback

Cambridge University Press has no responsibility for the persistence or accuracy of URLs for external or third-party internet websites referred to in this publication and does not guarantee that any content on such websites is, or will remain, accurate or appropriate.

Contents

Acknowledgements — page ix

Introduction — 1

PART I THE REASONABLENESS OF RELIGIOUS BELIEFS

1 Religious Epistemology — 11
 1.1 An Argument from Cultural Contingency — 12
 1.2 Epistemic Sources of Religious Beliefs — 17
 1.3 St Paul and the Pythia — 23
 1.4 Calibration of Epistemic Sources — 32

2 Science and Religion — 41
 2.1 The Place of the Earth in the Universe — 44
 2.2 The Time of Man and the Universe — 50
 2.3 From Laplace to Darwin and Beyond — 55
 2.4 Empirical Evidence against Theism — 61

PART II THE EVOLUTION OF RELIGION AND ETHICS

3 Religions: Origins and Evolution — 69
 3.1 Religious (Pre)history — 71
 3.2 Origins of Polytheisms — 76
 3.3 Transitions to Monotheisms — 86

4 Religion and Ethics — 97
 4.1 Religious Justifications of Moral Rules — 100
 4.2 Moralizing Religions Explained — 103
 4.3 The Earliest Expansions of Christianity — 109
 4.4 Global Warming, Population Growth, and Religion — 117

PART III APOLOGETIC STRATEGIES EVALUATED

5 The Decision Tree for Religious Believers   123
    5.1 Challenges for Religious Apologetics   125
    5.2 Apologetic Strategies Classified   129
    5.3 Religious Language Games   133
    5.4 Religious Confidentialism   136
    5.5 Involvement Evidentialism   145
    5.6 Personifying Evidence of God   151

6 Natural Theology   165
    6.1 Natural Theology: Descent and Revival   167
    6.2 Bare Theism and Bayesian Natural Theology   171
    6.3 The Semantic Challenge for Bare Theism   177
    6.4 The Predictive or Explanatory Power of Theism   180
    6.5 The Final, Epistemological Challenge   186

    Conclusion: The Two Interrelated Core Questions   189

Bibliography   203
Index   215

Acknowledgements

It was an honour to be invited by Paul Moser and Chad Meister, the volume editors of Cambridge Studies in Religion, Philosophy, and Society, to contribute a volume to this series. The invitation has been challenging as well, since in my earlier book on the philosophy of religion, *God in the Age of Science? A Critique of Religious Reason* (2012), I evaluated extensively (and critically) the many arguments in support of theism provided by excellent analytic philosophers of religion such as Richard Swinburne. Would I be able to write something really and radically new compared to my earlier endeavours? This is what I have tried to do in the following pages, at least to a large extent. I am most grateful to Chad and Paul for inviting me, and it has been a great pleasure to produce this book.

Since Dutch is my native language and I have been a university professor of philosophy in the Netherlands during over thirty-five years, my English often needs to be corrected. I am deeply indebted to my dear Oxford colleague and friend Peter M. S. Hacker, who not only commented critically on my arguments but also corrected numerous linguistic blunders.

Many other friends and colleagues have enriched my insights with regard to the many topics discussed in this book by commenting on some sections or on interrelated articles. Let me express my gratitude to Peter Barthel, Maarten Boudry, Gijsbert van den Brink, Frank van Caspel, John Cottingham, Willem Drees, Daan Dronkers, Hein Duijf, Louw Feenstra, Job de Grefte, Julia Hermann, Jeroen Hopster, Wouter Kalf, Michael Klenk, Eddie van de Kraats, Niels van Miltenburg, Paul Moser, Fred

Muller, Graham Oppy, Rik Peels, Emanuel Rutten, Richard Swinburne, and Franciscus Verbunt. My part-time assistant Nick Boerma traced tirelessly many articles published on topics discussed in this book, and checked the references.

After I had held a chair of philosophy at Leiden University since 1985, Utrecht University appointed me as a distinguished professor of philosophy in 2003. I am deeply grateful to the university board for this appointment, which gave me a lot of time for research. My greatest debts are to my spouse, Anthonya Visser, for abundant love and support. The book is dedicated to her.

Introduction

Let me roll out the red carpet for readers of this interdisciplinary book on religion, ethics, and evolution by telling an anecdote about a theological experience I once had. The story raises some of the main issues to be investigated in the following pages. Thereafter, the contents of the book are indicated, and I say a few words on its composition, title, and intended readership.

In the year 2000, I was one of the few non-Indian speakers at the Platinum Jubilee Celebrations-Conference of the Indian Philosophical Congress, held in New Delhi at the end of December. Nobel laureate Rabindranath Tagore and the later president of India Dr Sarvepalli Radhakrishnan established the congress in 1925 to enhance Indian philosophical self-confidence and intellectual independence. During the conference, prominent Indian philosophers or 'delegates' delivered lengthy lectures. Many of them were traditionally dressed Brahmans, or Brahman descendants. There was time reserved for discussions between individual participants after lunches and dinners, which were prepared on wood fires in the open air.

During one of these meetings, I chatted with a believing Hindu and expert on Tantric traditions, who tried to enlighten me about the complex personalities of Shiva and Kundalini Shakti. After a while, I could not help asking: 'But how many gods *are* there according to you?' He burst out laughing, and replied: 'At least fifty thousand!' Later I learned that according to popular versions of Tantra Hinduism, there are 33 *crore* deities, that is, 330 million gods.

In order to test or tease my interlocutor a little, I spelled out the well-known arguments from simplicity and parsimony of Jewish, Christian, and Muslim philosophers of religion to the effect that the truth of monotheism is more probable than that of any polytheism. My Tantra companion was unimpressed. 'Surely', he said, 'most philosophers and scientists agree that simplicity is not an indicator of truth, but at best a pragmatic intellectual virtue of theories. Reality may be very complex indeed!' He went on explaining to me that Indian religious traditions are not frightened of large numbers. They do not suffer from meganumerophobia, as he called it. Had this not been different in the monotheist mores of Judaism, Christianity and Islam?

His favoured illustration was the contrast between Christian and Hindu speculations about the age of the universe. Whereas Bishop Ussher's (1650) widely endorsed calculation on the basis of the Old Testament yielded the result that God's creation of the world had started on the evening of Saturday, 22 October of the year 4004 before Christ, present-day cosmologists have computed the age of the universe since the Big Bang at about 13.799 billion years. 'Of course', my friend said, 'this differs widely from pre-scientific Hindu estimates that our actual universe is in the 51st year of the present Brahma, that is, some 156 trillion years old'. But at least, he stressed, Hindus did not underestimate the age of the universe by framing it in terms of some childishly small numerical measure. Then he burst out laughing again and brought his peroration to its jocular climax. 'Indeed', he averred, 'monotheist believers are just like children. They cannot count further than three, and many of them not even beyond one.'

* * *

Jokes of debatable taste may raise crucial philosophical questions. If we interpret the endorsement by the faithful of a specific religious doctrine as holding it to be true, in the common sense of 'truth' as correspondence to reality, either Tantric polytheism or Christian (and Judaic, and Muslim) monotheism must be false, since on this interpretation they contradict each other. Surely, then, the facts of religious diversity raise an urgent issue of intellectual integrity for believers. Can they still be justified, warranted, or reasonable in holding on to their faith, if they are aware of the perplexing plurality of religions in the world? This is a central problem of Part I of the present volume, called 'The Reasonableness of Religious Beliefs' (Chapters 1 and 2).

One possible answer might proceed as follows. Reliable methods of religious research, or trustworthy primary sources of religious truth, have shown that a particular cluster of religious beliefs is true, whereas the competing clusters are all false. However, is there any reliable method of religious research, or a trustworthy source of religious truth? Chapter 1 on 'Religious Epistemology' provides a preliminary overview of religious methods or sources, such as revelations, prayer, possession rites, prophesies, and divine apparitions. After having examined two such sources, I argue that none of them can be validated as a reliable resource of religious beliefs, if at least these beliefs are interpreted as coherent claims to truth. In Chapter 2, 'Science and Religion', it is shown that for this very reason, traditional theological explanations of aspects of our universe have been eliminated gradually in the course of the history of scientific progress. In the sincere search for truth, scientific and scholarly methods have outcompeted religious methods, since the former could be validated whereas the latter could not. Shouldn't we conclude by means of a pessimistic induction that all religious claims to truth must be abandoned, at least if we aspire to intellectual integrity?

Part II of the book, entitled 'The Evolution of Religion and Ethics' (Chapters 3 and 4), starts from the provisional conclusion of Part I that religious beliefs do not rest on reliable epistemic sources or methods. If that is so, the fact that most humans endorse and cherish such beliefs is perplexing indeed. How should we explain it? Successful religions transfer their doctrines from one generation to the next, preferably by educating or indoctrinating children at an early age. What explains the fact that these beliefs arose in the first place? And which social or psychological functions are fulfilled by the endorsement of religious beliefs? During the last decades, so-called cognitive sciences of religion have made some progress in providing multiple answers to these questions.

Chapter 3, 'Religions: Origins and Evolution', starts from the fact that, as far as we know on the basis of historical and anthropological research, everywhere on Earth polytheist or animist religions preceded monotheist ones, if the latter arose at all. How should we account for this fact? Two different questions have to be answered. First: how to explain the ultimate origin of beliefs in the existence of supernatural beings? Various explanations are discussed briefly, from David Hume to the by-product hypothesis of a hypersensitive agent detection device, and their empirical credentials are assessed. Once originated, shared, stabilized, and institutionalized, religious beliefs may fulfil various psychological and communal functions. Religions are complex social systems, which have many different features. By appealing to some of these features and functions, one might try to answer the second question of this chapter: how can we explain the gradual cultural transition from polytheist religions to monotheisms? Two intermediate creeds are examined briefly. A Hume-inspired hypothesis about transitions to monotheism is developed and tested.

In Chapter 4, 'Religion and Ethics', many different topics are discussed. For example, how should we explain the contemporary dominance of so-called moralizing religions? According to cognitive anthropologists such as Nicolas Baumard and Pascal Boyer (2013), moralizing religions originated rather recently in human history, and they did so in relatively large-scale societies. I focus on the two moralizing monotheisms that have most adherents today, Christianity and Islam, and investigate some of the main mechanisms that explain their predominance. For example, it has been argued that by postulating an effective system of supernatural justice, human communities that endorsed one of these religions reinforced social cohesion and reduced free-riding more than competing communities. Other questions raised in this chapter are, for example, what explains the growth of the Jesus sect after Christ's crucifixion, and how should religious believers react to the urgent threat of human-induced global warming?

When we combine the results of the first two parts of this book, we will be inclined to conclude that they provide a debunking account of all religious beliefs. In other words, an argument to the best explanation of human religious creeds, together with background knowledge of various kinds, yields the conclusion that very probably these creeds are all false, if they are coherent and make any sense, or at least that endorsing them is objectively unjustified, to the extent that they posit the factual existence of a supernatural being. Monotheist believers will endorse this religious 'error theory' with regard to the gods worshipped by polytheist religions, whether bygone or still existing ones, such as Homeric, Germanic, Ancient Egyptian, Aboriginal, Hindu, Shinto, Tantric, voodoo, or traditionally Chinese faiths. However, they will reject it regarding their belief that only the god they worship *does* exist. Can monotheists justify such an exceptionalist position? That is: can one reasonably endorse faith in one particular god while being an atheist with regard to all the other gods humans have worshipped or still revere? In order to answer this question affirmatively, monotheist philosophers have developed many different apologetic strategies. Recent versions of such strategies are examined in Part III, 'Apologetic Strategies Evaluated' (Chapters 5–6).

Chapter 5, 'The Decision Tree for Religious Believers', starts by explaining why monotheists have developed so many different apologetic strategies. If a god really existed who is infinitely good, omnipotent, and omniscient, and who loves all human beings like a good father, one would expect, perhaps naively, that this god reveals himself openly to all human beings in their early childhood, as decent parents do. In that case, apologetic strategies would be superfluous. As we saw, however, the very idea of such a god arose relatively recently and only locally in human history. Even now, Her, His, or Their existence is not manifest to most of us. Given this fact of 'Divine hiddenness', one can understand that religious believers have developed many different apologetic strategies, since there is no easy and unambiguous access to the deity they worship. Wittgenstein-inspired philosophers of religion have even claimed that faith in God does not consist in, or rely on, a factual belief that a specific supernatural being exists at all. In my earlier book on the philosophy of religion, *God in the Age of Science? A Critique of Religious Reason* (2012), I classified these apologetic strategies by means of a Decision Tree for Religious Believers. Here I add new end nodes to the decision tree, and discuss the main non-argumentative strategies as exemplified in the oeuvre of prominent present-day religious philosophers.

Chapter 6 on 'Natural Theology' starts by summing up the history of Western natural theology, including its decline after the scientific revolution and its recent revival. It is the aim of this discipline to provide sound arguments and convincing evidence supporting a specific religious doctrine, such as the blend of monotheism called 'theism'. Since I criticized such arguments extensively in my (2012) book, and several other authors have refuted them as well, I do not discuss the many recently proposed versions of ontological, cosmological, fine-tuning, meta-ethical, etc. arguments for the existence of God. Rather, I focus on a number of structural difficulties, which show that the argumentative apologetic enterprise of natural theology is doomed to fail. As we will see, for example, the prior probability that a specific monotheistic god exists, such as Allah or God, is very low indeed, whereas it is problematic to attribute any predictive or explanatory power to theism.

The Conclusion of this book will function as Sundays do in some Western countries. Readers may take a rest and make up their mind about the existence of the many gods that humans have feared, adored, or still worship. If you decide to remain, or become, religious, will you prefer to believe in large numbers of gods, as many Tantric Hindus do, or restrict your faith to small numbers? If you are inclined towards the latter option, might it be not more reasonable to prefer zero to three or one? In other words, should Sunday still be considered to be the Day of the Lord? However this may be, we should enjoy it as the Day of the Sun, the *dies*

Solis, because there are no good reasons to doubt whether the Sun exists, and its presence is a crucial condition for life on Earth.

* * *

The two core questions of the book are the following. First, how likely or probable is it that any particular god exists? Is it not much more plausible to conclude that all gods are human inventions? This first question ultimately is a philosophical one, and it belongs to the philosophy of religion, although many results of empirical research are needed for answering it properly. Second, how should we account for the occurrence and the functions of religious beliefs in human societies and individuals? This second question mainly belongs to the social sciences, while disciplines of the humanities, such as historical inquiry, are also essential for answering it. One of the innovative aspects of this volume is that it combines research concerning these two core questions.

As I shall argue, the ways in which the second question should be answered essentially depend on the reply to the first, philosophical one. Many empirical studies of religion seem to deny this dependence, since they claim to be religiously neutral and purely scientific. The converse dependence also exists, since specific empirical explanations of the mental and social functions of religious beliefs may support sceptical doubts concerning the truth of these beliefs. This interdependence of the two core questions explains the global composition of the book. The philosophical Parts I and III flank the empirical and explanatory second part.

With regard to the cultural evolution of monotheisms, I develop a somewhat speculative empirical hypothesis, which is inspired by David Hume and David Sloan Wilson. According to this hypothesis, the historical transition from polytheisms to monotheisms has been due mainly to specific evolutionary mechanisms of selection, which explain why monotheist individuals and groups have had a greater 'fitness' than polytheist ones.

The topic of religion is of relevance to all of us, whether we are religious believers or not. One reason for this relevance is that although advanced societies have become more secular over the last century – the United States is an exception to some extent only – the whole of humanity is becoming more religious. As research on *The Changing Global Religious Landscape* published by the Pew Research Center in 2017 predicts, in 2060 the percentage of religiously affiliated humans on Earth will be 87.5 per cent, which is higher than today. The main cause of the former development is that higher education and the resulting secularization tend to diminish drastically human fertility rates where contraceptives are available. Consequently, most secularized countries have fertility rates below the replacement level, whereas the rates of traditionally religious countries and communities substantially exceed it (Norris and Inglehart, 2004). Since on average the fast-growing human population on Earth is still becoming more religious rather than less, knowledge of religions and their motivating powers is indispensable for those who want to understand what is happening in our world and to base their actions on real evidence. For example, would the United States US-led coalition have invaded Iraq in 2003, spreading 'shock and awe', if the politicians in charge had known more about the religious diversity in that country, among other things?

Reason and Religion is aimed at various types of readers. Of course, I enter into debates with academic colleagues in philosophy, theology, and the sciences of religion. Yet I have tried as well to explain the many complex issues involved to a wide readership, so that the book is accessible to students in all disciplines and of interest to the general public. I hope that each of you will read with pleasure the following pages, whether you are a religious believer, agnostic, or an atheist.

PART I

THE REASONABLENESS OF RELIGIOUS BELIEFS

I

Religious Epistemology

Can one be justified in endorsing as true a particular religious belief if one is aware of the striking diversity of religions that humans have embraced or still adhere to? This central question of religious epistemology is increasingly urgent today, since mass media, air travel, and extensive migration confront us ever more with the many aspects of religious diversity. Let me start (§1.1) by formulating an Argument from Cultural Contingency to the effect that holding a particular religious belief is illegitimate or unjustified if it is incompatible with the religious convictions of other human beings and if the believer is fully conscious of this incompatibility.

As we shall see, such an Argument from Cultural Contingency, or from religious diversity or pluralism, can be conclusive only if all mutually incompatible religious beliefs are epistemically on a par, that is, if none of them clearly relies upon better evidence, arguments, cognitive faculties, or sources of knowledge than the other, incompatible ones. In order to explore preliminarily whether this is the case, §1.2 provides an overview of the primary epistemic sources of religious beliefs. Having discussed two prominent examples of such sources in §1.3, I argue that the central credentials of religions that dominate the world today, such as Christianity or Islam, are not superior to those of religious beliefs that all of us reject as false. Nobody has validated any of the primary sources of religious faith, and none of the particular methods of testing the truth of religious beliefs has been calibrated. In other words, it has not been shown that any of these religious methods or sources is reliable (§1.4).[1]

If this argument is compelling, all well-educated and culturally informed human beings, that is, all of us who are aware of religious diversity, should abandon their religious beliefs, at least if one really cares about believing only what is true. Since many readers will be upset by this conclusion and find it unacceptable, it has to be tested carefully. I start doing so in §1.4 by showing that the Epistemological Argument from Cultural Contingency applies to all primary epistemic sources of religious beliefs, such as alleged revelations, miracles, investigative religious pathways of various kinds, authentic religious experiences, the so-called *sensus divinitatis*, and even to a 'More Humane Approach'.[2]

1.1 AN ARGUMENT FROM CULTURAL CONTINGENCY

Tourists who travel around the world today are able to admire majestic instances of religious diversity. One might attend Catholic ceremonies at the Vatican, revere the beauty of Hindu sanctuaries such as the Sri Ranganathaswamy Temple at Srirangam, or study the impressive architecture of the great Mosque of Eyüp in Istanbul. Erecting such monuments would not have been possible if the relevant communities had not been deeply convinced of the truth of their respective religious beliefs, since the expense of these endeavours was enormous.

There is no doubt, then, that without the diversity of religious convictions many cultural treasures would not have been created. If one wants to assess the value of such creeds, however, one should distinguish carefully between two different perspectives. On the one hand, firmly holding specific religious beliefs may fulfil multiple functions in both mental and social life, for instance by motivating actions such as building monuments, helping the poor, stimulating childbearing, or fighting unbelievers. If it would be feasible to add up and evaluate impartially all the good and bad effects of endorsing religious beliefs, one might attempt to calculate whether every impact taken into account, religious faith in general, or one religion in particular, is beneficial or detrimental to humanity.[3] On the other hand, one may focus on the contents of religious beliefs and wonder

---

[1] Cf. Philipse (2018) for a short German version of this chapter.
[2] Cottingham (2014), subtitle. Cottingham's and other epistemic justifications for holding a specific religious belief are evaluated in Part III.
[3] Cf. Philipse (2012, 2014), pp. 66–67, for scepticism as to whether this can be done.

how probable it is that a specific religious conviction about gods or God is true, or to what extent one might be justified or warranted to endorse it, if at least this belief is consistent and does make any sense.

Let me call the former aspect the *functional* one and the latter the *epistemological* perspective (the Greek word 'ἐπιστήμη' means knowledge). Endorsing beliefs that are false or unjustified may have positive functional results, as is shown by psychological research on attribution theory, for example.[4] Yet, doing so would be bad from the epistemological point of view, that is, concerning the search for truth and knowledge. In this first chapter, I focus on religious epistemology. Are religious beliefs to the effect that in fact a specific deity, spirit, devil, or ghost exists still intellectually acceptable for 'educated and intelligent people living in the twenty-first century'?[5]

Confronting the diversity of religious beliefs clearly raises an epistemological problem for the faithful. 'If I had been born and educated in a different religious tradition', they may wonder, 'would I have endorsed the content of that creed as devotedly as I am now subscribing to my own faith?' The problem is particularly pressing if the respective creeds are mutually incompatible, such as a polytheistic and a monotheist belief. Since only one of two incompatible beliefs can be true, one might confront a Christian or Muslim monotheist with the following counterfactual conditional: 'If you had been born and educated in the culture of Tantric Hinduism, for example, probably you would have been a profuse polytheist.' Or, more formally:

CC_{1a}. 'You are now believing that p, but if you had been educated in another cultural setting, you would have believed that q' (where p and q are mutually incompatible religious beliefs).

On the basis of such a first premise, various versions of the Argument from Cultural Contingency (CC) may be constructed.[6] The gist of such an argument is that given the premise of cultural contingency, it cannot be justified or legitimate to stick to one's own religious belief to the effect that a specific god exists. However, accepting premise CC_{1a} does not yet make it illegitimate or unjustified to endorse a religious belief that p. As

---

[4] Cf. the so-called self-serving bias: on average, we tend to attribute our successes to our own merits, whereas we explain our failures with reference to external factors that we cannot control. It is unlikely that all these attributions are true.

[5] The quote is from Plantinga (2000), p. viii.

[6] Cf. for example Baker-Hytch (2014). As Baker-Hytch argues, many of these versions are unconvincing. Unfortunately, he does not consider the version proposed in this section.

many critics have pointed out, CC_{1a} might be applied not only to religious beliefs but also to empirical or scientific ones. For example, you believe now that the Earth is both rotating around its axis and orbiting the Sun, but if you had been a well-educated intellectual in late medieval Europe, you would have held Aristotle's view, accepted by Christian authorities, that the Earth is the unmoving centre of a relatively small universe. Surely this counterfactual insight does not make it illegitimate to believe that the Earth is a planet rotating around its axis and orbiting the Sun. Well, why not?

The reason is, of course, that from Copernicus, Kepler, and Galileo onwards, preceded by Aristarchus of Samos, many pieces of empirical evidence and conclusive scientific arguments have been provided for the superiority of the modern views over that of Aristotle. Both the employment of novel instruments such as telescopes and the development of mathematically formulated theories that enabled scientists to derive and test new predictions have shown that Aristotle was wrong at this point. In other words, well-informed individuals, living in different cultural settings, may not be *epistemically on a par* with regard to the set of relevant beliefs, since in one of these settings the results of more advanced methods of discovery and of testing beliefs are available than in the other.

Hence, we have to reformulate as follows the first premise of an Argument from Cultural Contingency:

CC_{1b}. 'You now believe that p, but if you had been educated in another cultural setting, you would have believed that q' (where p and q are mutually incompatible religious beliefs *that are epistemically on a par*).

At this point, however, philosophically informed religious believers might indignantly reject premise CC_{1b} by claiming, 'there simply *are* no religious beliefs incompatible with mine that are epistemically on a par!' One reason they will adduce is that, as they contend, their own religious beliefs rely on an infallible epistemic source, such as the Qur'an and Sunnah according to many Muslims, or the *sensus divinitatis* postulated by Christians such as John Calvin or Alvin Plantinga, whereas conflicting religious beliefs allegedly cannot have been derived from such a well-functioning and reliable source of religious knowledge. In other words, against premise CC_{1b} they claim that 'my revelation is the true one, whereas all competing revelations are fake, at least to the extent that their content is logically incompatible with mine', or that 'my well-functioning *sensus divinitatis* yields true religious knowledge, whereas those who endorse an incompatible religious creed merely do so because their mental organ for religious knowledge is malfunctioning'. Consequently, the various conflicting religious beliefs would *not* be on a par epistemically.[7]

Let me explain briefly by way of illustration Plantinga's Calvinist model of religious knowledge, the subtleties of which I cannot discuss here.[8] Plantinga contends that *if* the omnipotent god (called God) he believes in really exists, this god or his Holy Spirit will have implanted out of grace the core doctrines of (Protestant) Christianity in the minds of Calvinists. As a consequence, strongly believing Calvinists would simply *know* that these doctrines are true, without needing any positive evidence or arguments to support their beliefs. Formulated in epistemological jargon, their religious beliefs would be 'properly basic', just like elementary beliefs about things we clearly perceive by our senses. Since this may be quite probable *if* the god Plantinga postulates really exists, given this assumption the religious beliefs of Calvinists will be 'warranted' in the sense of his 'externalist' epistemology, so that holding these beliefs amounts to knowledge. It follows that we can only call into question the existence and reliability of the *sensus divinitatis* postulated by Calvinists if we first argue convincingly that their god does *not* exist. And this, Plantinga claims, is a burden of proof that cannot be absolved convincingly.

Does this Calvinist objection to our premise CC_{1b} really refute it? Of course not, many readers (including you?) will answer, since those who endorse religious beliefs incompatible with Calvinism might put forward an argument that mirrors meticulously the Calvinist one. A Shaman will profess that during his states of trance he communicates with multitudes of malevolent spirits. *If* these spirits really exist, his religious experiences of them will amount to knowledge, so he will claim, since he perceives spirits by means of his Shamanist perceptual organ, that is, his *sensus divinitatis*. Calvinists informed about Shamanism will deny the existence of such spirits. As a consequence, they will argue, the states of trance of the Shaman cannot be reliable sources of religious knowledge. The Shaman is not sluggish, however, and, informed about Calvinism, he will reply by claiming that the god Calvinists believe in surely does not exist, so that the postulated *sensus divinitatis* of Calvinists must be either non-existent or malfunctioning.

---

[7] Various strategies developed in order to support this conclusion are discussed in Chapters 5 and 6.

[8] Cf. for a detailed discussion: Philipse (2012, 2014), chapters 3 and 4; Philipse (2013a); Plantinga (2000, 2011, 2015), and §5.4.

Let us briefly analyse the logic of this confrontation. Both parties claim that they possess a specific source or organ of religious experience, a *sensus divinitatis*, so to say, and that *if* the god or deities they believe in exist(s), this organ yields reliable basic (non-argumentative) knowledge about this divinity. However, they agree that their respective religious beliefs are logically incompatible: if Calvinism is true, Shamanism must be false, and vice versa. However, if an alleged source or organ of knowledge of some kind continuously yields incompatible results, we should not trust it. Hence, we should refrain from endorsing the religious beliefs allegedly delivered by this organ or source, unless we know of independent and convincing evidence or arguments for their truth.

Calvinists may reply that *if* their god exists, *their* organ for religious knowledge will be reliable, so that the Shamanist should first demonstrate that God does not exist. The Shaman will retort that *if* all the spirits he claims to perceive really exist, *his* organ for religious knowledge functions reliably, so that the Calvinist should first demonstrate that these spirits do not exist. In other words, as far as they can be aware of, the Calvinist and the Shamanist are epistemically on a par, or 'epistemic peers' in this respect, so that they cannot be justified to go on endorsing as true their mutually incompatible religious beliefs.[9] Hence, they should abandon them and become agnostic.

Whenever one and the same alleged source-type of religious knowledge continuously yields incompatible religious beliefs concerning the factual existence of gods or spirits in different religious communities, so that the overall truth-ratio of the beliefs that result from the supposed source is low, we might say that this fact functions as an 'undercutting defeater' of all the relevant beliefs. It shows that we should not endorse beliefs that allegedly rely on this type of source, unless we have other convincing evidence in their favour while equivalent evidence is lacking with regard to all incompatible beliefs.[10] Let's call such an alleged source of knowledge a 'sham-source', for short.

We may now formulate as follows a somewhat more sophisticated argument from cultural contingency or religious diversity:

---

[9] Cf. Philipse (2012, 2014), chapter 4, for a more detailed argument to this effect. Plantinga's conditional epistemology of Calvinist faith cannot be purely 'externalist' in the epistemological sense, if at least he wants to show how it can be legitimate to stick to one's faith when one is aware of religious beliefs that are incompatible with one's own. Cf. also §5.4.

[10] Cf. for various conceptions of epistemic defeaters: Philipse (2012), pp. 48–49. Many subtleties are omitted here in order not to overburden the reader.

CC_{1c} Holding religious beliefs is culturally contingent in the sense that, typically, the faithful would have endorsed another religious creed if they had been raised in another cultural context.

CC_2 Each specific religious creed, in the sense of a set of beliefs to the effect that specific supernatural entities (gods, spirits, angels, ghosts, devils, etc.) exist, is incompatible with some other religions. For example, monotheist religions deny the existence of deities that polytheistic religions believe in.

CC_3 Mutually incompatible religions are epistemically on a par, because they rely on the same types of alleged sources of knowledge about the supernatural, such as a *sensus divinitatis*, divine revelations, religious experiences, trance states, dreams, religious authorities or traditions, miracles, immersion in specific sects or religious communities, and so on.

CC_4 Since each of these alleged source-types of religious knowledge yields many mutually incompatible religious beliefs, their truth-rate is too low for being relied on in our search for truth, even if one of these beliefs were in fact true. From the epistemological point of view, they are sham-sources of knowledge, and this insight is an undercutting defeater of all religious beliefs.

CC_5 Consequently, no religious belief to the effect that a particular god or specific deities exist(s) is well founded or justified for culturally informed individuals. Hence, we should not endorse as true any such religious belief, at least if we aim at being intellectually conscientious.

One might call this the 'Epistemological Argument from Cultural Contingency', since premise CC_3 is essential for its soundness.[11] Because the premise is so important, it requires further elucidation and support, which is provided in §§1.2 and 1.3.

1.2 EPISTEMIC SOURCES OF RELIGIOUS BELIEFS

One cannot discuss properly sources of belief or knowledge without making some elementary conceptual distinctions. Let me first distinguish between secondary sources and primary ones.

If an inhabitant of Paris tells me that the Eiffel Tower is standing on the Champ de Mars, which is true, and I trust my obviously decent interlocutor in this respect, I acquire knowledge by testimony. A large amount of knowledge and beliefs we obtain is grounded in the secondary source of

---

[11] The epistemological argument from cultural contingency applies to all beliefs concerning matters of fact. Since moral beliefs are normative, those who would like to apply the argument to normative beliefs as well should show that the truth-conditions of normative beliefs are essentially similar to those of factual beliefs. However, I reject such versions of meta-ethical realism. Incidentally, although premise CC_{1c} expresses the original motive for developing the argument, it is not required for the logical validity of this epistemological version.

testimony, for instance when we read newspapers, watch news bulletins on television, believe what priests, pastors, pandits, pujaris, or parsons tell us about their god(s), or consult Wikipedia. Suppose, however, that I travel to Paris, take the Métro to station Bir-Hakeim, and walk to the Eiffel Tower. Now I see the tower with my own eyes, and, spotting a street sign, I discover that it is standing on the Champ de Mars. In this scenario my knowledge that the Eiffel Tower stands on the Champ de Mars is based upon a primary epistemic source: my visual perception of what my belief is about.

A source of knowledge or belief is a primary one if, in principle, using it can generate knowledge that is new, not only for a specific person but also for anyone else. Our sense organs are primary sources of knowledge and so are many scientific instruments and experimental setups. Let me mention for example the advanced LIGO detectors in Livingston, Louisiana and Hanford, Washington, USA, which measured gravitational waves for the first time, on 14 September 2015.[12]

Secondary sources of knowledge or belief, in contrast, are sources that transmit information which has been obtained already, either by other people or by oneself. Testimony is a secondary source of knowledge obtained by others, whereas memory functions as a secondary source of knowledge that the person who remembers may have acquired earlier from a primary source.[13] In most contexts, the distinction between primary and secondary sources is relative to a particular belief or instance of knowledge. The source of my knowledge that Donald Trump won the 2016 Republican Primaries was a secondary one, to wit my newspaper, but the original source of my knowledge that I read this in the newspaper was primary: the awareness of my reading experience.

Another distinction that is important for what follows is concerned with ways in which beliefs may be 'grounded' in their epistemic sources.[14] When I am waiting for a tram in Amsterdam, and I see a streetcar of line 5 approaching, my visual perception causes my belief that the tram will arrive in a moment at the stop.[15] This first manner in which the

---

[12] LIGO means: Laser Interferometer Gravitational-Wave Observatory. The gravitational waves were predicted by Einstein's 1915 general relativity theory, so it took one hundred years to detect them. Cf. Abbott et al. (2016).
[13] More strictly speaking, memory is not a 'source' of knowledge but rather a retention of knowledge previously acquired: a store of knowledge.
[14] Cf. Audi (1998), pp. 7–8.
[15] I am using the word 'belief' here in a somewhat technical sense that is common in epistemology. In our ordinary-language use of 'believe', I would say 'I believe the tram

functioning of an epistemic source may ground a belief might be called *causal grounding*. Typically, the perception also justifies the relevant belief, so that the causal grounding amounts to a *justificational grounding*.[16] But not all causal groundings of beliefs succeed in being justificational, at least not interpersonally. Suppose, for example, that while smoking marijuana and looking along the rail, Bill experiences a visual illusion or hallucination, which causes him to believe that tram 5 is approaching. When he tells his sober-minded spouse that he is seeing the tram arriving, she turns around to look along the railroad and discovers that no tramcar is in sight.

The distinction between causal and justificational grounding is crucial for what follows, but it is often overlooked. A possible explanation for neglecting it is that both types of grounding may be expressed by the same phrases. When Bill's wife asks him, 'Why do you believe that tram 5 is arriving?' and his answer is, 'Well, I see it!', this reply expresses both a causal and a justificational grounding of his belief. Furthermore, an experience may justify my endorsement of a specific belief from my subjective point of view, although it does not justify the belief in the objective sense of making it probable that the belief is true. Bill's visual experience of tram 5 justifies subjectively his belief that the streetcar is coming, if he is not aware that the experience is an illusion caused by cannabis, but it is not an objective justification.

In the subjective sense, the causal and the justificational grounding of a belief coincide, although what is caused is one's having the belief, whereas what is justified subjectively is the content of the belief. In the objective sense, however, causal and justificational grounding may come apart. In what follows I use the notion of justificational grounding in the objective sense only. Finally, when a belief is grounded in an epistemic source in such a way that this grounding guarantees the truth of the belief, so that the belief amounts to knowledge, one might speak of *epistemic grounding* in a strict sense. In a broader sense, epistemic grounding includes mere justificational grounding as a subspecies.

We may now reformulate conclusion CC$_5$ of §1.1 as follows. None of the alleged primary sources of religious beliefs ground them in the

---

is coming' only if I am not entirely sure it is coming and do not see it is. Cf. Hacker (2013), chapters 5–8, for a very instructive conceptual analysis of 'belief' and 'knowledge'.

[16] Strictly speaking, what is causally grounded is someone's believ*ing* something, whereas the justificational grounding is concerned with the contents of beliefs, that is, what is believed. Cf. Philipse (2012), p. 69.

justificational or epistemic sense, although they may have grounded them causally, at least to some extent. In order to provide further support for this conclusion, I first define 'religious beliefs' somewhat more precisely and see what their primary sources have in common. In §1.3, I discuss two examples of such primary sources. I argue in §1.4 that no primary source of religious beliefs grounds them in the justificational or epistemic sense, because the sources of religious beliefs could not be calibrated.

The term 'religion' functions on the basis of what philosophers call a family resemblance between the multi-dimensional phenomena we label religions. In other words, there is no essence of religion in the sense of one substantial set of properties that all religions have in common. At first sight, the same holds for our notion of religious belief. Prototypical instances of religious belief are convictions that specific gods, spirits, angels, or devils exist in fact, have specific intentions, and commit actions of some kind. But austere versions of Buddhism do not include such a belief in a god, for example, although they contain the idea that living beings are reborn after death as long as the cycle of suffering does not end in nirvana. Notwithstanding the diversity of religious beliefs, however, all of them do share an essential property. They are concerned with the *supernatural* in the sense of something that cannot be discovered by ordinary sense perception, by human interpersonal communication, or by applying the methods of the empirical sciences.[17] For this reason, religious beliefs may be defined broadly as beliefs that posit or presuppose the existence of supernatural conscious beings or properties in this sense.[18] Let us now investigate what are the epistemic sources that ground religious beliefs in the existence of gods, devils, spirits, angels, and the like.

The faith of most religious believers is grounded merely in secondary sources, such as religious traditions, authority, and testimony. As William James observed, however, '[i]t would profit us little to study this second-hand religious life', since the secondary sources of religious belief do not differ essentially from those of other beliefs, and their epistemic value is merely derivative.[19] If we want to assess the epistemic or justificationary grounding of religious beliefs, we should focus on their primary sources.

---

[17] The latter insight is not a priori or definitional but rather the result of the last four centuries of scientific research and progress. Cf. Chapter 2.
[18] Cf., for example, Morris (2006), p. 18. This definition excludes purely symbolical reinterpretations of religious beliefs.
[19] James (1902), p. 29.

These primary sources are the sources relied on by the original founders of religious traditions and by followers who claim to have personal access to the supernatural domain, that is, by those who have 'first-hand' religious convictions.

What are the primary sources of religious beliefs concerning gods and other supernatural beings? Since divinities, angels, devils, souls, etc. are conceived of as persons, these primary sources are not like the abstract arguments used to prove theorems in mathematics, for example. Rather, they are usually conceived to be communicative experiences of some kind. As is shown by worldwide anthropological research on religions, archetypical primary sources of religious belief are receiving divine revelations or messages, usually during dreams, trance states, possession rites, or oracle-experiences, or when undergoing spirit-possession, often during fever-induced deliriums or under the influence of hallucinogenic substances. For example, according to Ibn Ishaq's biography, Muhammad received his first revelation from the archangel Gabriel while he was dreaming in the cave of Hira on the mountain Jabal an-Nour.[20]

Since the primary sources of religious beliefs allegedly provide an epistemic grounding of beliefs about supernatural beings, it is not surprising that, typically, these sources differ from our common primary sources of knowledge about natural phenomena, such as sense perception.[21] Typically, beliefs about the supernatural are grounded in primary sources that somehow are not 'natural' either. In contradistinction to our normal perceptual experiences of the world around us, religious experiences of the founders of religious traditions are often 'abnormal' in a sense, as William James stressed already in *The Varieties of Religious Experience*:

> Even more perhaps than other kinds of genius, religious leaders have been subject to abnormal psychical visitations. Invariably they have been creatures of exalted emotional sensibility. Often they have led a discordant inner life, and had melancholy during a part of their career. They have known no measure, been liable to obsessions, and fixed ideas; and frequently they have fallen into trances, heard voices, seen visions, and presented all sorts of peculiarities which are ordinarily

---

[20] Cf. Husayn Haykal (2008), pp. 79–80.
[21] One might object that miracles are an exception, since a miracle should be defined as a natural event that in principle cannot be explained scientifically. Surely, if a miracle really occurred, we should be able to perceive it by our senses? Take Christ's alleged bodily resurrection, for example. However, if one perceives an event of which one thinks that it is a miracle, one is only justified epistemically to call it a miracle if one can show that a scientific explanation of the perceived event is impossible. And this one cannot perceive by sense experience.

classed as pathological. Often, moreover, these pathological features in their career have helped to give them their religious authority and influence.²²

Recent research concerning primary sources of religious belief seems to confirm James' classic on this issue. For example, three experts in clinical neuroscience from the Harvard Medical School have attempted to diagnose conscientiously the psychic sources that produced the seminal religious experiences of Abraham, Moses, Jesus, and St Paul (Saul of Tarsus), assuming for the sake of argument that the biblical accounts of their personality and religious experiences have at least some historical accuracy.²³ One motivation for this diagnostic investigation was that '[a]s many as 60% of those with schizophrenia have religious grandiose delusions'. This psychiatric fact raises the question whether and on what basis we can 'distinguish between the experiences of psychiatric patients and those of religious figures in history'. Should we not acknowledge 'that persons with [...] psychotic-spectrum disorders have had a monumental influence on civilization'? If so, '[h]ow do we explain to our patients that their psychotic symptoms are not supernatural intimations when our civilization recognizes similar phenomena in revered religious figures?'²⁴

Of course, neither William James nor our Harvard authors are allowed to answer these questions professionally, since by doing so they would overstep the frontiers of their psycho-medical disciplines. In principle, it might be possible that a supernatural being communicates with religious founding fathers or mothers via unnatural experiences of some kind, such as psychotic ones, or via dreams. Furthermore, if such a supernatural interference had occurred in fact, this would not refute the neuropsychiatric analysis of the relevant religious experiences. Add to this the sensitivity of public opinion in the United States concerning science-motivated criticisms of religion, and we understand the rationale of the following caveat:

Discussion about a potential role for the supernatural is outside the scope of our article and is reserved for the communities of faithful, religious scholars, and theologians, with one exception. It is our opinion that a neuropsychiatric accounting of behavior need not be viewed as excluding a role for the supernatural. Herein [i.e. in this article], neuropsychiatric mechanisms have been proposed through which behaviors and actions might be understood. For those who believe in omnipotent and omniscient supernatural forces, this should pose no obstacle, but

---

[22] James (1902), p. 29. [23] Murray et al. (2012).
[24] Murray et al. (2012), pp. 410–411, 424.

might rather serve as a mechanistic explanation of how events may have happened. No disrespect is intended towards anyone's beliefs or these venerable figures.[25]

It is one of the main jobs of philosophers, however, to develop an all-inclusive world-view that is justified epistemically; their task is not restricted to empirical research. For this reason, philosophers should not exert the caution expressed in the paragraph just quoted. At the end of §1.3, I return to the question whether and to what extent neuropsychiatric diagnoses and other secular explanations of the extraordinary experiences that functioned as primary sources of religious beliefs make it less likely that a supernatural being has played any role in causing these experiences.

1.3 ST PAUL AND THE PYTHIA

As Gustave Flaubert once wrote, 'Le bon Dieu est dans le détail' (The good God is in the detail).[26] For this reason, we should not discuss primary sources of religious beliefs in the abstract only. Without analysing the specific characteristics of particular sources, we cannot decide whether they have any epistemic value for grounding a religious belief. I have selected two representative examples of such primary sources, which played a crucial role in the respective religions: St Paul's conversion experience on the road to Damascus, and the communications of Apollo with the Pythia in the Oracle of Delphi. Let me start with Paul or Saul.

According to Acts 9:1–19, Saul of Tarsus was 'still breathing threats and murder against the disciples of the Lord' when he went on his way to Damascus. How should we explain that this prominent persecutor of Jesus' followers converted to the Jesus creed, so that, ultimately, he could become the principal founding father of the Christian religion? Let us not forget that more than half (fourteen) of the twenty-seven books of the New Testament have been attributed traditionally to St Paul. Without Paul's preaching among both Jews and Gentiles in the Roman Empire, the Jesus sect would never have developed into the world religion of Christianity.[27]

---

[25] Murray et al. (2012), p. 423.
[26] Unfortunately, I could not detect this famous quote in Flaubert's writings. I'll be delighted if a reader will provide the reference.
[27] According to current biblical scholarship, at least seven of Paul's epistles can be considered to be authentic.

The book of Acts answers our question as follows by describing Saul's conversion experience:

> Now as he journeyed he approached Damascus, and suddenly a light from heaven flashed about him. And he fell to the ground and heard a voice saying to him, 'Saul, Saul, why do you persecute me?' And he said, 'Who are you, Lord?' And he said, 'I am Jesus, whom you are persecuting; but rise and enter the city, and you will be told what you are to do.' The men who were travelling with him stood speechless, hearing the voice but seeing no one. Saul arose from the ground; and when his eyes were opened, he could see nothing; so they led him by the hand and brought him into Damascus. And for three days he was without sight, and neither ate nor drank.[28]

Let us assume for the sake of argument that this passage is historically reliable at least to some extent.[29] Then we might try to answer conscientiously three different questions. The first one (a) is concerned with the unnatural character of this revelation-experience, which is staged as the primary epistemic source grounding Saul's belief that he was elected to spread the word of Jesus/God among Jews and non-Jews. Can we give a neuropsychiatric or other scientific diagnosis of the four striking features of this experience, to wit, (1) a light from heaven flashing about him, (2) Saul falling to the ground, (3) hearing a voice, and (4) being without sight during three days? This is what the Harvard experts mentioned in §1.2 aimed to do, using the *Diagnostic and Statistical Manual of Mental Disorders* DSM-IV-TR published by the American Psychiatric Association.[30]

A second question (b) is concerned with the content of the alleged supernatural communication to Saul. What explains the fact that he attributed the voice he heard or seemed to hear to the resurrected Jesus, whose followers Saul was persecuting so brutally? And how should we explain that Saul thought to receive an assignment to convert radically from a Jewish persecutor of Jesus' followers to someone who should devote his life to proclaiming Jesus? In order to answer questions of this type, historical and psychological considerations are indispensable. Finally, we might wonder whether (c) the unnatural experience of Saul described in Acts 9:1–9 was merely a causal grounding of his belief that a supernatural figure was speaking to him, or whether it also amounts to a justificational grounding in the objective sense, as many believing Christians assume.

---

[28] Acts 9:1–9. Cf. also Acts 22:6–11, and Acts 26:12–18.
[29] Of course, these passages in Acts are 'Lucan expansions in narrative form of a few sober remarks which Paul himself makes in his letters', as De Jonge (2002, p. 43) observes, with reference to Gal. 1:13–17; 1 Cor. 9:1, and 1 Cor. 15:8–9.
[30] American Psychiatric Association (2000).

A traditional answer to question (a) concerning a diagnosis of Saul's experience on the road to Damascus is that he suffered from an epileptic attack, more particularly, that his religious experiences were symptoms of temporal lobe epilepsy.[31] According to the Harvard clinical neuroscientists, however, 'it is not necessary to invoke epilepsy as an explanation for these experiences'. They claim that there is 'lack of evidence for more common epileptic accompaniments' in Acts and Paul's authentic letters.[32] Since they hold that characteristic (4) of Saul's conversion experience, his blindness, should be interpreted metaphorically, they diagnose the experience from a psychiatric point of view as a symptom of 'paranoid schizophrenia, psychosis NOS, mood disorder-associated psychosis, or schizoaffective disorder'. As Saul preserved his ability 'to write and organize his thoughts', the authors favour a 'mood disorder-associated explanation for his religious experiences'.[33]

A very different account of what happened to Saul, and why he interpreted his experience as a supernatural occurrence, stresses features (4) combined with (1), that is, the 'great light from heaven' and the fact that Saul 'could not see because of the brightness of that light' (Acts 22:6–11), now interpreted literally. According to a recent paper by William Hartmann, co-founder of the Planetary Science Institute in Tucson, Arizona, the description of Saul's experience offers 'a strikingly good match' to eyewitness accounts of the 'explosive entry of an asteroid fragment over Chelyabinsk in 2013'.[34] Saul's temporary blindness may have been caused by exposure to the intense ultraviolet radiation resulting from a fireball event, that is, by what is now called photokeratitis. According to Acts 26:14, 'we had all fallen to the ground'. This can be

---

[31] Cf., for example, Nietzsche (1881), §68, and Landsborough (1987).
[32] Murray et al. (2012), pp. 415, 416.
[33] Murray et al. (2012), p. 417. The abbreviation NOS means: not otherwise specified. This diagnosis is based on an overview of biblical passages concerning Saul's personality. The authors use two different arguments to the effect that Saul's blindness should not be interpreted in the literal sense of visual blindness but rather metaphorically. First, they refer to a number of biblical passages in which those who do *not* accept the Christian creed are called blind metaphorically, such as Acts 28:26, Romans 11:8–10, or 2 Corinthians 4:3–5. But this argument is not very convincing, since according to Acts 9:1–9, Saul could not see anything during three days *after* his conversion experience. The second argument is that the description of Saul's conversion on the road to Damascus in Acts 26:9–18 does not mention any blindness of Saul. This argument is not convincing either, since two passages in Acts about Paul's conversion experience (Acts 9:1–9 and Acts 22:6–11) tell us that he could not see because of the brightness of the light, whereas only one passage (Acts 26:9–18) does not mention this.
[34] Hartmann (2015), p. 368.

attributed to the shockwave generated by an explosion of the meteoroid in the air. Of course, witnesses of such an overwhelming spectacle, which had not been experienced before, interpreted it in terms of the cultural conceptions prevailing at their historical epoch, as Hartmann argues with respect to Saul and his companions.

My motive for mentioning these two discrepant secular diagnoses of St Paul's conversion experience is twofold. In the first place, the diversity of possible explanations shows clearly to what extent they are somewhat speculative. The biblical sources they are relying on are not medical records, and the three accounts in Acts of Saul's conversion on the road to Damascus are slightly different. For example, in Acts 9:7, it is said that '[t]he men who were travelling with him stood speechless, hearing the voice but seeing no one', whereas according to Saul's own record in Acts 22:9, 'those who were with me saw the light but did not hear the voice of the one who was speaking to me'. One might try to confirm further the meteor hypothesis by searching for meteorites in and around Syria, but dating such an event will have an uncertainty margin of at least one century. In the second place, both of the diagnoses I mentioned explain convincingly the uncommon or unnatural character of Saul's experience. They account for the fact that he could honestly interpret what happened to him as an encounter with a supernatural person, given Saul's religious background and the fact that he lacked any expertise in modern psychiatry and/or astronomy.

Concerning the content of Saul's conversion experience, that is, with regard to our question (b), we have to interpret it in its cultural context of 35–50 CE. We should also attempt to explain psychologically why Saul converted so radically while or after undergoing his deeply shocking unnatural experience. Let me mention just one example from the long list of psychological accounts proposed during the last two centuries. As St Paul says in Galatians 1:13–14, before his conversion he 'persecuted the church of God violently and tried to destroy it', he 'advanced in Judaism beyond many of my own age', and was 'extremely zealous [...] for the traditions of my fathers'. According to the psychological diagnosis Friedrich Nietzsche proposed in 1881, it is Saul's extreme zealousness in trying to live up to Jewish law that explains his conversion to Jesus during or shortly after his world-shattering experience. The more Saul attempted to meet the demanding requirements of the Jewish law but failed to do so, the more he became conscience-stricken, so that subliminally he started to hate the law. During the ordeal on the road to Damascus, he may suddenly have apprehended subconsciously his final solution. Could he not annihilate the Jewish law if he converted to Jesus, and thereby liberate himself and everyone else from its exigent obligations?[35]

We now have to raise again question (c) as to whether the unnatural experience of Saul described in Acts was merely a causal grounding of his belief that a supernatural figure was speaking to him. Or does it amount to a justificational grounding in the objective sense, as many Christians assume? Before answering this question, I should discuss briefly my second example of a primary source of beliefs concerning the supernatural: the experiences of the Pythia in Delphi as a possessed medium of Apollo, the Greek god of prophesy.

At the time of St Paul's life, the Oracle of Delphi was still vastly more important in terms of cultural impact than the small sect of Jesus followers, which is a first reason for examining it. From its establishment in the eighth century BCE until it was closed down around 393 CE, when the Christian emperor Theodosius forbade 'pagan' temples to operate, the Delphic Oracle was the most eminent source of communication with the divine in Greek civilization. Delphi was called the *omphalos* (navel) of the Earth, that is, the centre of the world. The medium in Delphi was a female person, which is a second reason for selecting this example of a primary source. Unfortunately, around 400 CE fanatic Christians destroyed most of the buildings that still remained after plunders and earthquakes, in order to eliminate completely religions competing with their own. A third reason for singling out the Oracle of Delphi is that after the excavations at the end of the nineteenth century, its functioning has been investigated thoroughly, both from a theological and from a scientific point of view.

According to many classical sources such as Strabo (64 BCE–25 CE), the divine possession of the Pythia was triggered by a gas, vapour, or *pneuma*.[36] Being prepared once a month for her communication with Apollo by purification rituals such as fasting and bathing nakedly in the Castalian Spring, the Pythia would descent into the 'adyton' (the inaccessible), a cavern under the Delphi temple. Placed on a gilded tripod, she then inhaled the *pneuma*, which arose probably from a cleft in the rock below her, and which was thought to produce divine possession or *enthusiasmos*. According to Plutarch, who functioned as a priest in Delphi around 100 CE, the *pneuma* smelled like a sweet perfume, although the Greek verb πύθειν from which the name 'Pythia' was derived,

---

[35] Nietzsche (1881), §68.   [36] Cf. Hale et al. (2003) for what follows.

means 'to rot'. Clearly, in high concentrations the pneuma will not have smelled very pleasant.

Having inhaled this *pneuma*, the Pythia would transmute into a mild or sometimes ecstatic state of oracular trance, and would say or rave things that often were difficult to decipher. Priests then interpreted her pronouncements as prophecies communicated by Apollo, and formulated them in hexameters. One of the best-known examples of the historical impact that Delphic oracular pronouncements could have is the advice to King Croesus of Lydia when he asked the oracle whether he would win a war against the Persian Empire. Having received the reply that a great empire would be destroyed if he went to war, he confidently launched a campaign against Persia but was defeated and captured by Cyrus the Great around 546 BCE.[37]

According to all classical sources about the Delphic Oracle, the prophetic inspiration of the Pythia was triggered by her inhaling a vapour in the *adyton*. However, when French archaeologists excavated the Delphi site in 1892–1894, they did not notice clearly the fissures in the rocks under the temple, nor smell a *pneuma*. In 1904, a young British historian from French descent, Adolphe Paul Oppé, published an influential article called 'The Chasm at Delphi'.[38] He argued that all classical sources were erroneous, since there was neither a chasm in the rocks nor an *adyton* in the temple. Transcending the boundaries of his historical expertise, he also claimed that there could not have been a vaporous cleft, since the Delphi region was not volcanic, and that no natural gas could produce a state of trance that resembled spiritual possession. Because Oppé's article seemed to be persuasive among archaeologists during most of the twentieth century, many Delphi experts attempted to explain the spiritual possession of the Pythia by postulating merely psychological mechanisms.

However, recent geological, archaeological, and toxicological research by an interdisciplinary team has established that the classical authors were perfectly right. Quite probably, a gas mounting from a fissure did cause the trance states of the Pythia. In the 1980s, the American geologist Jelle Zeilinga de Boer discovered traces of fault lines both east and west of the temple, which he interpreted as symptoms of a fissure that continued under its foundations. Since his work was part of a development project of the United Nations to survey active faults in Greece along which earthquakes had been generated, and being ignorant of the Oppé

---

[37] Herodotos, *Histories*, I, 91.   [38] Oppé (1904).

orthodoxy in archaeology, he did not pay much attention to his finding. This changed when he met archaeologist John Hale more than ten years later in Portugal, who had asked him to investigate whether there was earthquake damage at a Roman villa. Over a bottle of wine they discovered that they disagreed about the presence of fissures or fault faces under the Delphi sanctuary and decided to compose a team of experts in order to do further research on the site.[39] The results of their investigations have been published in two articles of 2001–2002.[40]

First of all, the team discovered that the inner sanctum of the temple is both sunken and asymmetrical, as the *adyton* was according to classical authors. Since there also turned out to be a drain for spring water nearby, this confirmed ancient sources claiming that gas emissions had mounted with water. Second, another fault line was discovered, which ran northwest to south-east and crosses the east–west fault line exactly at the site of the oracle. If any gases had been emitted through water in these fissures, it is to be expected that the emission was most noticeable at their intersection, which would explain why the temple had been built exactly at this spot. In the third place, a chemical analysis of water samples from the Kerna spring in the sanctuary showed that they contained three gases, methane, ethane, and ethylene, which might have evaporated in the *adyton*. This seemed to confirm Plutarch's description of the *pneuma*, because ethylene smells sweetly. Finally, a toxicological analysis of ethylene shows that inhaling low concentrations may induce a pleasant trance state, whereas stronger concentrations might cause patients to utter incoherent cries and to move violently, which corroborates the accounts of how the Pythia behaved.

Clearly, then, one might explain the 'unnatural' character of the Pythia's revelatory trance experiences as a psychic effect of inhaling ethylene, which answers our question (a) with regard to the Delphi Oracle. It is interesting to note that these effects were attributed to Apollo only from the late ninth century BCE onwards, whereas the oracle itself probably dated already from around 1400 BCE. In order to account for the fact that the trance experiences of the Pythia were attributed to the god Apollo, and to explain their contents, we should rely on experts of Greek cultural history. Since the oracle functioned during more than a thousand years, I shall not try to answer question (b) here, that is, the explanatory question concerning the content of the alleged supernatural

---

[39] Cf. Hale et al. (2003) for an overview.
[40] Cf. De Boer et al. (2001) and Spiller et al. (2002).

communications of Apollo to the Pythia. There were simply too many of them. Instead, let me focus finally on question (c) concerning both Paul and the Pythia. Should we interpret their unnatural experiences merely as *causal* groundings of their belief that a supernatural figure was speaking to them, or did these experiences also amount to a *justificational* grounding in the *objective* sense?

The Delphi research team of Hale and De Boer concludes an overview of its results in the *Scientific American* by telling the reader how Plutarch attempted to reconcile science and religion. Being a priest of Apollo, he had to explain why Apollo used a gas in order to inspire the Pythia, instead of speaking to her directly, as undoubtedly He could have done. Why did Apollo need the *pneuma*, that is, the impact of ethylene? Our authors reply to this question as follows:

> Plutarch believed that the gods had to rely on the materials of this corrupt and transitory world to accomplish their works. God though he was, Apollo had to speak his prophesies through the voices of mortals, and he had to inspire them with stimuli that were part of the natural world. Plutarch's careful observations and reporting of data about the gaseous emissions at Delphi show that the ancients did not try to exclude scientific inquiry from religious understanding.[41]

However, the crucial question is the converse: does the scientific account that explains the trance states of the Pythia exclude, or at least render superfluous, the hypothesis that a god, Apollo, was speaking to the Pythia at the Delphic Oracle? Although our authors end their article by stressing 'how much we have to gain if we approach problems with the same broad-minded and interdisciplinary attitude that the Greeks themselves displayed', I do not assume that they, or any of the readers of this book, seriously consider the possibility that the god Apollo really exists, or at least existed, and in fact communicated with the Pythia. In other words, I assume that everyone today will deny that the unnatural experiences of the Pythia provide an objective *justificational* grounding of religious beliefs concerning Apollo and his prophesies, although they grounded them *causally* given the cultural context. We can explain very well how the primary source of beliefs concerning Apollo's prophesies worked without invoking any supernatural influence. Philosophically speaking, we should apply Ockham's razor or the *lex parsimoniae* and refrain from postulating a supernatural cause.

---

[41] Hale et al. (2003), p. 73.

I suggest that the same conclusion holds with regard to St Paul's conversion experience. Let me confess that my preferred answer to question (a) concerning the unnatural character of what happened to Saul on the road to Damascus is the hypothesis that an explosive entry of an asteroid fragment caused his ordeal, as William Hartmann argues convincingly. Such events were very rare – they occurred about once per century – and probably meteoritic phenomena were unfamiliar to inhabitants of the Palestine region. As a consequence, Saul would not have understood at all what happened to him when 'a great light from heaven suddenly shone', and an instant later he 'fell to the ground' (Acts 22:6–7), because a shockwave knocked the travellers off their feet. Since the entry of an asteroid may cause a thunderous sound, which in all versions of Acts is mentioned 'in the sentence *after* the celestial light flashes around them', Hartmann argues plausibly 'that the noise of a fireball could have been conceived by a zealous first-century partisan to be a divine voice speaking from heaven'.[42] Finally, Saul's blindness may have been caused both by the brightness of the event and because Saul may have stared at the fireball more intently than his companions, since he believed that it was a divine apparition. This resulted in severe photokeratitis, so that Saul could not see for about fifty hours.

As in the Delphi case, the content of Saul's conversion experience, that is, the answer to question (b), should be accounted for by relying on the cultural context and on psychological mechanisms, as indicated above. How should we answer question (c) concerning Saul's primary source of his belief in a divine Jesus? Should we interpret his unnatural experience on the road to Damascus merely as a *causal* grounding of his belief that the supernatural Jesus was speaking to him, or did the experience also amount to a *justificational* grounding in the objective sense? That is, did a resurrected Jesus really speak to Saul? *Prima facie* there is no reason to give an answer to this question concerning Saul that differs from our reply regarding the Delphi case. On the contrary, whereas Apollo was assumed to communicate with the Pythia thousands of times, whereas the resurrected Jesus revealed himself so clearly to Saul only once, the Delphi Oracle was a vastly more convincing primary source of religious belief than Saul's experience on the road to Damascus.

---

[42] Hartmann (2015), pp. 374–375.

1.4 CALIBRATION OF EPISTEMIC SOURCES

Let me summarize briefly the results of the first three sections of this chapter, before formulating the central problem to be discussed in the present, concluding section. In §1.1, an Argument from Cultural Contingency has been formulated to the effect that, given the diversity of mutually incompatible religions in the world, a culturally informed individual cannot be justified to endorse as true a religious belief that a particular deity exists. One might recapitulate this Epistemological Argument from Cultural Contingency as a simple *modus ponendo ponens*. (x) If two mutually incompatible religious doctrines (concerning the existence of god(s)) are epistemically equivalent, then endorsing one of them as true is unjustified. (y) With regard to their primary epistemic sources, all religious doctrines are epistemically equivalent or on a par, whereas each of them contradicts at least one rival religious doctrine. (z) Hence, endorsing any particular religious doctrine as true is unjustified.

In §1.2, it is argued that such mutually incompatible religious beliefs, like Christian Calvinism on the one hand and Shamanism on the other, are indeed epistemically on a par, at least at first sight, because they are grounded by the same types of primary epistemic sources. Since deities are supernatural beings, the primary epistemic sources of religious beliefs differ from epistemic sources such as sense perception, which provide access to natural phenomena. Typically, primary sources of beliefs concerning the supernatural are themselves not 'natural' epistemic sources either. This is illustrated in §1.3 by the examples of St Paul's religious experience on the road to Damascus, and the Pythia's communication with Apollo in the temple at Delphi.[43]

Although the Pythias and Paul will have thought sincerely that the relevant deity was communicating with them or him, we now have at our disposal completely secular or natural explanations of their extraordinary experiences. Hence, we do not need to postulate any deities in order to explain what happened. What is more, we should not postulate them in order to account for these experiences, because entities must not be multiplied beyond necessity (*Non sunt multiplicanda entia sine*

---

[43] From their subjective perspective, both Paul and the Pythias thought that they were having supernatural experiences. Objectively speaking, these experiences were 'unnatural' in a different sense. They were very exceptional, and neither Paul or the Pythias had the scientific knowledge needed to explain them. Hence, they had recourse to a supernatural explanation or interpretation of what occurred to them.

necessitate). This is yet another argument (Ockham's razor) for concluding that these primary sources do not epistemically ground the respective religious beliefs.[44]

Can we generalize this conclusion? That is, can we argue conclusively that none of the primary sources of religious convictions epistemically grounds any positive religious belief concerning supernatural beings, so that these beliefs are also epistemically on a par in this negative sense, at least with regard to their primary sources? I think we can, and I spell out the argument in the present section. It consists of the following steps or theses. (1) We can rely legitimately on a primary source of beliefs only if this source has been validated or calibrated epistemically, that is, if it has been established that this source usually yields knowledge or beliefs with a high probability of being true. (2) Of the many primary sources of religious beliefs, such as revelations, religious experiences, or dreams, none has been calibrated epistemically. Hence, (3) we cannot rely legitimately on any primary source of religious beliefs. Let me call this the 'Calibration Argument'.

Since gods or deities are supernatural persons of some kind, the direct evidence for their existence has been conceived of traditionally in most religions as consisting in forms of unnatural communication, as the examples of Paul and the Pythias illustrate. Apart from such typically religious sources of belief concerning the supernatural, so-called rational or natural theologians have attempted to argue that there is a particular god by also adducing more indirect and purely secular evidence, such as the existence of the universe or the alleged fine-tuning of constants in laws of nature. As I said in the Introduction, the merits of natural theology are evaluated briefly in Chapter 6. In my (2012, 2014) book *God in the Age of Science? A Critique of Religious Reason*, I argued extensively that given the total natural evidence adduced in favour of and against the existence of the god defined by theism, it remains very improbable that such a god exists, if the definition is coherent and makes any sense at all. This is why I focus at present on the direct and primary sources of religious beliefs.

Let me develop the Calibration Argument. Usually, the term 'calibration' refers to methods of establishing the reliability of measuring instruments within specific ranges. Here, I use the word in a broader sense, for

---

[44] Of course, such an Ockham's razor argument to the effect that theism is an unnecessary hypothesis for explaining specific phenomena does not and should not (yet) aim at showing that God does *not* exist. Cf. van Inwagen (2005), and Glass (2017).

tests of epistemic reliability concerning primary sources of beliefs in general, and I employ 'validation' as an equivalent term. The first premise of the argument will appear to be self-evident to most of us:

CA_1. We can rely legitimately on a primary source of beliefs only if this source has been validated or calibrated epistemically, that is, if it has been established that this source usually yields true beliefs or beliefs with a high probability of being true.

We may classify primary sources of belief at different levels of abstraction. At a very high level we might say, for example, that the ultimate primary source of all our beliefs about the natural world is sense perception, often assisted by the use of scientific instruments. At the lowest level, however, the specification of primary sources may be very specific. The primary source of my belief that the doorbell is ringing is my hearing the familiar sound, and the primary source of a physician's belief that 'dense bodies' appear in the blood of a patient is that a low-powered electron microscope reveals it.[45]

At whatever level of abstractness we classify primary sources of belief, we always apply explicitly or implicitly, and should apply, the following three rules for calibrating them.[46] First (a), repeated and mutually independent uses of the same source, both by ourselves and by others, should yield results that are consistent and informative. If results are mutually inconsistent, we should be able to discover in general which one is correct by applying the source anew. Furthermore (b), we should examine whether using different primary sources or detection methods that can be applied independently to the same issue yields the same result. This second rule relies on an argument from coincidence. If different and mutually independent primary sources yield identical results, it would be an unlikely coincidence if these results were contaminated by their sources rather than informing us objectively about the items investigated. Finally (c), if the primary sources are theory laden, as is typically the case when we are using scientific instruments, for example, theoretical understanding of the sources will be essential to their validation or calibration, and the relevant theories should be well confirmed by evidence of various types.

It is sometimes suggested that calibration rules do not apply to sense perception and other types of experience, such as religious experiences, because we cannot but start relying on the primary sources of belief.

---

[45] Cf. Hacking (1983), pp. 200ff. for this latter example.   [46] Cf. Philipse (2013a).

Hence, we are justified in doing so until we are confronted by defeating considerations. For example, Richard Swinburne has argued that there is a fundamental principle of rationality, which he calls the Principle of Credulity, according to which what we take ourselves to perceive or experience is probably so, unless there are defeaters.[47] In other words, in the absence of defeaters we should 'take the way things seem to be as the way they are', so that 'in the absence of special considerations, all religious experiences ought to be taken by their subjects as genuine'.[48]

However, the Principle of Credulity does not exclude the need to calibrate the primary sources of our beliefs, since occasionally we are confronted by defeaters that undermine beliefs based upon each of these sources. Hence, we have to calibrate them in order to establish to what extent they can be trusted. Take sense perception, for example. Swinburne is right in that we cannot acquire any knowledge about perceivable things unless we start by trusting our senses to some extent, as we do instinctively. But we would stop doing so in cases where we failed to validate their particular uses. In fact, we are calibrating our sense organs continuously. For example, if we appear to see a stork flying towards us, but when it approaches it seems to be a grey heron, we should look again from nearby in order to identify the bird (rule a), and learn about the range within which we can distinguish reliably between these types of wading birds. Furthermore, if we think the glass door at the entrance of our office is closed, but we cannot see it properly because the Sun is blinding us, we might check our visual impression of the closed door by touching it (rule b). Finally, a neighbour of mine told me that he was hearing a sharp sound all the time and thought that his pacemaker produced this noise. As I did not hear anything, I advised him to have it investigated. Medical research indicated that he suffered from tinnitus, so that he seems to hear a particular noise when no external sound is present (rule c).

Since we can legitimately rely on a primary source of beliefs only to the extent that this source has been calibrated, we should apply this first premise of the Calibration Argument to the primary sources of religious beliefs. As I mentioned in §1.2, for example, Prophet Muhammad allegedly received his first revelation from the archangel Gabriel while he was dreaming in the cave of Hira on the mountain Jabal an-Nour. According to both the Old and the New Testaments, dreams are often

---

[47] Cf. Philipse (2012, 2014), p. 317, note 23.
[48] Swinburne (2004), pp. 303–304, and Philipse (2012, 2014), §§15.4–15.7.

used by God as means of divine communication. Can we calibrate the reliability of dreams during which it seems that someone is appearing or speaking to us? Although I have not consulted statistical research on this issue, it is obvious that very often the individual persons or animals appearing in dreams don't exist, such as monsters or exceptionally attractive sex partners with wings, and that if they exist, they do or say things that would never be done or said in reality.[49] Consequently, dreams do not pass the calibration test, and the same holds for the other primary sources of religious beliefs, such as miracle-appearances or interaction with the divine during prayer.[50] Hence, it seems safe to generalize and endorse the second premise of the Calibration Argument:

CA_2. Of the many primary sources of religious beliefs, such as revelations, religious experiences, or dreams, none has been calibrated epistemically.

From premises CA_1 and CA_2, conclusion CA_3 follows deductively (*Modus Tollendo Tollens*):

CA_3. We cannot rely legitimately on any primary source of religious beliefs.

This Calibration Argument supports further premises CC_3 and CC_4 of the Epistemological Argument from Cultural Contingency stated in §1.1. The primary sources of religious beliefs are not only on a par epistemically. They have not been calibrated either, so that one should not rely on them in endorsing as true specific religious beliefs, at least if one aims at endorsing only beliefs that are well grounded. Let me finish this chapter by discussing an objection.

Some contemporary Christian philosophers have argued that both the traditional conception of 'modes of access to the divine' and the purely rational approach of natural theology are too narrow-minded or misdirected.[51] Rather, we should engage in what has been called an 'epistemology of involvement', and realize that epistemic evidence for the existence of God will be provided only to those who are committed deeply and wholeheartedly to a particular kind of religious life. In other words, the

---

[49] In investigating the content of dreams, one should use basic classificatory and statistical principles of dream content analysis, as developed by Schredl (2010), for example. Interestingly, Aristotle already denied that dreams are foretelling or sent by a divine being.

[50] Cf. Philipse (2012), §6.3 on prayer, and §§10.2–10.5 on miracles. Cf. Edis and Boudry (2014) on the question as to whether a validation of oracle pronouncements is possible in principle.

[51] Cf. Cottingham (2014), pp. 68–69 and *passim*.

evidence for God's existence is not objective, like scientific evidence or results of sense perception. It is given only to those who practise 'a voluntary act of openness to divine grace', which is 'a lifelong process' and involves 'a *radical moral change*',[52] or to those who engage in 'volitional theism', that is, who are trying seriously to become themselves 'personifying evidence of God' by 'learning to love as God loves'.[53]

Of course, many Christian traditions have preached that God is free to provide evidence of His existence by Grace to humans of his choice only, and that Original Sin explains the fact that many of us do not receive such evidence.[54] According to the authors quoted above, Divine evidence will be provided, if at all, only to those who engage deeply in Christian life for quite some time, so that the investment needed for obtaining such evidence may be huge. It is also suggested that those who realize the Christian ideal of practising charity become themselves evidence of God's existence. What should we think of these approaches, which advertise themselves as being 'more humane'?

The fact that it may be costly and complicated to acquire evidence for the existence of a specific entity or phenomenon is in itself no objection. Let me mention again the example of the interferometric detectors in Washington State, the use of which enabled physicists for the first time to observe directly gravitational waves of cosmic origin on 14 September 2015. The LIGO observatories each support an L-shaped ultra-high-vacuum system, which extends 4 kilometres on each side, and contains interferometers. The gravitational waves which physicists intend to detect originated tens of millions of light years away from Earth. Since they will distort the 4 kilometre mirror spacing only about 10^{-18} metres, the measuring instruments should be sensitive to distances of about one thousandth of the charge diameter of a proton. It is no wonder, then, that after Einstein published his general theory of relativity in 1916, it took nearly a century to develop the super-sophisticated technology for observing gravity waves and to observe them for the first time. Might one not argue that contacting God will be even more difficult than detecting gravitational waves, since He is conceived of as an infinitely powerful, wise, good, and free purely spiritual being?

Clearly, the very nature of the being or phenomenon for the existence of which one would like to acquire evidence should explain how costly

---

[52] Cottingham (2014), pp. 70, 149, 157, 159; and §5.5.
[53] Moser (2010), pp. 263, 266; and §5.6.
[54] Cf., for example, §5.4, on Alvin Plantinga's religious confidentialism (my label).

and difficult it is to obtain such evidence, given our human resources. The physical conception of cosmic gravitational waves on the basis of Einstein's general theory of relativity satisfies this requirement. Is this also the case for those who argue that it takes years of involvement in a religious community in order to make the acquaintance of the Christian god, for example? One might object that if indeed this god is infinitely wise, powerful, and morally good, as traditional Christianity claims, and if he is like a loving father for all humans, he should unambiguously reveal himself to all of us early in our earthly lives, as decent fathers do. Since this did not and does not happen to most humans, clearly such a god does not exist. The many attempts by believing Christian philosophers to account for this divine hiddenness, that is, to explain why God does not reveal himself to all of us, or why he started to reveal himself to humanity only about two or three thousand years ago and very locally, or why it is so difficult to acquire communicative evidence of his existence, are not very convincing.[55]

However this may be, the Epistemological Argument from Cultural Contingency applies as well to the more humane approaches within religious epistemology. Just as Paul Moser or John Cottingham argue that Christian religious life is a 'continuous process of learning', during which one should open oneself sincerely to all the relevant resources of human experience,[56] the Tantric Hindu I met in 2000 held that only those who practise *Ishta devata* meditations during many years will experience *darshan*, that is, a vision of some gods and goddesses. One should then internalize these divinities during rituals that resemble sexual courtship and consummation. Different religions tell their believers that only if they engage wholeheartedly and permanently in the relevant religious practices will they experience a 'personal call to allegiance' from the relevant deity or deities, which is 'addressed not to the analytic mind but to the heart'.[57] Unfortunately, however, a monotheist will hold that the 330 million Tantric deities do not exist, and a Tantric believer might say the same about the Christian or the Islamic god.[58]

Since the central theological beliefs of these diverse religions are mutually contradictory if they make any sense at all, whereas no reliable

---

[55] The so-called hiddenness argument against the existence of the god of theism has been defended recently by J. L. Schellenberg (2006, 2015). Cf. Chapters 5 and 6 for an extensive analysis of various apologetic strategies.
[56] Cottingham (2014), p. 174.   [57] Cottingham (2014), p. 170.
[58] Of course, polytheists are more liberal than monotheists in this respect.

methods of religious research have been developed that might enable us to find out which ones are true and which ones false, they are epistemically on a par. Hence, intellectually decent people who really care about truth should not endorse any positive religious conviction concerning the existence of a divinity.

In this chapter, I have focused on the epistemology of religious beliefs. Clearly, however, although different and mutually incompatible sets of religious beliefs concerning the supernatural are epistemically on a par, one of them may be much more attractive than another from the functional or the moral perspective.

If a polytheistic religion preached passionately that according to its gods one should love all humans as much as one can, pursue impartial scientific research, embrace human rights including the freedom of religion, and do what is needed in order to solve urgent problems of humanity, for instance by curbing population growth and preventing effectively and very soon further humanly induced global warming, such a religion would be morally meritorious. Nevertheless, concerning its belief to the effect that there are many gods, it would be on a par epistemically with the morally somewhat less attractive versions of monotheism.

Take, for example, the variety of Islam elaborated in *The Book of Healing* (*Kitab Ash-Shifa bi ta'rif huquq al-Mustafa*), written by Qadi 'Iyad ibn Musa (1083–1149), one of the seven saints of Marrakech.[59] According to part 4, chapters 1 and 2 of this authoritative book, which many Muslims still read today, all unbelievers should be killed, just like believing Muslims who disparage the Prophet. Morally decent Muslims will reject this imperative. I mention it merely because it illustrates and confirms further the fact that mutually incompatible religions are epistemically on a par. Since there are no well-calibrated epistemic methods of research that will enable us to discover that one of the many mutually contradictory religious doctrines is true, some of those who intend to convince unbelievers of the truth of their theology but fail to do so cannot think of any other solution to the problem of religious diversity than killing the unconverted.

Let us not forget that even during the Enlightenment in Europe, those who openly lacked respect for the Christian faith could receive the death penalty. This is shown by the notorious case of François-Jean Lefebvre de La Barre, for example, who was tortured and beheaded in 1766 after his

---

[59] Quadi 'Iyad ibn Musa (1149).

sentence had been confirmed by the Paris Parliament. Should I apologize to my readers for referring to these cases of religious criminality? I mention them merely in order to stress that an apology for endorsing a religious belief according to which it is morally *good* to do so even if one cannot know that one's belief is *true* may be quite unconvincing.

2

Science and Religion

How are science and religion interrelated? These two cultural domains are of great complexity. In our times they consist of many different instances, that is, multiple scientific disciplines and numerous religious movements or religions, respectively.[1] Furthermore, instances of the scientific domain may be related, or unrelated, to specific aspects of religions in diverse ways. For these reasons, the subject of the present chapter is restricted severely. As in Chapter 1, I adopt the epistemological point of view and wonder to what extent religions and the sciences can, and do, contribute to the human search for truth.

Historians of science will emphasize that religious beliefs have contributed to the quest for truth quite often, because their endorsement motivated scientists to investigate things and sometimes even to formulate specific hypotheses.[2] This holds for quite some founding fathers of the scientific revolution in Europe, from Copernicus and Galileo to Kepler, Descartes, Boyle, and Newton. Our topic is not motivation or inspiration, however, but method. In §1.4, I argued that if we search seriously for truth, we cannot rely legitimately on the primary epistemic sources of religious beliefs, such as revelation experiences, a *sensus divinitatis*, or lifelong religious involvements, because these sources have not been calibrated or validated.

If one defines the scientific enterprise in the broadest sense as the human search for truth by means of well-validated epistemic methods

---

[1] I am using the term 'science' in the very broad sense of the German 'Wissenschaft', so that it includes the social sciences and the humanities.
[2] Cf., for example, Brooke (1991) and (2006).

and sources, which is the definition to be preferred in this context, it follows that science rules out any endorsement of religious beliefs (as defined in §1.2).³ In this specific sense, then, there is a methodological conflict between science and religion.⁴ By definition, scientific claims to truth are claims that can be tested and supported by validated methods of research, and are based upon calibrated primary epistemic sources, whereas there are no such sources and methods that can legitimize religious truth-claims to the effect that a specific god or other supernatural being exists or acts in certain ways.⁵

The thesis that there is this conflict of method between science and religion in their search for truth is confirmed by the historical fact that after the scientific revolution in sixteenth–seventeenth-century Europe, religious considerations, predictions, and explanatory hypotheses have been eliminated gradually from all sciences.⁶ Time and again, religious predictions or explanations of phenomena turned out to be epistemically inferior to non-religious ones, both in terms of empirical testability or confirmation and with regard to their predictive power. For instance, none of the Christian predictions of the so-called End of Times so far has turned out to be correct.⁷ Furthermore, the conviction of early followers of Jesus that He was resurrected physically after his crucifixion can be explained better by cultural factors than by assuming that the resurrection really happened.⁸ In the present chapter I discuss briefly some well-known examples of the removal of religion from science, which confirm the conclusion of the Calibration Argument stated in §1.4.

The fact that this elimination has been a historical and gradual development shows that the separation between science and religion is not just a conventional matter, as some so-called methodological naturalists claim

---

³ That is, beliefs that posit or presuppose the existence of supernatural conscious beings or properties. If religious believers reinterpret these beliefs in a purely symbolical sense, for example, their beliefs do not meet this definition.
⁴ Cf. Philipse (2013a) for an elaborated argument to this effect, contra Plantinga (2011).
⁵ Cf. Barbour (1998) for an overview of many different views of religious believers concerning the relations between science and religion.
⁶ How did modern science come into the world? See Cohen (2012) and Weinberg (2015) for an encompassing historical analysis. Of course, in many ancient traditions of research in mathematics or astronomy, there was no role for religious arguments either.
⁷ There have been innumerable predictions of the end of the world by Christian authorities. For example, in 1284 CE, Pope Innocent III predicted that the world would end 666 years after Islam had arisen, and Martin Luther claimed that the world would end not later than in 1600. Cf. Wikipedia, 'List of dates predicted for apocalyptic events', https://en.wikipedia.org/wiki/List_of_dates_predicted_for_apocalyptic_events.
⁸ Cf. Philipse (2012, 2014), §§10.3–10.5.

today. It is not an issue of a priori principles either, as Immanuel Kant argued at the end of the eighteenth century.[9] The strict separation between science and religion resulted rather from a cultural learning process. The better we managed to calibrate our methods of research, and to develop reliable and well-tested procedures for discovering truths and evaluating hypotheses in any domain whatsoever, the more we realized that all primary sources of religious beliefs are unreliable and cannot be trusted as sources of truth. For example, scientific research has discredited many biblical contentions concerning God's accomplishments, so that biblical claims of this kind cannot be regarded as reliable sources of truth.

Let me start in §2.1 by indicating briefly the scientific progress with regard to the place of the Earth in the universe, from Genesis up to the present. We then move from space to (space-)time (§2.2), and discuss how plausible it is to assume that an omnipotent, omniscient, and infinitely good god would have created the universe in which our Earth is situated by causing the Big Bang. Having explored space and time, I shall examine two more specific examples of scientific progress in which religiously inspired explanations of empirical phenomena have been eliminated by superior and purely secular scientific theories: Laplace versus Newton, and Darwin versus Paley. Generalizing from these illustrious instances I conclude not only that whenever religious believers claim that in fact there is a god, and that this hypothesis might explain some empirical phenomena, they commit the well-known fallacy of God-of-the-gaps. I also contend that if one avoids this fallacy but endorses factual religious beliefs nevertheless, one acts in an epistemically irresponsible manner (§2.3). Moreover, many empirical discoveries made during the last four centuries of scientific progress yield strong arguments against the existence of all gods, including the deities of Judaism, Christianity, and Islam. It is not only the case that 'there is no evidence to favour the God Hypothesis', there also is much empirical evidence against it, if at least this hypothesis is coherent and makes any sense at all (§2.4).[10]

I apologize to readers for focussing on Christianity in the present chapter. This is unavoidable, however, because the scientific revolutions that established science as a continuing and institutionalized cultural enterprise of humanity occurred mainly in Europe during the sixteenth–

---

[9] Cf. Philipse (2012, 2014), chapter 2, for a historical overview of the epistemic status philosophers attributed to factual religious beliefs.
[10] Quote from Dawkins (2006), p. 59.

nineteenth centuries. It is an interesting historical question why these revolutions happened in Europe and not with equal impact in Islamic civilizations or in India, China, or Japan, even though numerous contributions to scientific progress originated in these areas.[11]

The conclusion of the chapter is the following. In our times, no legitimate epistemic grounding of religious beliefs on the basis of their primary sources is possible any more.[12] Even worse, the factual contention that a particular god exists is quite implausible given many aspects of scientific progress. The only way in which religious believers may escape from the methodological conflict between science and religion is to strip their religious beliefs from all factual claims to truth, and to reinterpret these beliefs as purely symbolic in some sense. Stephen Jay Gould advocated such a compatibilist strategy when he argued that science and religion are, or should be, non-overlapping magisteria (the NOMA principle).[13] According to Gould, the religious area of research is restricted to values, whereas matters of fact can be investigated by the sciences only (in the wide sense of the German *Wissenschaften*, and including common sense), that is, by using well-calibrated methods of research.

Many religious believers will reject this elegant solution to the conflict between science and religion, however, because it forbids them to believe that in fact their god(s) exist(s). In Part III, I discuss and evaluate various apologetic strategies developed recently by theists in order to legitimize their religious beliefs within our science-informed cultural context. Atheists repudiate Gould's resolution as well, since they deny that an epistemically legitimate foundation or exploration of human values can have a properly religious dimension.

2.1 THE PLACE OF THE EARTH IN THE UNIVERSE

What is the place of the Earth in the universe? In order to answer this question today, we should begin by disambiguating the word 'place'. It might mean here either the Earth's location or its relative importance

---

[11] Cf. Cohen (2012) and Weinberg (2015) for well-researched answers to this question. The invention of printing played an important role in the history of science in Europe, for example.
[12] Unless, of course, a real miracle would happen, the occurrence of which would be established scientifically. In order to do so, one would have to show that no future scientific explanation of this event will be possible, which is quite a demanding burden of proof.
[13] Gould (1997, 1999, 2002).

given the size of the universe. Although these two meanings of our question were intimately connected originally, they should be distinguished clearly in the light of contemporary cosmology.

If we wonder where in the universe the Earth is located, present-day cosmologists will argue that this question is either trivial or unanswerable, depending on how we interpret the term 'universe'. If we are talking about the observable universe, planet Earth is located at its centre by definition, because the 'observable universe' is defined as the region of the universe that is perceptible to us humans as terrestrial observers.[14] If, however, we are talking about the universe in itself, as it evolved after the Big Bang, there are no reference points with regard to which we can determine the place of the Earth, because the evolving and expanding universe has neither centre nor edge. We can locate the Earth only in specific subdomains of the universe, such as the solar system, the Milky Way galaxy, or the Virgo supercluster. Nevertheless, we might still answer our question in its second sense. The cosmic importance of the Earth and, consequently, of mankind has dwindled drastically during recent progress in cosmology.[15] This aspect of scientific advancement counters the traditional monotheist conviction that divine creation culminated in the genesis of mankind.[16] Let me explain, starting with Genesis.

At the historical period in which the biblical book Genesis originated from earlier Mesopotamian myths, nobody conceived of earthly surfaces on which people were living as parts of a planet, the Earth. According to Genesis 1, God (Elohim) called the dry land he created 'Earth', and separated it from the seas during the third day of creation (Genesis 1:9–10). How there could be 'days' before God produced 'lights in the firmament of the heavens to separate the day from the night' during the fourth day is a puzzle I shall not try to resolve here (1:14). God created these lights, that is, the Sun, the Moon, and the stars, in order 'to give light upon the earth' (1:16–18). Interestingly, God also created light already during the first day of creation by saying 'Let there be light' (1:3). In spite of the many exegetical problems that will bewilder readers of the first

---

[14] In this context, the term 'perceptible' refers to all objects from which electromagnetic radiation had the time to reach the Earth since the beginning of cosmic expansion.
[15] What I mean here by 'the cosmic importance' of the Earth is its size relative to the size of the universe. Similarly, the criterion for the cosmic importance of mankind assumed here is the size of its habitat relative to the size of the universe.
[16] Cf., for example, Psalm 8:5–6: 'Yet thou hast made him [man] little less than God, and dost crown him with glory and honor. Thou hast given him dominion over the works of thy hands; thou hast put all things under his feet', etc.

creation story in Genesis, one thing is clear. Divine creation reached its supreme climax when on the sixth day God made man in his own image. God created man both male and female and gave them dominion over all animals and plants living in the sea, in the air, and upon the earth (1:26).[17] In other words, God created humans in order to be masters of the cosmos, in which they occupied a central position.

Let us stride with big steps through the history of Western Christianity and science in order to summarize what happened to man's self-situating in the universe during and after the scientific revolution. The significance of mankind as marked by its place relative to the size of the universe diminished rapidly. As a consequence, the belief or myth that a god, such as Elohim or God, had created the universe primarily in order to house humanity became ever more implausible. Given our scientific knowledge of the universe today, the claim that such a god exists and has created the universe for us humans in particular is altogether far-fetched.

According to the narrative of Genesis, the cosmos contains a flat disc of earth in its centre, surrounded by waters, an underworld for the dead below, and a firmament 'in the midst of the waters', above which are waters as well (1:6–7). Both during the Hellenistic era and in medieval Europe, this picture of the world was replaced by more precise models of the cosmos invented by Greek philosopher-scientists such as Aristotle and Alexandrian mathematical experts like Claudius Ptolemy. Let me summarize briefly Aristotle's view of the universe as expounded in his treatise *On the Heavens* (Περὶ οὐρανοῦ, *De Caelo*) of about 350 BCE, since Islamic authors such as Averroes and Christian authorities like Thomas Aquinas largely endorsed it. Philosophers and theologians in the West gave up Aristotle's cosmology only after it had been refuted empirically during the scientific revolution.

Aristotle held that the 'ouranos', cosmos, or universe is a spatially finite, spherical, and eternally existing entity, which consists of many layers or spheres. The outermost layer contains the fixed stars and is also called 'ouranos'. Beyond this all-embracing layer, there is nothing whatsoever apart from the divine: no space, time, void, or place. Since Aristotle thought that there can be no void within the universe either, he assumed that all the other moving heavenly bodies we perceive, such as the Sun, Moon, and planets, are fixed in rotating lower and transparent spherical layers. Hence, the visible movements of each of these heavenly bodies had

---

[17] I am quoting from *The New Oxford Annotated Bible* (May and Metzger 1973), in which 'earth' is sometimes printed with a capital ('Earth') and sometimes not.

to be explained mechanically by postulating rotations of several crystalline spheres. The circular movements of the spheres would be perfect and eternal, since heavenly bodies are ungenerated and indestructible.

Inside the most inner layer, the sphere of the Moon, there are no infinite and perfect movements, however. Sublunary entities and phenomena are perishable, and are composed of four elements at most – fire, air, water, and earth – which have their natural places in this order from the Moon downwards to the centre of the spherical universe. Aristotle's doctrine of natural places would explain both that nearly all earth occupies the centre of the universe, on which earth we humans are living, and that things which consist predominantly of one of these elements tend to move to the element's natural place. For example, flames of a fire move upwards, stones that we drop fall down, air bubbles up in water, and so on. Aristotle developed these ideas in great detail and tried to support them by providing empirical evidence.

There are notable differences between Aristotle's earth-centralist cosmology and the allegedly revealed views expressed in Genesis, as Christians interpreted them later on. For example, the universe is eternal according to Aristotle, whereas traditional Christians and Muslims believe that God created the world. Nevertheless, we can understand well why scientifically interested religious authors endorsed Aristotelian cosmology for so many centuries. Both according to Aristotle and to traditional Christianity and Islam, mankind on earth occupies the central and immovable place in a surveyably small universe, so that one could conceive of God as our 'heavenly father'. Indeed, many biblical texts state explicitly that our Earth or world will or can 'never be moved'.[18] Let me now indicate briefly how scientific progress has transformed radically our conception of the universe and the place of man, focussing on two crucial moments only.

From the sixteenth century onwards, astronomers such as Copernicus and Kepler developed various heliocentric views, according to which the Earth is a planet that orbits the Sun. Initially, these views were often presented to the wider public merely as mathematical models, which predicted the perceived positions of stars and planets better than geocentric models. By stressing the traditional distinction between physical and mathematical astronomy one could pretend to protect the Aristotelian-Christian geocentric conception of the universe against empirical

---

[18] Cf. Psalm 93:1, 96:10, 104:5; 1 Chronicles 16:30.

refutations.[19] However, after Galileo started to use a refractor telescope and (claimed to have) observed phenomena such as the phases of Venus and moons orbiting Jupiter, he defended heliocentrism explicitly as a superior physical theory in his *Siderius Nuncius* of 1610.

It is a complex historical question what triggered the Roman Catholic Inquisition in 1616 to have the case investigated by so-called Qualifiers, a committee of ten theologians (cardinals). They concluded both on scientific and on biblical grounds that heliocentrism is 'foolish and absurd in philosophy' and 'formally heretical since it explicitly contradicts in many places the sense of Holy Scripture'.[20] Although perhaps Galileo was allowed to use heliocentrism as a purely mathematical model or calculating device, the Inquisition condemned him finally for heresy on 22 June 1633. The main ground was that in Galileo's *Dialogue Concerning the Two Chief World Systems* of 1632, the character called Simplicio defended geocentrism quite clumsily, whereas much more convincing empirical arguments were put forward for heliocentrism as a physical theory and against the Aristotelian-Christian view of the world. Lifelong house arrest was the moderate price Galileo had to pay for this science-inspired courage.

The cosmic importance of the Earth and, consequently, of mankind has dwindled drastically during more recent progress in cosmology. In Galileo's times, experts in astronomy such as Tycho Brahe still argued that the Earth does not orbit the Sun because no stellar parallax could be discovered. If the Earth orbited the Sun, one should be able to detect a difference between the angles under which one observes a star from different positions, say from opposite sides in the Earth's yearly orbit. Of course, the farther away from Earth a perceived star is located, the smaller this difference of angle will be. When in 1838 Friedrich Bessel measured a parallax for the first time in astronomical history, for star 61 Cygni, the parallax angle turned out to be much smaller than someone like Tycho Brahe or Galileo could imagine. Indeed, Brahe underestimated drastically the dimensions of the universe and the distances of stars from Earth. As we know now, the star nearest to Earth apart from the Sun is

---

[19] Cf. the editor's preface to the first official edition of Copernicus' *De Revolutionibus Orbium Coelestium* of 1543, and Kuhn (1957), chapter 5, the first two sections.

[20] These English translations are quoted from Wikipedia, Galileo Galilei, 'controversy over heliocentrism', https://en.wikipedia.org/wiki/Galileo_affair. Cf. Finocchiaro (2005), chapter 1, for many historical details concerning the condemnation of Galileo.

Proxima Centauri, a red dwarf, which is situated today about 4.25 light years away from the Sun.

Distances measured in light years far exceed what ordinary humans can imagine. One light-year is about 9.5 trillion kilometres (= 5.88 trillion miles), that is: 9,461,000,000,000 kilometres, which is the distance that light travels in a vacuum during 365.25 days.[21] Let me just remind the reader that light travels from the Sun to the Earth in about 8.32 minutes. How large is our observable universe, measured in light years? In order to stimulate the reader's understanding, let me mention, for example, that the large galaxy cluster that is nearest to our Milky Way, the Virgo cluster, is already about fifty-nine million light years removed from us.

The observable universe is defined as the spherical region of the universe the contents of which can be observed or detected, in principle, from Earth at the present time. Contents at great distance can be 'observable' because, in spite of cosmological expansion, electronic radiation emitted long ago from these contents can still reach us on Earth. In order to indicate the size of our observable universe we might multiply by two the radius of this spherical region of the universe. The radius can be calculated in light years (ly) by multiplying the age of the universe since the Big Bang with an assumed spatial expansion rate of the universe up till now, that is: $13.8 \times 3.315 = 45.7$ billion light years (45.7×10^9 ly). Hence, the diameter of our observable universe today is in the order of 2×45.7 billion light years, that is, 91.4 billion light years. The observable universe contains at least 2 trillion galaxies, while astronomers estimate that there are between 100 billion and 400 billion stars (or solar masses) in our spiral galaxy alone, the Milky Way.

According to various versions of cosmic inflation theory, the present size of the entire universe is much larger than that of the observable universe, although estimates of the former size provided by cosmological experts differ drastically and cannot be confirmed by empirical research. Some experts believe that at present the entire universe is about 250 times larger than the observable universe, whereas others have proposed an impressively higher estimate, such as 6×10^{23} times larger.[22]

However this may be, given what we know today about the size of the observable universe on the basis of recent cosmological discoveries and

---

[21] My apologies to British readers for using the terms 'billion' (1,000,000,000) and 'trillion' (1,000,000,000,000) in American English and not in their traditional English meaning.

[22] Cf. for an accessible overview: *Wikipedia*, 'Observable universe', https://en.wikipedia.org/wiki/Observable_universe.

calculations, the idea that the universe was created by a God-father primarily in order to house humanity has lost its credibility completely. The relative importance of planet Earth and of our solar system compared to the size of the observable universe is much smaller than that of one grain of sand relative to all the sand on Earth.[23] Many other aspects of the universe would be incomprehensible if traditional theism were true. For example, why would God have created spaces of the size cosmologists have discovered recently, such as the so-called Giant Void, which measures about 1.3 billion light years across?

If devout readers reply that we, small-minded humans, cannot fathom God's mental infinity, they should conclude that we cannot attribute legitimately to God any intention to create man either, so that one cannot infer the existence of God from our presence on Earth. Indeed, is it not somewhat hubristic to assume that a perfect god would have created the immense universe in order to house humanity, among other things?

2.2 THE TIME OF MAN AND THE UNIVERSE

As we saw, scientific progress concerning the place of the Earth in the universe debunks drastically the traditional monotheist doctrine that there is a god, called God, who created the world as a home for us humans. This conclusion of §2.1 is supported further when we compare briefly the biblical chronology of man's lineage with results of scientific research concerning the age of the Earth, of mankind, and of the universe. Let me start with biblical chronology.

If one takes narrative biblical texts to be divine revelations, they have to be interpreted literally unless a metaphorical or poetic meaning is clearly intended. This is why many Christians assumed that the world, plants, animals, and mankind were created during six days, as Genesis 1 describes, until scientific progress refuted this assumption.[24] Endorsing it, Christian theologians of the past have attempted to calculate the amount of time that has elapsed since creation on the basis of biblical chronologies of generations from Adam to Abraham (Genesis 5 and 11), adding the estimated period from Abraham to their own epoch. One of

---

[23] Cf. Blatner (2014), who suggests this comparison.
[24] However, on the basis of Psalm 90:4 ('For a thousand years in thy sight are but as yesterday when it is past'), some Christian experts interpreted each biblical day of creation as one thousand years. Cf. Jackson (2006), p. 29.

their motives was undoubtedly that they wanted to learn when the Last Judgement would occur.

It is no wonder that biblical scholars from Theophilus of Antioch (second century CE) until James Ussher (1580–1656 CE) obtained somewhat different results from their calculations, since perplexing problems had to be resolved. Should one take seriously, for example, the claims of Genesis 5 that Adam lived 930 years, Seth 912 years, Enosh 905 years, and so on, and that they got their first sons at ages of 130, 105, and 90 years, respectively?[25] Furthermore, various versions of the Bible present different chronologies, such as the Hebrew Masoretic text or the Septuagint version. Nevertheless, the results of these biblical calculations were taken seriously until well into the eighteenth century, and some Christians still do so today. Many Christian authorities endorsed the conclusion of Archbishop Ussher, published in his *Annales veteris testamenti* of 1650, that divine creation had taken place in October 4004 BCE. The creation date of 4004 BCE was printed in the margins of copies of the King James Bible published in 1701.[26]

Already during the second half of the seventeenth century, however, scientific research in geology seemed to refute Bible-based calculations of the age of the universe. For instance, the discovery of seashell fossils high up on Italian mountainsides inspired Benoît de Maillet (1656–1738) to form the hypothesis that sea levels on Earth had fallen in the past at a rate of about three inches per century because of the evaporation of ocean waters. Given the height of the fossils above sea level, he calculated that the Earth had to be over two billion years old.[27] Although Maillet's hypothesis has turned out to be mistaken, his estimate was in the right order of magnitude. Today, scientists have computed the age of the Earth on the basis of radiometric dating of meteorite material. Many of such dating techniques have been developed and tested since the 1960s. Planet Earth turns out to be approximately 4.54 ± 0.05 billion years old, an estimate that is confirmed by radiometric dating of the oldest known terrestrial and lunar materials, such as small zircon crystals. Of course, there is no such thing

---

[25] According to the Septuagint edition, the ages at which these patriarchs got their first son are 230, 205, and 190, respectively.

[26] It is difficult to prove historically, however, that the decision to do so was based upon Ussher's book. For an overview of biblical chronologies and an analysis of Ussher's result, see Jackson (2006), chapter 2.

[27] Jackson (2006), pp. 64–65.

as the exact age of the Earth, since planet Earth resulted from a process of accretion which lasted some tens of millions of years.

Before the discovery of radioactivity and of solar nuclear fusion, physicists such as William Thomson, the first Baron Kelvin, thought that the age of the Earth had to be calculated by estimating the cooling time of its near-surface to its present temperature, assuming that the Earth had started as a completely molten entity.[28] However, the result of his calculations published in 1862, to the effect that the Earth was between 20 and 400 million years old, seemed to be incompatible with the time that biological evolution would have taken. As Charles Darwin had already argued, the process of random heritable variations and natural selection from the origin of life to the emergence of complex mammals such as man needed much more time. According to present-day biologists, the beginning of life on Earth must have taken place between 4.2 and 3.5 billion years ago. The discovery of radioactivity and the development of radiometric dating techniques resolved the contradiction between calculations of the age of the Earth on the one hand and estimates of the timescale of biological evolution on the other. Since radioactive decay continues to heat the Earth and nuclear fusion continues to heat the Sun, their age cannot be calculated on the basis of cooling time assumptions, as Kelvin believed.

Biblical chronology has been refuted as well by prolific research regarding the evolution of mankind, which involves many scientific disciplines, from physical anthropology and molecular biology to genetics. Numerous fascinating problems have been tackled. For example, why did bipedalism evolve in the hominid family of great apes about seven million years ago? Which fitness-enhancing factors explain the gradual evolution of human brains, which are much larger than the brains of other primates, so that brain growth has to be postnatal in part? Would the human species have originated at all if the population of non-avian dinosaurs on Earth had not been extinguished by the impact of an asteroid approximately sixty-six million years ago? Here, we are interested only in the timescale of human evolution, however. On the basis of many results of empirical research, such as genetics with regard to mutation rates, and the discovery and dating of fossils, experts have calculated that the evolutionary lineages of hominins and of chimpanzees will have split during the Late Miocene, some eight to five million years BCE. The transition from

---

[28] Dalrymple (1994), pp. 14–17.

Homo erectus to *Homo sapiens* occurred much later, between 350,000 and 260,000 years ago. Just as in the case of the place of man in the universe, scientific research on the temporal origin of mankind shows that the biblical account is completely mistaken in this respect, if it is interpreted as a historical record. If so, it is nothing but a primitive product of a pre-scientific culture and not revealed to humanity by an omniscient deity.

Let me finish this section by saying a few words about cosmology. Today, all cosmological experts endorse a version of the so-called Big Bang theory with regard to the development of the universe. Since in 1929 Edwin Hubble concluded from his analysis of galactic red-shifts that the universe is expanding, and after Georges Lemaître suggested in 1931 that an expanding universe might have originated from one extremely high-density spatial point – a 'Cosmic Egg' or 'primeval atom'– empirical evidence for a Big Bang scenario has accumulated. Applying Einstein's theory of general relativity, the model offers a unified explanation of many empirical phenomena, such as the cosmic microwave background radiation that Penzias and Wilson discovered accidentally in 1964 and the large-scale structures of space and the universe, so that it is well confirmed empirically.[29] Based upon many sophisticated measurements of its expansion rate, calculations of the chronology of the universe differ drastically from James Ussher's conclusion that the world has been created in 4004 BCE. Today, cosmologists date the initiating expansion of our universe at around 13.8 billion years ago.

Unsurprisingly, both the original proposal of a Big Bang scenario for the universe and its later empirical confirmations triggered hot-tempered discussions in the philosophy of religion.[30] Should Big Bang theory be interpreted as a scientific confirmation of the Christian creation story, even though their timescales are vastly different? Does the theory imply that our universe has been created out of nothing? However, when Pope Pius XII proclaimed in 1951 that Lemaître's theory on the origin of the universe offered a scientific validation of the Christian creation story, Lemaître disagreed. Although he was a Belgian Catholic priest apart from being a prominent astronomer, he insisted that science and religion had to

---

[29] Cf. Kragh (1999) for an overview, which is somewhat outdated because of the discovery of dark energy.

[30] Cf. Philipse (2012), §§12.6–12.7 for an analysis of arguments proposed by Richard Swinburne and Quentin Smith.

be disconnected.[31] What should we think of the relation between the Big Bang model of the universe and Christian theism if we focus on the temporal dimension?

Let me mention merely two reasons for concluding that if the omniscient, omnipotent, and infinitely good god postulated by traditional Christian theists existed, it is quite unlikely that he would have created the universe we are living in by producing a Big Bang singularity. First, when the earliest stars originated some 150–200 million years after the Big Bang, life as we know it could not have existed in the universe. Heavier chemical elements such as carbon and oxygen did not yet occur, whereas they are essential materials for life. These elements originated when the first generation of stars imploded and they were scattered into space by supernova explosions. As a consequence, only when second- or third-generation star systems came into being about four billion years after the Big Bang could life start to exist on some of their accreted planets. Humans evolved on Earth more than 13.7 billion years after the Big Bang. Surely, however, an omnipotent god as postulated by theism would have created a universe in which life could exist from the very start, if at least creating life was his main intention, as many Christians and other religious believers assume.

A second reason for concluding that our present cosmological knowledge with regard to the Big Bang genesis of the universe makes it very unlikely that God exists and produced the Big Bang is related to recent insights with regard to cosmic expansion. Although Big Bang cosmologists often assumed that the cosmic expansion from the Big Bang onwards would slow down due to gravitational effects, it was discovered in 1998 that in fact the expansion of the universe is accelerating.[32] Most cosmologists assume today that the expansion of the universe has been speeding up during about five billion years, since the universe entered its so-called dark energy-dominated era.[33] According to plausible cosmological models, the universe will go on expanding exponentially with time. Since mass density will decrease over time as well, finally all objects will dissipate away and a cold death will occur, the so-called Big Freeze. This dark state of the universe will never cease. Hence, the fraction of the total time of the universe since the Big Bang during which life is possible

---

[31] Cf. Singh (2010), p. 362.
[32] This has been discovered independently by two research projects: the Supernova Cosmology Project and the High-Z Supernova Search Team.
[33] Frieman et al. (2008).

equals a finite time divided by infinity, that is, it approaches zero. No omnipotent god would create such a weird universe, I assume, if at least this god intended to invent a cosmos mainly in order to enable life to exist. The more we learn about the spatial and temporal dimensions of the universe by studying recent scientific insights, the less plausible becomes the religious belief that in fact there is an almighty god who created this universe.

2.3 FROM LAPLACE TO DARWIN AND BEYOND

In Chapter 1, I argued that if we are aiming at truth, we cannot rely legitimately on the primary sources of religious beliefs, since these sources have not been validated. It follows that if the scientific enterprise in the broadest sense is defined as our human search for truth by means of well-validated epistemic methods and sources, there is a methodological conflict between science and religion. A core thesis of the present chapter is that from the scientific revolution in Europe onwards, expert consensus to the effect that this conflict exists arose only gradually. In other words, religiously inspired explanations of phenomena have been eliminated step by step from the world-views of experts, so that the 'Warfare of Science with Theology in Christendom' has had a long and fascinating history.[34]

Let me mention merely two well-known examples in order to illustrate my thesis of the gradual religious retreat from science: Laplace versus Newton, and Darwin contra Paley.[35] We know today that Isaac Newton (1643–1727) wrote more pages on religion than the *Principia* and *Opticks* contain, taken together. He did not publish most of his religious writings, since he realized that his radical and revolutionary anti-trinitarian views on Christianity would put him at risk.[36] What interests us here is not Newton's theology as such, however, but the role religious explanations still played in his science of nature. Of course, Newton believed like Descartes and Leibniz that the omnipotent Christian god had created the universe. In contradistinction to them, Newton also thought that given the laws of his classical mechanics, some specific

---

[34] Cf. White (1896) for an early, famous, and controversial historical overview. The quote is from his title.

[35] Cf. also Philipse (2012), §10.1.

[36] Most experts hold that Newton rejected the trinitarian view, according to which God is *both* one *and* consists of three persons: the Father, the Son, and the Holy Spirit. Cf. Westfall (1981), pp. 25, 103.

natural phenomena could be explained only with reference to particular Divine interventions.

For example, Newton held that two aspects of our planetary system should be explained by assuming that 'an intelligent Agent', that is, God, had intervened in order to produce them. First, 'blind Fate could never make all the Planets move one and the same way in Orbs concentrick'. This 'wonderful Uniformity in the Planetary System must be allowed the Effect of Choice'.[37] In other words, according to Newton the fact that all planets move around the Sun in the same direction and in concentric orbits cannot have a purely physical explanation. It had to be accounted for by assuming that God installed these orbits. Second, because of the gravitational interactions of planets such as Jupiter and Saturn, 'considerable Irregularities' would be caused in their orbits, 'which will be apt to increase, till this system wants a Reformation'.[38] Newton assumed that God had intervened in the past in order to sustain the stability of the solar system and that this 'intelligent Agent' would have to do so in the future as well.

Only twenty-five years after Newton had published these remarks in Query 31 of his *Opticks*, Immanuel Kant produced his *Allgemeine Naturgeschichte und Theorie des Himmels* (1755), in which he argued that the existing galaxies and our solar system originated from contracting nebulas.[39] This hypothesis would explain the unidirectional orbits of the planets around the Sun. Forty-one years later, the prominent French astronomer and mathematician Pierre-Simon de Laplace (1749–1827) provided purely physical explanations of both the unidirectional orbits of the planets and the relative stability of the solar system. In book 5 of his *Exposition du système du monde*, of which he published five editions from 1796 to 1824, he suggested like Kant that the unidirectional rotations of planets around the Sun could be explained by what is now called the Kant–Laplace nebular hypothesis. When the atmosphere of what became the Sun had contracted because of gravity, planets were formed by condensations in the plane of the solar equator. The contraction caused a rotation of the atmosphere so that all produced planets rotate around the Sun in the same direction.[40]

Furthermore, Laplace demonstrated by careful recalculations published in technical papers that variations in planetary orbits caused by gravitational attraction between existing planets such as Jupiter and

---

[37] Newton (1730), query 31, p. 402.   [38] Newton (1730), query 31, p. 402.
[39] Kant (1755).   [40] Cf. Gillespie (1997), pp. 173–175 for details.

Saturn do not threaten the stability of the solar system, because these variations remain within restricted limits. Hence, no divine intervention was needed in order to preserve the existing solar system in a long-term equilibrium.[41] According to a well-known anecdote about Laplace and his former pupil Napoleon, the latter wanted to read a volume of Laplace's *Celestial Mechanics* (*Traité de mécanique céleste*) and asked Laplace during a meeting in 1802: 'Monsieur Laplace, où est Dieu dans votre système?' (Mr Laplace, where is God in your system?). Laplace would have answered: 'Sire, je n'ai pas besoin de cette hypothèse' (Your Majesty, I do not need this hypothesis). Historians still debate whether Laplace was an atheist or rather a deist of some blend. Clearly, however, he publicly professed that within physics and astronomy there was no role whatsoever for a supreme being.

In the beginning of the nineteenth century, prominent and philosophically informed Christian apologists such as William Paley (1743–1805) concluded that astronomy 'is *not* the best medium through which to prove the agency of an intelligent Creator'.[42] For this reason, Paley focused mainly on plants and animals in his celebrated book *Natural Theology*, first published in 1802. He used the well-known watchmaker analogy many times in order to argue that the functional complexity of living beings and their parts, such as the eye, could be explained only by assuming that God had created the first instances of each species. Charles Darwin was an admirer of Paley from his student time onwards, when he had to read Paley's *Evidences of Christianity* for an examination in Cambridge. As one biography of Darwin declares: 'Paley's "logic" so delighted Charles that he learnt it by heart'.[43] It is no wonder, then, that in *The Origin of Species* of 1859, Darwin felt the need to refute repeatedly theories of special creation when he argued for his evolutionary biology, according to which the origins and ramifications of biological species are explained by the mechanisms of genetic variation and natural (including sexual) selection. With regard to the evolution of eyes, for example, Darwin wrote: 'If it could be demonstrated that any complex organ existed, which could not possibly have been formed by numerous

---

[41] Cf. Hahn (2005), pp. 78–80.
[42] Paley (1802), p. 199 (Paley's italics). However, in chapter 22 of his book, Paley still endorses Newton's claims that God is needed both to form and to uphold planetary systems.
[43] Desmond and Moore (1992), p. 78.

successive, slight modifications, my theory would absolutely break down. But I can find out no such case.'[44]

Darwin's own intellectual development is a striking illustration of my thesis that scientific progress eliminated religious beliefs only gradually. Whereas at first Darwin aimed at becoming a clergyman, endorsing Paley's views as a Cambridge student, his many biological discoveries during the voyage on the *Beagle* raised doubts already with regard to the claim that biological species are fixed. Furthermore, the discovery of religious diversity during this trip made him wonder whether not all religious convictions are equally (in)valid.[45] Although in *The Origin of Species* Darwin radically rejected species creationism à la Paley, he ends this book nevertheless by asserting that a 'Creator' originally breathed powers of life 'into a few forms or into one'.[46]

Later on, Darwin probably became agnostic and held that there is no reliable evidence for any religious belief. He was also impressed by the amount of natural evil implied by his well-confirmed evolutionary theory. If a process of blind mutations and natural selection has produced the diversity of species existing today, suffering, death, and extinction have been crucial to the gradual genesis of animal species and of man. Does this not exclude an omnipotent, omniscient, and perfectly good god's creating mankind by means of an evolutionary process? Clearly, Darwin's theory of evolution 'gave the problem of evil a new twist'.[47] It implies a novel and powerful argument from 'natural' evil against theism, as Darwin realized. Admittedly, 'Evolutionary theory does not prove that there is no God', since arguments from evolution against theism might be counterbalanced by arguments supporting theism. It does not follow, however, that 'like other scientific theories, it is neutral on this question', since the theory of evolution implies this new argument from natural evil against theism.[48]

In *The Descent of Man*, published in 1871, Darwin does not deny explicitly the existence of God.[49] Nevertheless, its general summary rejects the popular idea that we humans have an instinctive belief in God, which should be explained by assuming that God exists and has implanted the creed in our minds. Let me quote Darwin's refutation of this argument for theism from universal religious belief:

---

[44] Darwin (1859), p. 154.   [45] Darwin (2002), pp. 49–55.   [46] Darwin (1859), p. 396.
[47] Sober (2008), p. 186.   [48] The quotes are from Sober (2008), pp. 187–188.
[49] Historians assume that Darwin did not do so because he did not want to endanger his marriage with his very devout spouse. Cf. Darwin (2002), pp. xxi–xxii.

I am aware that the assumed instinctive belief in God has been used by many persons as an argument for His existence. But this is a rash argument, as we should thus be compelled to believe in the existence of many cruel and malignant spirits, only a little more powerful than man; for the belief in them is far more general than in a beneficent Deity. The idea of a universal and beneficent Creator does not seem to arise in the mind of man, until he has been elevated by long-continued culture.[50]

Darwin not only anticipated arguments against theism in this passage that have been developed in detail today, such as the arguments from religious diversity, from divine hiddenness, or from locality (cf. §2.4). He also seems to endorse a purely naturalist explanation for the human belief in God when he indicates the positive social functions which such a belief may have. For example, Darwin suggests that 'the conviction of the existence of an all-seeing Deity has had a potent influence on the advance of morality', because such a belief stimulates moral behaviour even when no other members of one's group are present.[51] Since in *The Descent of Man* Darwin was concerned 'only with truth as far as our reason permits us to discover it', he abstained from endorsing any religious belief in this breathtaking book.[52] Hence, in 1871 Darwin completed the elimination of religion from biology.

After Darwin's hypothesis of blending had been corrected in the early twentieth century by the rediscovery of Gregor Mendel's rules of inheritance, and the theory of evolution was integrated with mathematical population genetics, the so-called modern evolutionary synthesis developed ever more quickly.[53] Mathematical modelling and derivations of testable predictions transformed the theory of natural selection into a prominent scientific research programme. Many scientific advancements have improved the modern evolutionary synthesis in the twenty-first century as well, such as progress in microbiology and genomics. As in most paradigm cases of scientific progress, the increase of scientific knowledge in evolutionary biology raises ever more interesting questions to be answered and problems to be solved. However, no expert in this field has argued that we should undo the elimination of religion from biology in order to solve these problems.

One might object that one crucial biological problem raised by Darwin has not been solved yet, and that a theological solution would be acceptable: the problem of the origin of life on Earth. Biologists agree that all life

---

[50] Darwin (1871), p. 682.   [51] Darwin (1871), p. 682.   [52] Darwin (1871), p. 689.
[53] Cf. Fisher (1918); Huxley (1942).

existing today on Earth evolved by common descent from a single primitive form, as Darwin had already suggested, and has been confirmed by recent DNA sequencing. This original form of life probably started to develop between 4.2 and 3.5 billion years ago, when organic molecules arose from inorganic matter or perhaps when it arrived on Earth in meteorites from elsewhere. Many scientific hypotheses are proposed with regard to the origin of life on Earth, and the actual empirical evidence is still insufficient for deciding which hypothesis is most likely to be true. Would it not be epistemically legitimate, then, to consider as one possible explanation the theistic hypothesis that God created the most primitive form of life on Earth, thereby starting evolutionary history? Are DNA molecules not so complex that the assumption of a divine intervention is plausible?[54]

Critics of such an argument reply that it contains the so-called God-of-the-gaps fallacy, that is, a specific version of an argument from ignorance. As the evangelist Rev. Prof. Henry Drummond urged already in his Lowell Lectures at Boston in 1893, one should not argue for the truth of theism on the basis of empirical phenomena which science has not yet explained. Such so-called God-of-the-gaps arguments for theism run the risk that they will be eliminated by future scientific progress. The gradual removal of religious explanations from science has been illustrated by the two examples in this section.[55]

Of course, one should wonder why, exactly, scientific progress eliminated religious explanations of empirical phenomena again and again. As I argued in §1.4 on the Calibration Argument, the answer is that religious explanations and beliefs (as defined in §1.2) do not rely on well-validated methods of discovery. 'Science' in its broadest sense should be defined as the search for truth by means of well-validated methods of investigation. Since religious beliefs do not rely on research that employs such methods, as researchers realized gradually during the history of science, there is an epistemic conflict between science and religion. Hence, epistemically conscientious and well-informed human beings should not endorse as true any religious belief, if at least they take seriously their search for truth. Accordingly, they should reject a religious explanation of the origin of biological evolution on Earth, for instance.

It follows that prominent Christian scientists such as Francis Collins (who led the Human Genome Project) are facing a difficult dilemma,

---

[54] Cf., for example, Gingerich (2006), pp. 43–80 and Behe (2007).
[55] Drummond (1896), chapter 10, p. 426.

because they intend to combine their scientific attitude with a religious conviction. *Either* they are aiming at truth with regard to their religious beliefs, such as the belief that God exists and created the cosmos, *or* they are not aiming at truth. If they aim at truth, they should rely on well-validated methods of research or discovery with regard to their religious convictions. However, the history of science and religion confirms the conclusion of Chapter 1 that there are no well-validated methods of religious research or reliable sources of religious truth. If, however, these scientists do not aim at truth with regard to their religious beliefs, there is no reason whatsoever for taking these beliefs seriously from the epistemic point of view. Let us ask Francis Collins which horn of this dilemma he prefers when he claims that the truth of his 'BioLogos' version of Christianity can be tested only by a 'spiritual logic of the heart, the mind, and the soul'.[56] Does he really think that this 'logic' is truth-conducive and can be distinguished somehow from wishful thinking?

2.4 EMPIRICAL EVIDENCE AGAINST THEISM

Religiously committed readers will assume that the gradual elimination of religion from science does not amount to a refutation of theism, the belief in God. They may admit that there are neither any validated methods of discovery with regard to religious convictions nor any reliable theism-based predictions, and that, as a consequence, we should strictly separate science and religion. Even so, they might object, wouldn't it be blasphemous to think that we have to detect God's existence by means of humanly invented methods of research? Can religious believers not claim legitimately that their religious creed is warranted because God implanted it in their minds by an act of divine grace, for example?

As we saw in §1.1, however, the Epistemological Argument from Cultural Contingency suggests that we cannot legitimately endorse as true *any* religious belief to the effect that there is a god. Should we then become agnostic with regard to the existence of all gods, including God, and admit that we simply don't know whether they do exist or not, if at least the description of such a god makes sense? Monotheists might object that belief in gods such as Apollo, Varuna, Woden, or Wyrd should be eliminated from our world-view, because the explanatory functions of these gods have been overtaken by scientific research. Hence, with regard

---

[56] Collins (2006), chapter 10.

to these gods we should not be agnostic but rather endorse atheism. Many monotheists hold, nonetheless, that the elimination from science of their own god, called Elohim, Yahweh, Allah, or God, does not amount to a refutation of theism. The strict separation of science and religion would rather have the advantage for monotheists that science is completely neutral with regard to the existence of God. From the scientific point of view there would be no legitimate empirical arguments either *pro* or *contra* theism.

As we have seen in §§2.1–2.3, however, this thesis of the neutrality of science with regard to theism is untenable. Scientific progress has yielded many empirical arguments against theism, that is, against the religious belief that an omniscient, omnipotent, and perfectly good god exists, and created the universe in order to house humanity. If we assume that the notion of God as defined makes sense at all, and add up these arguments, we should conclude that God's existence is improbable indeed, unless one can counterbalance them with convincing arguments in favour of theism.[57] Let me finish the present chapter by summarizing briefly some of the many empirical arguments against theism that result from scientific progress. Apart from such empirical reasons for rejecting theism, there are purely logical ones as well, as I indicate at the end of this section.

In §2.1 we saw that present scientific knowledge about the spatial size of the universe already refutes the religious conviction that God created the world primarily in order to house mankind on Earth. Given the diameter of our observable universe – today more than 91.4 billion light years – the cosmic importance of planet Earth has been reduced nearly to nil. Many other spatial aspects of the universe count against the hypothesis of theistic creation, such as the existence of the Giant Void. The size of the universe is also relevant in another respect. It is sometimes argued that the spontaneous origin of life on Earth is extremely improbable. Hence, we should assume that God created the first DNA molecules. This conclusion does not follow, however, if one takes into account the number of planets in the universe. Suppose that the spontaneous origin of life on a planet is extremely improbable indeed, so that the odds are 1 to 100 billion that life starts on a planet. Since there are at least 100 billion galaxies in the universe, and if on average each galaxy contains 100 billion

---

[57] Cf. Chapter 6 for a critical evaluation of such an apologetic argumentative strategy.

planets, which is not implausible, life would start nevertheless at least on 100 billion planets. It is no accident that we are living on such a planet.[58]

Scientific information about the timescale of our universe and of life yields further arguments against theism, as we noticed in §2.2. If God had created the universe in order to house man, being omnipotent and omniscient He would not have created a world that would last well over 13.7 billion years before mankind evolved. Furthermore, the recent cosmological predictions with regard to a heat death or 'Big Freeze' of the universe also amount to a strong argument against the hypothesis that God created our universe. Since this dark state of the universe will last infinitely long, the fraction of the total time of the universe in which life can occur approaches zero. God as defined would never have created such a world. It follows again that God does not exist. Finally, we saw in §2.3 that the theory of evolution implies a new and convincing argument from natural evil against theism.

Progress in other scientific disciplines has yielded many further empirical arguments against the assumption that God exists. For example, the god of theism is defined as a bodiless spirit with supreme mental capacities such as being omniscient and perfectly good. Quickly progressing research in the neurosciences shows, however, that all mental powers and performances depend on structures and the functioning of brains. As a consequence, it is impossible, or at least very improbable, that a bodiless spirit such as God exists, if this claim makes any sense at all. It would be an unconvincing ad hoc reply to answer that the dependence of mental functions on the brain holds only for the world God created.[59]

Other examples of empirical arguments against theism rely on anthropological and historical research. During his voyage on the *Beagle*, Darwin observed that the Christian god was unknown among South American tribes. Of course, Columbus had discovered already around 1500 that native inhabitants of the Americas were ignorant of the Christian God. As a consequence, European colonial empires staged conversion policies, which often were exceedingly cruel. Furthermore, archaeological and historical investigations have revealed that all ancient religions were polytheistic, such as early Hindu faiths, the Minoan civilization on Crete, or Ancient Egyptian beliefs. Although one Egyptian pharaoh, Amenhotep IV or Akhenaten, established a version of

---

[58] Cf. Dawkins (2006), p. 138, for a similar argument. As I noticed in §2.1, the observable universe already contains at least two trillion galaxies.
[59] Cf. Philipse (2012), §§ 11.5–11.10 for further discussion.

monotheism around 1351 BCE, his successors abolished it (cf. §3.1). It follows that if He exists, God was hiding himself from many human beings, and that He remained completely hidden from humanity for a very long period. Even biblical authors complained that 'thou art a God who hidest thyself' (Isaiah 45:15). Since God is conceived as a good father for all humans, and good fathers would never hide themselves from their children, it follows that God does not exist.[60]

A special version of this 'Argument from Divine Hiddenness' has been called the 'Argument from Locality', or the 'Argument from the Demographics of Nonbelief'. Since according to theism God is eternal and omnipresent, one would expect that he would reveal himself everywhere on Earth, to all human beings and cultures. However, according to the monotheist religions of Judaism, Christianity, and Islam, God revealed himself only locally. This limited locality of alleged divine revelations also amounts to strong empirical evidence against the truth of theism, since God would be blatantly unfair if he revealed himself to a subset of humans only.[61] Even worse, according to the Old Testament, God seems to be a tribal deity of the Jews who orders his people to 'utterly destroy' all the males of rival tribes because they worship other gods and to take the women, children, and cattle of these tribes 'as booty for yourselves' (Deuteronomy 20:10–18). As we shall see in Chapter 3, these and other disconcerting texts can be explained very well from a purely secular and scientific perspective. They would be an enigma, however, if one assumes that theism is true and that biblical books are divinely inspired, so that God revealed himself in misleading and deeply immoral manners, if he revealed himself at all.

In this chapter, I argued that during the last four centuries, religious explanations have been eliminated gradually from the sciences in the broadest sense of the term, including the humanities. This has happened in all scientific disciplines because researchers realized ever more sharply that there are neither any reliable sources of truth for religious beliefs nor well-calibrated methods of religious research and discovery. The resulting separation of science from religion does not imply, however, that all scientific results are religiously neutral. On the contrary, many empirical discoveries yield convincing arguments against the truth of theism and of other religious beliefs, as I indicated succinctly in this section.

---

[60] Cf. Schellenberg (2006, 2015), for detailed versions of the 'argument from divine hiddenness'.
[61] Cf. Maitzen (2006).

Even worse for religious believers, the progressive elimination of religion from science amounts to empirical evidence against theism as well. If the omnipotent god of theism existed and had created the universe, it would be plausible to expect that scientific progress would reveal ever more indications of His divine presence and activities. In other words, if theism were true, scientific progress would probably increasingly yield empirical confirmations of theism, and theism would be included in science rather than eliminated from science. As a consequence, the elimination of religion from science during scientific progress amounts to yet another argument against the truth of theism at a meta-level.

Finally, one should wonder from a semantic and logical point of view whether theism makes any sense. As has been pointed out already, the traditional definitions of God in terms of omnipotence and omniscience imply various so-called paradoxes. The best-known paradox of omnipotence arises when one wonders whether an omnipotent God would be able to create something He cannot destroy. Both the affirmative and the negative answers imply that there is something, defined consistently, that God cannot do, so that He is not omnipotent. A popular version of this paradox is raised by the question as to whether God can create a stone he cannot lift or cause to rise.[62] If He can create it, He cannot lift it, so that He is not omnipotent, but if He cannot create it, He is not omnipotent either. Since the predicates 'omnipotent' and 'omniscient' imply such paradoxes, nothing can be defined consistently in terms of these predicates unless their omni-domains are restricted.[63]

Given these arguments, we may conclude provisionally that theism either does not make conceptual sense as a claim to truth, or that it is false if it can be defined consistently, as are all other religious beliefs to the effect that specific gods exist.[64] However, if each religious belief to the effect that god(s) exist(s) is either incoherent or false, or at least holding it does not result from a reliable epistemic source, how should we explain the fact that so many human beings endorse religious beliefs? This explanatory question is the topic of Part II.

---

[62] Cf. Howson (2011), pp. 45–46.
[63] Cf. Swinburne (1993), pp. 157–166; (2016), pp. 166–168, for a problematic solution to this paradox.
[64] In Part III, sophisticated apologetic strategies will be evaluated.

PART II

THE EVOLUTION OF RELIGION AND ETHICS

3

Religions

Origins and Evolution

Part I was devoted to religious epistemology. Are there any reliable primary sources of truth for beliefs to the effect that a deity, angel, ghost, spirit, or devil exists? I argued in Chapter 1 that there are no such epistemic sources. Since scientists became ever more sharply aware of this fact, and because pious predictions turned out to be false many times, religious beliefs have been eliminated gradually from the scientific enterprise defined broadly, that is, as the human search for truth by means of well-validated methods of research. The resulting separation between science and religion does not imply, however, that science is religiously neutral. On the contrary, there are many convincing science-based arguments to the effect that God (as defined by theism) does not exist, as I indicated in §2.4. The same holds for the innumerable other divinities humans have conceived of.

Let us acknowledge, then, that in fact there are neither any gods nor other supernatural beings, such as angels, devils, or spirits and souls of the deceased. In consequence, all human beliefs to the effect that such a supernatural being exists are illusory. If so, it is an intriguing question what explains the widespread occurrence of religious convictions. According to an investigation of the global religious landscape on Earth conducted by the Pew Research Center, 84 per cent of humanity was religiously affiliated in 2010.[1] Since on average religious believers have more children than unbelievers and educate them religiously, a later investigation of the Pew Research Center published in 2017 predicts that

---

[1] Pew Research Center (2012).

in 2060 the percentage of religiously affiliated humans on Earth will have risen to 87.5 per cent.[2] It is plausible to assume that most religious believers endorse the idea that the supernatural being(s) of their religion do(es) exist in fact. How can we account for this surprising worldwide spread of false beliefs?

Although the last sentence may sound as if it raises a simple question, the issues involved are complex, and the bulk of the relevant scholarly and scientific literature is immense. Accepting religious beliefs and publicly displaying religious commitments may have many functions, both at the individual level and at the group or societal level. Furthermore, religions in a broad sociological sense are complicated cultural institutions, of which religious creeds are merely one aspect among many.[3] It is no wonder, then, that there is a great diversity of empirical disciplines in which religious phenomena are studied, like archaeology, history, cultural anthropology, psychology, brain sciences, sociology, evolutionary biology, and recently developed subdisciplines such as the so-called cognitive science of religion.[4] My focus in this chapter is on two central questions only.

As we shall conclude from the overview of religious (pre)history in §3.1, it is plausible to assume that everywhere on Earth the earliest religions were animist or polytheist, in the sense that adherents believed in the existence of many gods and other supernatural beings.[5] Gradual transitions from polytheistic religions to monotheisms occurred in various cultures but not universally. If so, how should we explain the origin of polytheist or animist beliefs, given the fact that they are all false? What are the mental and social functions of these convictions? Various answers to this first and complex core question are discussed in §3.2. Furthermore, what accounts for the transitions from polytheist creeds to monotheisms? This is the second main question of this chapter, to which §3.3 is devoted.

Both of these questions were originally raised a long time ago, and various answers have been provided. Many philosophers will have read David Hume's classic *The Natural History of Religion*, which was first published in 1757. Since Hume's times the empirical sciences of religion

---

[2] Pew Research Center (2017).
[3] It does not follow from the cultural complexity of religions, however, that it would be 'pointless to evaluate religions as though they offer objective truth claims', as Richard Sosis and Jordan Kiper contend (Bergmann and Kain (2014), p. 257), because many religious believers endorse such claims to truth.
[4] Cf. Watts and Turner (2014) for an overview of cognitive sciences of religion. Cf. also Eyghen et al. (2018).
[5] Even Christian authors, such as Karen Armstrong (1994), have endorsed this account.

have made some progress, so that we may have to update his answers. Let me stress again that although the two core questions of this chapter are empirical and explanatory, it depends on the results of the philosophical Part I which answers to these questions will be correct.

For example, if it is plausible to assume that divinities such as Aphrodite or Apollo really exist(ed) and congregated with ancient Greeks, the beliefs of the latter concerning the former may be explained with reference to reliable perceptual experiences that acquainted them with these gods, and which were expressed in works of art. However, if it is very unlikely that such gods exist(ed), a different explanation of the relevant religious beliefs will be appropriate. Clearly, then, the empirical sciences of religion should rely on the upshot of philosophical arguments about the existence of gods, as spelled out in Part I. They cannot be 'neutral' with regard to the issue whether these gods exist in fact, although some empirical experts tend to pretend that they can be and are.[6]

3.1 RELIGIOUS (PRE)HISTORY

It is customary to distinguish between the prehistory and the history of religions, using as a criterion the invention of writing. Since writing developed gradually at different times in various cultural regions on Earth, the transition from prehistory to history should be dated differently as well, depending on the region in which it occurred. For example, in Mesopotamia and in Egypt writing developed some 5,200 years ago, whereas in Mesoamerica it occurred only around 300 BCE.

If we want to speculate about the origins of the oldest religious beliefs in prehistory, we may rely on two types of empirical evidence. First, we might investigate the earliest burial sites and rock or cave paintings in order to discover whether they contain any indications of particular religious convictions. For example, Philip Lieberman concluded from anthropological and archaeological research concerning a Neanderthal burial site in Croatia, which probably dates from approximately 40,000 BCE, that cultures of the Middle Palaeolithic or Middle Stone Age may have endorsed beliefs in a rebirth and afterlife of ancestors.[7] With regard to more recent

---

[6] Cf., for example, Scott Atran (2002), p. ix: 'I do not intend to refute such nonscientific explanations of religion, nor do I pretend that they are [...] intellectually unjustified'.
[7] The so-called Krapina site was discovered in 1899. Cf. Philip Lieberman (1991). Cf. also Devièse et al. (2017) on the dating of the Vindija Cave. According to some sources, the Krapina remains date to about 130,000 years ago (Cf. www.britannica.com/topic/Krapina-remains).

burial sites, this conclusion is confirmed by the fact that many ancient graves entombed food and other gifts to the dead. Second, some scholars have assumed that the earliest religions on Earth may have resembled those of hunter-gatherers living today, such as Australian Aboriginals for example, many of whom still believe in a number of distinct deities.

Of course, each of these two types of empirical evidence may be regarded as deeply problematic. Prehistoric graves and paintings do not contain texts referring to gods or other supernatural beings, so that we 'can only guess at the ideas and rituals that underpinned these great artistic endeavours'. For example, do the Palaeolithic paintings of bison, deer, and horses in the Lascaux Cave represent the surviving spirits of these animals, which were hunted for food? Furthermore, during the more than fifty thousand years that Aboriginal communities have lived in Australia, their religious beliefs may have changed numerous times. After European explorers discovered Australia from 1606 CE onwards, missionaries converted many Aboriginals to Christianity.[8] It follows that with regard to prehistoric periods, 'questions about the origin of religion are guesswork', at least to some extent.[9] Nevertheless, it is plausible to conjecture on the basis of these two types of evidence that all early religious beliefs of human groups were polytheistic in the sense that each group or tribe endorsed the existence of many different gods, spirits, or other supernatural beings.[10] When gods were distinguished somehow from other supernatural subjects such as spirits of the dead, each of these prehistoric cultures was probably polytheistic in the stricter sense as well.[11]

If we move from religious prehistory to the history of religions, this hypothesis is confirmed by the fact that each of the earliest documented religious beliefs was polytheistic.[12] The oldest surviving religious texts,

---

[8] As far as we know, the Dutch navigator Willem Janszoon was the first European who landed in Australia, in 1606. Originally, the Australian continent was called New Holland.
[9] Both quotes in this paragraph are from Smart (1998), p. 35.
[10] Of course, the prehistorical primacy of animism or polytheism is denied sometimes by Jewish, Christian, and Islamic scholars, whose scholarship is influenced by their religious beliefs.
[11] In some languages, such as Chinese, there is no word that is clearly equivalent to 'god' or 'deus'.
[12] In what follows I shall employ terms such as 'polytheism' and 'monotheism' with reference to beliefs in the existence of god(s) only, abstracting from beliefs in other supernatural beings. In this sense, a 'monotheist' may endorse beliefs in many supernatural beings apart from one god, such as devils, spirits of the deceased, or angels. How god (s) is (are) distinguished from other supernatural beings will depend on the particular religious creed, if it contains such a distinction at all.

carved on walls and sarcophagi of the Saqqara pyramids in Egypt around 2400 BCE, mention various gods, such as the deity Osiris, and are meant to guide deceased pharaohs and their queens to an afterlife. According to the Old Babylonian version of the Epic of Gilgamesh, which dates back to the eighteenth century BCE, there are many gods as well, such as Shamash, who supports Gilgamesh. Let me also refer to the Minoan civilization on Crete, which flourished from around 2500 BCE onwards until volcanic eruptions and Mycenaean conquests destroyed it in about 1400 BCE. Although its language written on clay tablets (Linear A) still remains undeciphered, cultural historians have concluded from seal impressions and other depictions that the Minoans mainly worshipped some female goddesses, such as a mother goddess of fertility and a distaff divinity of animals.

The hypothesis of the historical priority of polytheisms is confirmed further by ancient Greek sources, such as the *Iliad* and *Odyssey*, or Hesiod's *Theogony*. After the Roman Republic conquered Greece around 146 BCE, the many Roman gods were identified with traditional Greek deities: Jupiter amalgamated with Zeus, Juno with Hera, Neptune with Poseidon, Venus with Aphrodite, and so on. The historical priority of polytheism holds for Hinduism too, since early Vedic texts such as the Rigveda (1500–1200 BCE) glorify many gods, although some of its hymns may also suggest either atheism or the idea that all gods and human souls or selves (*Atman*) are ultimately identical. When writing emerged in ancient China around 1250 BCE, sources such as Shang dynasty oracle texts reveal beliefs in a pantheon of more than 200 divinities, presided by king-god Shangti.[13]

Although in the sixteenth century the Spanish conquerors of the Inca Empire burned all written records the Incas kept, it is clear from many sources such as iconography on pottery and surviving legends that the peoples of the Inca realm worshipped many different gods as well. Germanic peoples were polytheistic until Christians converted them from late antiquity onwards, and there are many traces of polytheism in the Old Testament. According to Psalm 89:6–7, for example, the Lord (Yahweh) is 'a God (El) feared in the council of the holy ones', and in Exodus 18:11, Jethro claims to know 'that the Lord (Yahweh) is greater than all other gods (elohim)'. These and many further pieces of historical evidence confirm what David Hume wrote in the first chapter of his

---

[13] Cf. Eno (2008).

Natural History of Religion (1757): 'As far as writing or history reaches, mankind, in antient times, appear universally to have been polytheists'.[14]

Historians of religion who study the transitions from polytheisms to monotheist convictions distinguish several varieties, or rather precursors, of the latter. In the strict sense, monotheism is the belief that only one god exists.[15] Religious systems according to which one's own group of believers worships one god, whereas it is accepted that different groups each worship other gods with similar validity, are called 'henotheisms' (ἑνός θεός, one god). Sometimes the term 'monolatry' (μόνος λατρεία, one worship) is used as well, which designates religious beliefs to the effect that many gods exist although it is legitimate to worship one of them only.[16] Let us now wonder when the earliest historical transitions from polytheisms to henotheism, monolatry, and monotheism occurred.

In his notorious book *Der Mann Moses und die monotheistische Religion* (1939), Sigmund Freud classified the theological revolution brought about in 1344/1342 BCE by the Egyptian pharaoh Amenhotep IV as monotheist.[17] Today, the Atenism this pharaoh propagated is mostly called monolatry. When Amenhotep changed his name to Akhenaten (which means 'agreeable to Aten'), and a few years later decided that the solar deity Aten was the only god of Egypt, he did not deny explicitly the existence of other gods. Some scholars still celebrate Atenism as the earliest recorded version of monotheism in history. We should be somewhat reluctant in this respect, however, not only because Atenism has to be classified as a version of monolatry but also since it survived merely for about twenty years. After Akhenaten's death traditional Egyptian polytheism was restored, and his successors destroyed the new capital he had built.

Similar reluctance to apply the term 'monotheism' may be legitimate with regard to Zoroastrianism, which has also been glorified as the first instance of monotheism in history. The prophet Zarathustra or Zoroaster probably lived at some period during the second millennium BCE and

---

[14] Hume (1757), p. 26.
[15] Of course, most traditional monotheist theologies distinguish between their only god and many other supernatural beings, such as spirits, angels, a devil, etc., the existence of which is often endorsed as well.
[16] Unfortunately, terms such as 'henotheism' and 'monolatry' are defined in various ways. For example, 'henotheism' has also been defined as 'the belief in *one* god over and above *other* gods that exist' (in the entry 'Monotheism' of the *New World Encyclopedia*).
[17] Freud's book was translated into English immediately, in 1939, as *Moses and Monotheism*.

founded a religious movement that in the sixth century BCE became the dominant religion in ancient Persia. Since Zoroastrianism remained the official religion of Persian empires until the seventh century CE, when Muslims conquered the country, its historical importance cannot be denied. Even today there are Zoroastrians, both in Iran and in India. After the 1979 Iranian revolution, this religion revived to some extent among those who disapproved of the theocratic-republican Shia regime.

Zarathustra is considered to be the author of hymns such as the Gathas and the Yasna Haptanghaiti, written in his native language Old Avestan, which are the main sources with regard to his life and religious beliefs. Whether Zoroastrianism is a monotheist religion in the strict sense has been questioned at least on two grounds. First, its supreme god Ahura Mazda is opposed by the bad or destructive Angra Mainyu or Ahriman, although the latter is interpreted often as a principle and not as a god, which has to be eliminated in the course of time.[18] Furthermore, according to Zoroastrianism there are many Amesha Spentas or holy 'divine sparks'. They are often described as divinities, which would imply that Zoroastrianism is a blend of polytheism. Perhaps it is more plausible, however, to assume that the Amesha Spentas were conceived of as aspects of creation. Some central doctrines of Zoroastrianism may have inspired Judaism, Christianity, and Islam, such as its belief in free will, in heaven, and in hell.

When exactly Judaism developed from polytheistic ancient Semitic religions into monotheism is a difficult historical question about which experts disagree. As indicated already, many passages in the Hebrew Bible rather reveal monolatry, such as Exodus 15, according to which the Lord (YHVH) 'is a man of war' (15:3) who clearly is the strongest and most majestic 'among the gods' (15:11). That the ancestors of tribes we call Jewish were polytheists before becoming monolotrists is shown by some early texts as well, such as Judges 10:6: 'the people of Israel [...] served the Baals and the Ashtaroth, the gods of Syria, the gods of Sidon, the gods of Moab, the gods of the Ammonites, and the gods of the Philistines'. It is plausible to assume, then, that the religious beliefs of the Israelites also developed from polytheism to monotheism via henotheisms and monolatry of various blends. According to many historians, this may have happened during the Babylonian captivity of the sixth and fifth centuries BCE (cf. §3.3).

---

[18] Cf. Boyd et al. (1979).

Similar gradual transitions from poly to monotheisms occurred locally in classical Greece and in some versions of Hinduism, for example. Let me focus on ancient Greece here, since the Hindu history is too complex to be summarized briefly. Greek philosophers such as Xenophanes of Colophon (c. 570–c. 475 BCE) or Aristotle (384–322 BCE) are often classified as monotheists. Whereas this is dubious in Xenophanes' case, whose surviving quotes reveal a belief in one greatest pantheistic god among many other deities, Aristotle argued in book XII of his *Metaphysics* for the existence of one eternal and perfect thinking being, called 'god' (θεός), who is the final (teleological) cause of all movements in the universe.[19] If one does not interpret the 'divine bodies' Aristotle also mentions in book XII as divinities, Aristotle endorsed monotheism in this book.[20] It is no wonder, then, that Aristotle's theology inspired both Islamic philosophers such as Avicenna and Christian thinkers like Thomas Aquinas.

Generalizing from these examples, it is legitimate to confirm David Hume's thesis that all monotheist religions gradually grew out of polytheist or animist ones. As Hume wrote in *The Natural History of Religion*, 'polytheism or idolatry was, and necessarily must have been, the first and most antient religion of mankind'.[21] Let us now focus on the first core question of this chapter and wonder how we can explain most plausibly the origins of polytheist beliefs.

3.2 ORIGINS OF POLYTHEISMS

Why did early humans invent and endorse polytheistic or animist beliefs? Let me start by clarifying this question before discussing some answers. First, as I argued in Chapters 1 and 2, there are no objective epistemic groundings of religious beliefs that a specific supernatural being exists. Furthermore, it is very improbable that in fact there are any supernatural beings whatsoever. Jewish, Christian, and Muslim monotheists will accept these claims with regard to the many gods of polytheisms: they are atheists with regard to these divinities. Hence, they will agree that all polytheistic beliefs to the effect that specific gods exist are false, and that holding them is being subject to illusions. Our first explanatory core question is concerned with the origins of these illusions. How should we

---

[19] *Metaphysics*, XII, 1072b.   [20] *Metaphysics*, XII, 1074a.   [21] Hume (1757), p. 26.

Religions: Origins and Evolution

explain that they arose? We focus on explanations that can be tested empirically in principle by means of well-calibrated methods of research.

Second, many illusory beliefs of human individuals are given up shortly after they originated. For example, when I take subway B at 81st Street in New York in order to go to Washington Square, and discover that my coach stops at 86th Street, it is obvious that I took the train in the wrong direction, and my belief that I got on the right coach has proved wrong. The same thing may happen with beliefs to the effect that a specific supernatural being exists, if these convictions can be disproved easily. Millions of such beliefs occur to individual minds and are abandoned soon afterwards, since the specific expectations they implied were rebutted.[22] Let me focus here on religious beliefs that could not be refuted easily, because they were somehow immunized against rebuttal.[23] Quite often, human groups or tribes endorsed such beliefs after they originated, and publicly acknowledging them fulfilled important social functions. Apart from explaining the origins of religious beliefs, one should also account for the fact that individuals and human groups went on holding them to be true, at least for some time.

Finally, it is not my aim to develop and confirm empirically a new answer to the first core question of this chapter, since I am a philosopher and not an empirical scientist of religion. Let us try merely to evaluate some of the most prominent answers provided by empirical experts on religions from different disciplinary backgrounds, such as psychology, anthropology, evolutionary biology, or the cognitive sciences of religion. How are these answers interrelated? To what extent have they been confirmed empirically? And finally: is there any scientific progress with regard to traditional explanations of the origins and functions of polytheistic beliefs?

In order to answer this last question, we would have to summarize the state of the art in the sciences of religion compared to which we intend to evaluate whether there is any scientific progress, say from the year 1880 CE onwards. Since some authors have provided such a summary, however, I refer readers to their accounts.[24] Let me merely mention at this

---

[22] Cf. Dennett (2006), p. 101: 'Two or three religions come into existence every day, and their typical lifespan is less than a decade. There is no way of knowing how many distinct religions have flourished for a while during the last ten or fifty or a hundred thousand years, but it might even be millions, of which all traces are now lost forever.'

[23] Cf. Barrett (2004), p. 22, on 'minimally counterintuitive concepts'.

[24] Cf., for example, Wilson (2002), chapter 2. For an overview of recent empirical research on the origin and functions of religious intuitions, see McKay and Whitehouse (2015).

point David Hume's explanation of the origin of polytheistic beliefs, as developed in *The Natural History of Religion* of 1757, because in this classic he already raised the two core questions of the present chapter and provided plausible replies.

According to Hume's account, polytheistic beliefs arose because of 'the various and contrary events of human life' such as storms, sunshine, wars, famine, sickness, births, pestilence, and death. These natural events triggered 'incessant hopes and fears, which actuate the human mind'.[25] Polytheist beliefs are not grounded in reason or intellect, Hume argued, but rather in 'the ordinary affections of human life', such as 'the anxious concern for happiness, the dread of future misery, the terror of death, the thirst of revenge, the appetite for food and other necessaries'.[26] How did these affections give rise to polytheist beliefs according to Hume? The core of his answer is that since the natural causes of most events crucial for human life were still unknown, early humans postulated supernatural causes on an anthropomorphic model.

As Hume says, '[t]here is an universal tendency amongst mankind to conceive all beings like themselves'.[27] Therefore, it is '[n]o wonder [...] that mankind, being placed in such an absolute ignorance of causes, and being at the same time so anxious concerning their future fortunes, should immediately acknowledge a dependence on invisible powers, possest of sentiment and intelligence'.[28] In order to account for the 'variety of events', the postulated supernatural beings had to be 'vastly multiplied', so that 'every place is stored with a crowd of local deities'.[29] All these deities are represented 'as intelligent, voluntary agents, like ourselves; only somewhat superior in power and wisdom'.[30] Polytheists, or 'idolaters' as Hume called them, tried to influence their divinities in many different ways in order to change their own destinies. Hume supports this explanation with a wealth of empirical evidence, mainly based upon early Greek and Latin sources from Homer onwards.

If we want to classify Hume's account of polytheist beliefs in modern terms, we might call it both psychological and pluralistic. It is psychological because he focuses on non-rational 'principles of human nature, which enter into religion', and it is pluralistic since many of such principles are indicated, between which there might exist 'a kind of contradiction'. For example, '[o]ur natural terrors present the notion of a devilish and malicious deity: [o]ur propensity to praise leads us to acknowledge an

---

[25] Hume (1757), pp. 30–31.   [26] Hume (1757), p. 32.   [27] Hume (1757), p. 33.
[28] Hume (1757), p. 34.   [29] Hume (1757), p. 35.   [30] Hume (1757), p. 48.

excellent and divine'.[31] Hume does not probe deeply into the social functions of endorsing religious beliefs, although he stresses the 'evident advantage' of polytheisms in that they 'naturally admit the gods of other sects and nations to a share of divinity'. Whereas various polytheisms are mutually compatible, as many Roman conquerors realized, each version of monotheism tends to exclude both polytheisms and rival monotheisms.[32]

Today, there is a wide spectrum of scientific explanations concerning the origin and functions of polytheist beliefs. To what extent is there any intellectual progress compared to Hume's account? One source of this progress might consist in the global theoretical perspective adopted. Nowadays, many experts attempt to explain the origins and functions of polytheist beliefs, and of religions in general, within the conceptual framework of evolutionary theory. Since Darwin's theory of evolution was reconciled with Mendel's theory of genetics during the 1920s, various more recent versions of the 'modern synthesis' have been developed. Furthermore, many mental and social characteristics of humans are explained today within the framework of a 'dual inheritance' theory, that is, by accounts that refer both to genetic and to cultural variation, to heritability or cultural transmission, and to various types of fitness consequences or mechanisms of selection.[33] This cultural evolution of evolutionary theory opens up numerous conceptual possibilities for explaining the origin, spread, and stability of specific religious beliefs. Let us adopt the evolutionary outlook for a moment in order to map the many explanatory options.[34]

From an evolutionary perspective, religions may be considered as complex cultural systems consisting of numerous different traits, both at the individual and at the social level. Although a comprehensive notion of religion is a family resemblance concept, most religions have many features in common, such as rituals, symbols, music, myths, moral convictions, taboos, and commitments to supernatural agents and an afterlife.[35] From a logical point of view, there are various different explanatory options within an evolutionary framework. Let me classify them as follows on the basis of four different types of distinctions.[36]

---

[31] Hume (1757), p. 82.   [32] Hume (1757), p. 59.
[33] Cf., for example, Henrich (2015) and Norenzayan (2013).
[34] Cf. Wilson (2002), p. 45.   [35] Cf. Sosis and Kiper (2014), p. 262.
[36] Cf. Godfrey-Smith (2009) for a more complex classification. With regard to each of the explanatory options I mention, one might distinguish between Tinbergen's Four Whys,

First, we have to distinguish between (A) trait-specific explanations and (B) trait-cluster explanations. Whereas in (A), the origins and evolutionary advantages of one specific trait are accounted for, defendants of (B) with regard to a specific cluster of traits will argue that only if conjoined within this cluster can the relevant traits make sense or be fitness-enhancing. With regard to religions, an A-explanation might focus on the endorsement of one specific religious ritual, social construct, or belief, whereas B-accounts are based upon the conviction that '[r]eligious beliefs emerge from within a cultural system and [...] must be understood within that system', so that a religious belief 'cannot be analyzed independently of the system in which it is embedded'.[37] Explanatory particularism (A) and explanatory holism (B) may be conceived of as the opposed limits of a continuous scale.

Second, one has to specify for each specific evolutionary explanation what are the units of selection, that is, which are the bearers of the relevant trait(s), whose fitness may be enhanced if they possess the trait(s). If the trait consists in (endorsing) a specific religious belief, the relevant unit of selection may be located at three different levels. In principle it is possible (1) that groups or tribes of human beings are relatively more fit in the biological sense if they share a specific set of religious beliefs, whenever sharing these beliefs enhances the cohesion and reproductive fitness of this group or tribe compared to competing tribes. If so, endorsing such a set of beliefs and transferring it to the children by means of obligatory instruction might be adaptive at the group level, and specific mutations in these beliefs might be fitness-enhancing for groups even if they are fitness-diminishing at the individual level.[38] Another option (2) is that individual human beings will be more fit in the evolutionary sense if they adopt a specific religious belief or cluster of such beliefs. This fitness advantage may have various causes. Holding specific religious beliefs might make one more attractive as a sexual partner, or it may motivate one to have more children, for example. Finally (3), specific religious ideas may spread easily between human beings even if they do not enhance the fitness of human groups, kin, or individuals. Considered from an evolutionary perspective, such ideas are sometimes called 'memes', the 'fitness' of which is greater to the extent that they spread

---

that is, between two types of proximate explanation and two types of ultimate, evolutionary explanation. In the text, I focus on ultimate explanations. Cf. Tinbergen (1963).
[37] Sosis and Kiper (2014), p. 272.
[38] Cf. Wilson (2002), chapter 1, on multilevel selection.

more easily than rival ideas. Richard Dawkins once invented this notion of memes as a cultural analogue of genes.[39] To what extent it amounts to more than a misleading metaphor is a matter of fierce debate.[40]

In the third place, as option (3) illustrates already, the criteria for measuring fitness may be diverse within the context of evolutionary accounts of religions. One may just use (a) the biological fitness criterion, which is the proportional rate of increase contributed to the demographic size of a population. Depending on whether one endorses (1) or (2), one will measure this contribution either at the level of groups or of individuals. However, criterion (a) is irrelevant if one defines the relevant units of selection merely in terms of cultural constructs or endorses a meme approach (3). Within the context of (3), one would have to specify clear criteria of identity for the relevant cultural items, or for memes, and develop (b) standards and methods for measuring their spread or 'fitness'. Up till now, no author has succeeded in doing so.[41]

Finally, with regard to each of the consistent combinations of A–B with 1–3 and a–b, one may develop and test empirically various hypotheses. It may be (i) that the trait or set of traits has been adaptive in a specific past environment and still is adaptive in present contexts, or (ii) that it originally was a by-product or spandrel, which has become adaptive in a later period, (iii) that it once was adaptive but is not so later on, although it continues to exist, or (iv) that it has been and still is a spandrel, that is, a by-product of psychological or social mechanisms that evolved independently. Let us now try to classify in terms of these categories (A, B; 1, 2, 3; a, b; i, ii, iii, iv) some well-known explanations of religious beliefs if applied to polytheisms.

One of the central hypotheses of the cognitive science of religion is the assumption that human minds or brains contain a so-called Hypersensitive (or hyperactive) Agent Detection Device (HADD).[42] The

---

[39] Dawkins (1989), pp. 192ff.
[40] Dennett (2006) endorses a '(relatively) sober version of the concept' of memes (p. 81), and distinguishes between religious memes that are (fitness-enhancing) mutualists, (fitness-neutral) commensals, and (fitness-reducing) parasites. Other experts on the evolutionary landscape of religion are more sceptical with regard to memetics. According to Scott Atran (2002), p. 241, it is a 'serious challenge to the possibility of memetics' that unlike genes, 'ideas rarely copy with anything close to absolute fidelity'. As Bennett and Hacker argue (2003, pp. 433–435), there is no coherent and meaningful notion of memes at all, and the ways in which Dawkins, Dennett, and others use the term 'meme' is deeply confused.
[41] Cf. Bennett and Hacker (2003), pp. 433–435.
[42] Cf. Barrett (2004, 2012); Boyer (2001); Boyer and Barrett (2005); Nola (2018).

evolutionary selection of this 'device' has been explained as follows. When our early hominid ancestors lived in African jungles, it was crucial for their survival to discern predators or enemies as quickly as possible. Those of our ancestors whose brain functions for detecting predators happened to be somewhat oversensitive, so that they fled swiftly not only from actual predators but also from a merely imagined predacious animal or enemy, had a greater fitness in the biological sense than fellow tribe members whose detection devices were undersensitive. The former hominids were more likely to survive and reproduce than the latter, who risked overlooking a real predator. Since possessing perfect sensitivity is highly improbable, it was to be expected that oversensitive detection modules would have evolved in the brains of hominids. Because these hominids were less likely to be devoured by predators, it is from them that humans descended and inherited the detection module. When they were endowed with such an over or hypersensitive detection device, human individuals who could not discover the predators supposed to be present may have presumed that apart from perceivable predators or enemies there also were invisible ones. Consequently, they imagined what we would now call hidden evil spirits or deities.

Strictly speaking, this HADD hypothesis should be classified as A2aii or A3aiv. It explains primarily the origin of human beliefs in specific devilish deities (A). The device itself would have been adaptive at the individual level (2), although it still is an open question whether the resulting religious beliefs in evil deities became adaptive for individuals as well (if not: 3). Furthermore, the hypothesis uses (a) the biological fitness criterion. Finally, although originally believing in an evil deity was merely a by-product of an oversensitive predator detection device, such a belief may have become evolutionarily advantageous later on, an 'exaptation' (so: ii or iv). Within the evolutionary framework of the cognitive science of religion, the HADD hypothesis is one of the core doctrines.[43] Let us now wonder to what extent it is scientifically superior to David Hume's explanation of human beliefs in evil polytheistic gods.

As I said already, one alleged advantage of the HADD hypothesis consists in its evolutionary context. Another aspect of possible progress since Hume is that, in principle, the HADD hypothesis may be tested by

---

[43] According to the usual criteria for scientific superiority, the HADD hypothesis conjoined to naturalism provides a better explanation of religious beliefs than any religious explanation. Hence, the HADD explanation of religious beliefs also provides an inductive argument to the best explanation against religious truth-claims, as Nola (2018) argues.

brain research if the neural networks are identified within which the postulated agent detection device is functioning. If so, one might attempt to investigate, for example, whether in the same types of situations the HADD activation levels are higher in the brains of religious believers than in the brains of agnostics and universal atheists, that is, of humans who do not believe that any supernatural being exists. As far as I know, there is no such brain research yet.[44]

Suppose, however, that it existed, and that its results confirmed the hypothesis that HADD activation levels are higher in the brains of religious believers. Let me stress that this predicted outcome of empirical brain research would not show that the lower activation level *explains* why some persons are prone to universal atheism whereas others endorse beliefs in supernatural agents. Establishing an empirical correlation does not amount to an explanation. Religious believers may be tempted to conclude from such an empirical result that the brains of unbelievers are malfunctioning to some extent. Atheists will reply, correctly, that they have concluded from the relevant empirical evidence that there are no gods or other supernatural beings (cf. Chapter 1). This result of rational reflection would explain their lower HADD activation levels when they think about worldly phenomena to which religious believers mistakenly ascribe some supernatural significance.[45]

As long as there is no specific brain research underpinning the postulated HADD explanation of the endorsement of religious beliefs, scientific progress from Hume onwards with regard to this explanation of polytheisms is minimal. Hume also hypothesized that various types of threat for humans motivated them to imagine supernatural agents, and one might wonder to what extent the HADD hypothesis makes any sense at all. Let me finish this section by discussing briefly some other contemporary explanations of polytheisms. Most of these accounts are mutually compatible, so that we should be theoretical pluralists in this respect. Whereas some explanations focus on the origin of polytheistic beliefs, others attempt to account for the endurance of these convictions by studying their mental and social functions.

---

[44] Cf. Hood (2010) and Norenzayan (2013) for an overview of recent experimental research.
[45] Cf. Saler and Ziegler (2006) for further hypotheses about the 'variance in vulnerability to theism or to atheism across individuals in a population' (p. 29). Empirical research has shown, however, that a higher HADD activation level can predict conspiracy mentality, for example (van der Tempel and Alcock 2015).

With regard to the origins of polytheistic beliefs, that is, how they may have arisen originally, some (or many) tens of thousands years ago, the following explanations have been proposed repeatedly and are plausible indeed. First, as we all experience, it is very difficult to accept the death of our beloved ones. Their deceasing confronts humans with an agonizing dilemma. One the one hand, we cannot delete easily from our hearts and minds the affections and habits of communication with regard to the deceased person. On the other hand, corpses of the deceased are possible sources of contamination and disease. This dilemma has been resolved in human cultures by combining complex burial rituals with the spontaneous belief that the deceased survive somehow their human death, as souls or spirits in an afterlife or elsewhere. Quite often, the souls of important persons were adored as gods or goddesses. Let me leave it to the reader to decide whether this explanation has to be classified as A2ai or otherwise.

Second, it is vital for humans and many types of animals that they are able to attribute intentions and other mental properties. This capacity is often called their 'theory of mind'. The terminology is misleading, however, since one can only endorse a theory if one has linguistic abilities and is able to formulate one's views explicitly.[46] One might prefer, therefore, to call the capacity of attributing mental properties the 'intentional stance', an ability that numerous animals have as well.[47] Clearly, such a capacity is fitness-enhancing in many ways, since it enables us to cooperate and to expect reliably the behaviours of both enemies and friends on the basis of experience. Furthermore, most humans share the tendency to adopt the intentional stance somewhat more widely than would be justified from a scientific point of view. That is, they attribute mental properties to entities that do not possess these properties, such as deceased human beings, and to many natural phenomena that strike them somehow, such as the Sun, stars, or a thunderstorm. In other words, the human intentional stance often is hyperactive as well, so that we may speak of an

---

[46] Adherents of the 'theory of mind' jargon justify it by arguing that one has no direct access to the minds of other human beings. Our conviction that other individuals have a mental life would be an explanatory hypothesis based upon our perception of their behaviours. However, this quite Cartesian view has been refuted by many philosophers, such as the later Wittgenstein.

[47] This terminology is due to Daniel Dennett; cf. Dennett (2006), pp. 109ff. and Dennett (1987). Cf. on attributing an intentional stance to chimpanzee's and other animals: De Waal (2006, 2019). For a critical philosophical analysis of Dennett's rather confused notion of an intentional stance, see Bennett and Hacker (2003), pp. 419–427.

HIS, a hyperactive intentional stance.[48] Explanations of the origins of polytheist beliefs with reference to the human HIS do not differ drastically from Hume's account, although they presuppose the evolutionary framework. They may be classified in various ways, such as A2ai, depending on the details of these explanations. The HIS is stimulated as well by the human tendency to interpret natural phenomena in teleological terms, that is, as serving some aim or purpose. This is sometimes called our 'teleological bias'.[49]

A third set of plausible accounts is concerned with the many specific functions polytheistic beliefs have had and still fulfil. For example, during the prehistory of mankind both individuals and tribal communities had to take difficult decisions, the consequences of which could be death and destruction. Should one flee from an inimical tribe or rather attack it? Would it be acceptable to consume the scarce amount of food one possesses, hoping that hunting would be successful during the next days, or not? The decisional stress and responsibility would be diminished considerably if one could delegate such decisions to superhuman beings that were supposed to know more about the future. This specific function of religious beliefs has been performed by many cultural practices and institutions, such as oracles and other ritualized decision procedures. My favourite example is the Oracle of Delphi, which probably originated in prehistoric times and functioned until it was shut down in 381 CE during the Christian persecution of so-called pagans under emperor Theodosius I (cf. §1.3). Oracles may have been evolutionarily adaptive in various respects, at the level of both individuals and cultural groups. For instance, their ritualized decision procedures may have diminished the risk of civil wars, in which case they should be classified as B1aiii.

As historical, psychological, and anthropological research has shown, many other functions have been, and still are, fulfilled by polytheist beliefs and practices. Religious rituals and prayers may be aimed at motivating divinities to procure things humans cannot deliver, such as sunshine, rain, or a bumper crop. Another function is to legitimize the rule of a sovereign or different forms of governance. Furthermore, implanting religious credulity into one's children may increase filial obedience, whereas teaching ancestor worship might fade out the fear of being forgotten. Threats of posthumous punishments for crimes or other forms of misbehaviour can

---

[48] As empirical research reveals (Riekki et al. 2014), religious believers evaluate random movements of geometric objects as more intentional than religious sceptics do.

[49] Cf., for example, Kelemen and Rosset (2009) and Kelemen et al. (2013).

make people more peaceful and law-abiding. In order to cope with incurable illnesses, countless cultures interpreted them as supernatural sanctions, whereas sacred medical ceremonies are often meant to create hope by pleasing the gods. Other religious rituals function as reinforcements of remembrance by means of countless repetitions of the same moral rules. Finally, if specific religious beliefs and rituals reinforce social cohesion and stimulate procreation, large groups of humans that endorse a specific religion may be more fit in the evolutionary sense than competing groups. Of course, each of these functions of polytheistic beliefs should be spelled out precisely and be investigated empirically in order to classify them in terms of the four types of distinctions specified above.[50]

For the moment, however, enough has been said by way of an answer to the first core question of this chapter. The rise and spread of polytheistic beliefs on Earth has had multiple origins, and endorsing such beliefs publicly fulfilled many different mental and social functions. As Daniel Dennett and others have argued, much more empirical research is needed in order to explore 'how religions have become what they are'.[51] Let us now attempt to answer the second core question of this chapter.

3.3 TRANSITIONS TO MONOTHEISMS

What accounts for the cultural transitions from polytheistic creeds to monotheisms? As we saw in §3.1, these transitions have often been gradual, that is, they proceeded via intermediate stages like henotheism and monolatry. Furthermore, the transits occurred to some extent in various cultures, such as the Egyptian civilization under pharaoh Akhenaten or in Zoroastrianism, and they may have taken place independently of each other. However, the religious evolution from poly to monotheism did not happen everywhere on Earth in all cultural contexts. Many polytheistic religions are still practised today, such as versions of Hinduism, Shinto or kami-no-michi, and traditional Chinese religions. Hence, we may wonder whether transitions from polytheism to monotheism are just cultural contingencies, which should be explained merely by accidental factors, or whether there also is some inner logic that is linked to specific external causes. Inspired again by David Hume, I argue in this

---

[50] Of course, monotheist religions may have many of these functions as well. For an overview of recent research on the moral functions of religions, see McKay and Whitehouse (2015) and Norenzayan (2013).
[51] Dennett (2006), p. 103.

section that there is such an inner logic, and that applications of this logic have been triggered by specific external stimuli.

Let me start by mentioning again one of the best-known accounts of a gradual transition from polytheism to monotheism via henotheism and monolatry: the historical development of the ancient Israelite religion according to 2 Kings.[52] Whereas a king of Judah such as Manasseh clearly is represented as a polytheist, since he 'worshiped all the host of heaven, and served them' (2 Kings 21:3), as did his son Amon, their successor Josiah imposed radical religious reforms quite violently, which resulted in a strict version of henotheism or rather monolatry (2 Kings 22). Unfortunately, Josiah's reign collapsed because 'Pharaoh Neco slew him at Megiddo' (2 Kings 23:29). After Nebuchadnezzar, king of Babylon, had conquered Jerusalem in 587 BCE and 'brought captive to Babylon all the men of valor' (2 Kings 24:16), a congregation of exiled priests may have developed a monotheist notion of YHWH (Yahweh).[53] They hoped, I suppose, that this powerful god would become their liberator from exodus.[54] Clearly, the context within which Judaic monotheism originated according to the second book of Kings was one of wartime.

How does this example fit in with David Hume's explanation of transitions to monotheism? According to Hume's classic *The Natural History of Religion*, when in human cultures monotheisms arose gradually from polytheisms, this occurred not on the basis of 'any [...] argument' but rather because of 'irrational and superstitious' mental processes.[55] Let me first quote a passage in which Hume sketches plausible transitions from polytheisms (which Hume called 'idolatries') to henotheisms or monolatries:

It may readily happen, in an idolatrous nation, that, tho' men admit the existence of several limited deities, yet may there be some one god, whom, in a particular manner, they make the object of their worship and adoration. They may either suppose, that, in the distribution of power and territory among the gods, their nation was subjected to the jurisdiction of that particular deity; or reducing heavenly objects to the model of things below, they may represent one god as

---

[52] Cf. Smith (2001). To what extent the two books of Kings are historically reliable is a complex issue. The books have been compiled from many sources, and their main intentions were not historical but moral and religious. Let's assume for the sake of argument, however, that they are historically reliable at least to some extent.

[53] I say 'may', since the relevant sources may also be interpreted as expressions of monolatry. See below.

[54] Cf. Gnuse (1997), p. 223.   [55] Hume (1757), §6, p. 51.

the prince or supreme magistrate of the rest, who, tho' of the same nature, rules them with an authority, like that which an earthly sovereign exercises over his subjects and vassals.[56]

Using again 'the model of things below', religious believers may then engage in attempts to obtain a profitable bargain by bootlicking this god. As Hume says, it does not matter whether the god is 'considered as their peculiar patron, or as the general sovereign of heaven'. In both cases, there is a mentally motivated logic that gradually transforms polytheism into monotheism. Hume starts to describe this logic as follows:

Whether this god, therefore, be considered as their peculiar patron, or as the general sovereign of heaven, his votaries will endeavour, by every act, to insinuate themselves into his favour; and supposing him to be pleased, like themselves, with praise and flattery, there is no eulogy or exaggeration, which will be spared in their addresses to him. In proportion as men's fears or distresses become more urgent, they still invent new strains of adulation; and even he who out-does his predecessors, in swelling up the titles of his divinity, is sure to be out-done by his successors, in newer and more pompous epithets of praise.[57]

Having read Hume up to this point, you may wonder why this psychological or social process of magnifying ever more one's adulated divinity would lead gradually from polytheism to monotheism. Although Hume does not explain explicitly this transition, he suggests its logic in the next sentence: 'Thus they proceed; till at last they arrive at infinity itself, beyond which there is no farther progress.'[58]

As I would propose, the logic of transition from polytheism to monotheism is the following. If all properties of a supreme god postulated by polytheists are deemed to be infinite qualities, so that this god is said to be infinitely powerful and infinitely knowledgeable, for example, there will seem to be no real room left any more for other gods. All effects that were attributed originally to the actions of many different gods now turn out to be direct or indirect impacts of the infinite omnipotence possessed by the postulated super-god. Although strictly speaking it would not be contradictory to combine polytheism with a belief in one super-god each of whose positive properties is infinite, there will seem to be no need any more for postulating other gods. Hence the increasing flattery that Hume sketches will finally result in monotheism or 'theism', since 'this notion of a supreme deity [...] ought naturally to lessen every other worship, and abase every object of reverence'.[59]

---

[56] Hume (1757), §6, p. 51. [57] Hume (1757), §6, pp. 51–52.
[58] Hume (1757), §6, p. 52. [59] Hume (1757), §6, p. 52.

Whether this monotheism can be a stable creed is another matter. Strictly speaking, we ordinary humans cannot understand the infinite properties attributed to the super-god. As Hume stresses, 'human conception' must 'fall short' of God's 'infinite perfections'.[60] This human incapacity to comprehend the notion of a god whose defining properties are said to be infinite explains why 'the principles of religion have a kind of flux and reflux in the human mind'. On the one hand, human cultures have 'a natural tendency to rise from idolatry [that is, polytheism] to theism'; but on the other hand, they tend 'to sink again from theism into idolatry'.[61] Because their infinite monotheistic god is incomprehensible, theists are inclined to postulate many 'inferior mediators or subordinate agents, which interpose betwixt mankind and their supreme deity'.[62] Hume does not refer explicitly to the canonized saints of Catholicism at this point, or to Jesus and Maria, since he was well aware of the dangers of religious persecution in the eighteenth century. The various transitions from populist Catholicism to Protestantism are hinted at in the following passage: 'But as these idolatrous religions fall every day into grosser and more vulgar conceptions, they at last destroy themselves, and, by the vile representations, which they form of their deities, make the tide turn again towards theism'.[63]

Summing up Hume's account of the gradual transitions from polytheism to monotheism, one might say that he mentions both an inner logic of magnifying the properties of a divinity until they are conceived of as infinite and a mental or social mechanism: praise or flattery, driven by human fears and distress. I endorse Hume's account of the inner logic, which obviously is correct. Yet I propose the following amendment with regard to the mechanism. Hume indicates nation- or tribe-internal practices of praise and flattery with reference to which he explains the fact that in many cultures the properties of a supreme god are magnified ever more. These practices are analogous to the flattery-competition between the courtiers or subjects of a king or monarch. I assume, however, that the motives for aggrandizing the properties of one's chief divinity are even stronger in tribe-external contexts, mainly when there is a military contest going on.

In situations of intertribal warfare, it was thought initially that a particular god of the polytheist ensemble was supporting one's military

---

[60] Hume (1757), §7, p. 56. [61] Hume (1757), §8, pp. 56–57.
[62] Hume (1757), §8, pp. 57–58. [63] Hume (1757), §8, p. 58.

endeavours. Let me mention, for instance, the Ancient Egyptian or Nubian goddess Menhit, whose name means 'she who massacres'. Early Berbers adorated Agurzil as a war deity who supported their struggles. Allegedly, the Icenic war goddess Andrasta bolstered up the Celts when they tried to prevent the Roman occupation of Britain around 60 CE. According to Irish mythology, the war goddess Badhbh appeared as a crow causing fear to enemies in order to let her side win the battle. Somewhat better known are military gods such as the Roman deity Mars, after whom the month of March has been named, or his Greek predecessor Ares.[64]

With regard to all these war-gods, the following historical hypothesis is plausible. Given the assumption that one's own war deity (if venerated properly) would wish one to defeat the enemy and would willingly support one's warfare, each of the adversaries will have thought that the probability of winning the war would increase if their own god were more mighty and knowledgeable than the enemy's war-god. Consequently, there will have been a competition of aggrandizement between military adversaries with regard to their martial divinities. As in the scenario of flattery-competition, the logical limit of this upgrading is reached when all positive properties attributed to one's god become infinite, such as limitless omnipotence, omniscience, infinite goodness (with regard to one's own tribe), omnipresence, and eternal existence.[65]

My amendment to Hume's explanation of the transitions from polytheism to monotheism can be summarized as follows. Apart from the inner logic of magnifying the properties of a divinity, there are two main mechanisms driving this logic. In addition to the tribe-internal practice of praise or flattery mentioned by Hume, there is the tribe-external rivalry of magnifying the properties of one's god in competition with one's military opponents. The underlying presumption of the latter mechanism is that the probability of winning would be greater if one's war deity is more powerful and intelligent than the inimical god. Both of these mechanisms may motivate tribal religious authorities to attribute ever greater properties to their gods until these features are claimed to be infinite. What is the empirical evidence for the presence of this second

---

[64] Cf. *Wikipedia*, 'List of war deities', https://en.wikipedia.org/wiki/List_of_war_deities.
[65] Mathematicians will stress today that there are several notions of infinity. Georg Cantor has argued that the infinity of God is the Absolute Infinite, which transcends other types of infinity. Cf. Nagasawa (2011), p. 111.

mechanism? Let me mention merely some of the many instances in order to trigger further research.[66]

Earlier in this section, I referred to one example from the ancient Israelite religion, spelled out in 2 Kings 21–24. Another well-known instance of the assumption that one's more powerful god will warrant one's victory can be found in Deuteronomy 20:1–4, which has been written before Josiah's religious reforms of 621 BCE. This text starts as follows: 'When you go forth to war against your enemies, and see horses and chariots and an army larger than your own, you shall not be afraid of them; for the LORD your God is with you, who brought you up out of the land of Egypt.' Some sentences further on, a priest is quoted, who says that 'the LORD your God is he that goes with you' in order 'to give you the victory'. If the Israelites were victorious over an inimical city that does not surrender itself, they had to 'put all its males to the sword' and 'take as a booty for yourselves' the women, children, cattle, and everything else (Deuteronomy 20:12–15). Psalms of David provide other cases in point, such as number 144, according to which 'the LORD [...] trains my hands for war, and my fingers for battle' (144:1–2).

Further evidence for the hypothesis that attributing ever greater power to one's own god has been motivated by military challenges is provided by Moses' father-in-law Jethro, priest of Midian, as presented in Exodus 18:11. According to this text, Jethro concluded the following from the successful Jewish flight out of Egypt and the victory over Amalek: 'Now I know that the LORD is greater than all gods, because he delivered the people from under the hand of the Egyptians, when they dealt arrogantly with them.' Earlier in Exodus (15:3–6), a 'song to the LORD' is cited, in which Moses and the people of Israel proclaimed that 'The LORD is a man of war', whose 'right hand, O LORD, shatters the enemy'. That their god is conceived of as greater than gods of competing tribes is revealed clearly in the following verses (Exodus 15:11): 'Who is like thee, O LORD, among the gods? Who is like thee, majestic in holiness, terrible in glorious deeds, doing wonders?'

Passages like these in the Hebrew Bible (or in the Old Testament) should still be classified as expressions of monolatry and not of monotheism as defined above. Yahweh is conceived of as the only God whom the Israelites should worship, not as the only god there is. Inimical tribes

---

[66] Cf. Longman III and Reid (1995) for many other instances.

adored other gods whose existence is not denied in many biblical texts, such as Deuteronomy 20:16–18:

> But in the cities of these peoples that the LORD your God gives you for an inheritance, you shall save alive nothing that breathes, but you shall utterly destroy them, the Hittites and the Amorites, the Canaanites and the Perizzites, the Hivites and the Jebusites, as the LORD your God has commanded; that they may not teach you to do according to all their abominable practices which they have done in the service of their gods, and so to sin against the LORD your God.

The monolatry interpretation is confirmed further by the fact that according to Deuteronomy 6:14–15, Yahweh would be jealous of other gods if Israelites worshipped them, because one can be jealous only of beings one believes to exist: 'You shall not go after other gods, of the gods of the peoples who are round about you; for the LORD your God in the midst of you is a jealous God; lest the anger of the LORD your God be kindled against you, and he destroy you from off the face of the earth.'

Yahweh is conceived of as superior to other gods in many respects apart from His unrivalled power. For example, He is said to be the first god who ever existed, the creator of the heavens and earth, and there will be no god after Yahweh.[67] It has been argued that for these reasons the terms 'henotheism' or 'monolatry' do not apply to the creed propagated in the Hebrew Bible. Applying these categories presupposes that Yahweh and the other gods mentioned belong to one and the same kind or species: the species of gods in general. However, the attribution of properties that belong to Yahweh only, *by definition*, would make Him 'species unique' in the sense that there cannot be an encompassing species or genus to which Yahweh and the other gods belong.[68]

I do not think that this argument is convincing, however. Admittedly, in the Hebrew Bible various properties are attributed to Yahweh only and not to other gods. But how can we know whether these properties are definitional or not? There is no distinction made in any of these texts between definitional and non-definitional properties of Yahweh, whereas the Hebrew equivalent of 'god' or 'supernatural being' is used for many other divinities as well, such as in Deuteronomy 32:16–17.[69]

---

[67] Isaiah 43:10: 'Before me no god was formed, nor shall there be any after me.' I suppose that texts such as Isaiah 44:6 should also be interpreted as stating the superiority of Yahweh over other gods: 'I am the first and I am the last; besides me there is no god'. Cf. Isaiah 45:5, 21–22, and 46:9; 2 Samuel 7:22; 1 Chronicles 17:20; etc.
[68] Heiser (2008), §3.   [69] Cf. Heiser (2008), note 63.

Consequently, I would still classify the Hebrew Bible as mostly monolatrious and partly henotheistic. It is argued again and again that the people of Israel should serve Yahweh only, and not the Ba'als and other gods 'from among the gods of the peoples who were round about them' (Judges 2:12). In many passages, the existence of these other gods is not denied, so that the relevant texts are not strictly monotheistic in the modern sense of this term. For example, in Psalm 95:3 it is proclaimed that 'the Lord is a great God, and a great King above all gods'. According to Psalm 97:9, the Lord is 'exalted far above all gods'.

The earliest texts of the New Testament, such as the first letter of Paul to the Corinthians, are expressions of monolatry as well. For example, in 1 Corinthians 8, it may seem to be suggested initially that God is the only existing divinity, because 'we know that "an idol has no real existence", and that "there is no God but one".' However, the continuation of this passage is monolatrious, I would claim, since it reads as follows: 'For although there may be so-called gods in heaven or on earth – as indeed there are many "gods" and many "lords" – yet for us there is one God, the Father' (1 Cor. 8:5). Other passages in the New Testament should also be interpreted as expressions of monolatry, if at least our methods of interpretation are purely historical and not religiously motivated.

As my Hume-inspired hypothesis says, real monotheism resulted only when infinite properties were ascribed explicitly to the god one believed in, such as infinite power and omniscience, so that, from a logical point of view, there was no room any more for competing gods. However, neither in the Old nor in the New Testament is infinite omnipotence or omniscience attributed to God. Admittedly, God is called 'eternal' in passages such as Deuteronomy 33:27: 'The eternal God is your dwelling place, and underneath are the everlasting arms. And he thrust out the enemy before you, and said, Destroy.' But the eternal existence of God does not imply infinity. Even if it did, God's presence during an infinitely long time would not exclude the existence of other gods. This logic of exclusion is implied only by ascribing explicitly to God properties such as infinite omnipotence and infinite omniscience. Translating 'El Shadai' as 'God Almighty' in texts such as Genesis 17:1 or Revelation 4:8 is strongly misleading, because originally 'El' was the name of the god at the head of the Canaanite pantheon, whereas 'Shadai' meant something like 'of the Mountain', or 'the Mighty'.

The cultural history of the concepts of infinity is complex. After Alexander III of Macedon (356–323 BCE) had been educated by Aristotle, among others, and became Alexander the Great when he conquered large domains in Asia and north-east Africa, Greek philosophy influenced ever more the religious traditions of these areas. The resulting Hellenization of the Near East explains why the original texts of what became the New Testament have been written in a *koine* (κοινή: common, ordinary, vulgar) version of Greek. Furthermore, key concepts of Greek philosophy started to penetrate early Christian traditions ever more, among which various concepts of infinity began to appear (ἄπειρον). The first Christian theologian who conceived of God as infinite may have been Clement of Alexandria (Titus Flavius Clemens) who lived from about 150 CE to 215 CE, mostly in Alexandria, and who was inspired by monotheistic Middle-Platonist philosophers such as Plutarch (45–120 CE).[70] The erudite Gregory of Nyssa (c. 335–c. 395 CE) argued more explicitly that God's properties are infinite or limitless, and that for this reason God is essentially incomprehensible to our finite minds.[71]

According to my Hume-inspired hypothesis, what motivated theologians such as Clement or Gregory to attribute infinite properties to their god was both the inner logic of magnifying God's qualities ever more and the tribe-internal practice of praise or flattery. My favourite illustration of the tribe-external incentive to magnify one's god would consist in emperor Constantine's official conversion to Christianity, if at least this conversion did occur in fact. As Constantine's father, Flavius Constantinus, was an officer in the Roman army, Constantine's education may have been mainly military. When emperor Diocletian appointed Flavius Constantinus as a Caesar in 293 CE, Constantine was educated at Diocletian's court and fought during many military raids in Asia, Syria, and Mesopotamia. Returning to Nicomedia from the eastern front, he witnessed Diocletian's 'Great Persecution' of Christians and in 305 CE joined his father's military campaigns in Britain beyond Hadrian's Wall. After his father's death in 306, Constantine was proclaimed Augustus and became emperor of the north-western Roman Empire.

As Constantine's coinages reveal, at first the Roman god Mars was his patron during many military endeavours. From 310 CE onwards, Constantine seems to have preferred Apollo, conceived of as *Sol Invictus*. According to contemporary Christian sources such as Lactantius' *Liber de Mortibus Persecutorum* (c. 314 CE) and Eusebius of Caesarea's Βίος Μεγάλου Κωνσταντίνου (*Vita Constantini*; about 339 CE), in 312 CE Constantine could win the crucial battle of the

---

[70] Cf. his *Stromata*, V, 81ff. referred to in Ritter et al. (2001), Band 11, p. 141.
[71] Cf. Weedman (2010) on Gregory's context.

Milvian Bridge against his Roman competitor Maxentius because he had a vision of the Christian cross with the message that he would triumph under this sign (ἐν τούτῳ νίκα, translated as: *in hoc signo vinces*).[72] Having been victorious later on in warfare against his competitor Licinius, Constantine became the sole Roman emperor. Symbolizing the integration of the eastern territory into the empire, the city of Byzantium was transformed into Constantinopolis, and numerous figures of traditional Greek gods were replaced by Christian statutes and symbols. For the first time in the Roman Empire, Christianity was legalized.

According to Christian sources, Constantine declared himself a Christian and attributed his military successes at least in part to God's omnipotent protection.[73] If this historical record is reliable, Constantine's conversion to Christianity confirms my Hume-inspired hypothesis with regard to military motives for magnifying one's god. According to Lactantius, at the Milvian Bridge battle Maxentius' army was twice as large as Constantine's. If Constantine and his army were convinced that because of their conversion the omnipotent Christian God supported them, this may have helped them somewhat to become victorious, since they will have thought that Maxentius was assisted merely by Mars, who was a much less powerful deity than God. Let me stress the 'if's in this paragraph, however, because there are no conclusive historical sources showing that Constantine really converted to Christianity before the battle at the Milvian Bridge.[74] Nevertheless, the contemporary Christian accounts concerning Constantine's conversion corroborate my Humean hypothesis, since they express the conviction that converting to an omnipotent god might help one to win a war.

Inspired by David Hume, I argued in this section that the gradual transitions from polytheism to monotheism follow the inner logic of magnifying the properties of one's gods until infinity has been reached. When the positive properties of one god are conceived of as infinite there will be no logical room left any more for other gods, so that monotheism will emanate. Apart from this inner logic, I distinguished two different motivations for applying it. On the one hand, there is the tribe-internal motive of praising and flattering one's preferred deity ever more in order

---

[72] It is interesting to note that in the volume of his Church History (Ἐκκλησιαστικὴ ἱστορία) that appeared in 315 CE, Eusebius does not mention the alleged Christian vision that Constantine would have experienced before the Milvian Bridge battle.
[73] Cf. Brown (2003), p. 60.
[74] Cf. Lendering and Hunink (2018), chapter 10; Kirsch (2004), chapter 5.

to enhance the divinity's goodwill and generosity. On the other hand, the tribe-external incentive to magnify one's god ever more arises whenever one's tribe or nation is at war and one assumes that the likelihood of winning a battle is greater if one's deity is more powerful and knowledgeable than the enemy's god. Of course, emperor Constantine would never have converted to Christianity if this cluster of religious sects had not amplified itself already within the Roman regions before his conversion. In §4.3, we will wonder what explains the surprising proliferation of the newborn Christian religion within the chaotic Roman Empire after St Paul's proselytization.

4

Religion and Ethics

It has often been argued that human ethics or morality requires religion. Many authors approvingly quote Dostoevsky, who is claimed to have written in *The Brothers Karamazov*: 'If God does not exist, everything is permitted.'[1] Numerous Americans tend to advocate this celebrated credo as well. For example, Laura Schlessinger once said that '[i]t is simply impossible for people to be moral without religion or God'.[2] As statistics of the Pew Research Center (2007) reveal, most US citizens endorse the conviction that morality needs a belief in God, and, as a consequence, they often associate atheists with immorality.[3]

We may interpret these claims in two different senses, however, only one of which is relevant to the central sections of this chapter. It is contended either that (a) only if God exists can moral norms be valid and legitimate, or that (b) in fact only religious believers really tend to endorse moral values and act morally well. Whereas (a) is a philosophical thesis, (b) is a factual claim to be checked by empirical research in the social sciences and cultural history.

If none of the supernatural beings postulated by human monotheist or polytheist creeds in fact exist, as I argued in Part I, no religious belief to the effect that there is a particular god or spirit can be legitimate in an objective epistemic sense, since all such beliefs are false. This philosophical conclusion already refutes each and every religious justification of

---

[1] Dostoevsky, (1990). The original Russian work was published as a serial in 1879–1880. The quote occurs to some extent in part 4, book 11, chapter 4 ('A Hymn and a Secret').
[2] Quoted in Zuckerman (2008) and in McKay and Whitehouse (2015).
[3] Cf. McKay and Whitehouse (2015) for further references.

morality. As I argue in §4.1, even if a specific god were to exist, such as the divinity Christians call 'God', it will not be valid to justify specific moral rules and ideals with reference to this deity.[4] Hence, the claims cited above are false if interpreted as (a) justifications of moral norms. Fortunately, there are many convincing non-religious vindications of moral rules and values.[5]

Since all religious beliefs to the effect that some divinity exists are false, the question as to what explains the endorsement of such beliefs by most human beings becomes a fascinating problem to be investigated by the empirical sciences of religion. In Chapter 3, some answers to this explanatory question have been provided, both with respect to polytheist religions and regarding the gradual rise of monotheisms. In the present chapter, we focus on so-called 'moralizing' religions. Adherents to moralizing religions hold that the superhuman agent(s) they believe in prescribe(s) specific moral norms for interpersonal human behaviour instead of merely promulgating rules for adoration. What explains the origin and historical spread of moralizing religions?

According to cognitive anthropologists Nicolas Baumard and Pascal Boyer, usually the spirits and gods postulated by tribal societies are not conceived of as providing moral prescriptions. The same would hold for most organized religions that emerged in large-scale cultures, such as the polytheisms of classical antiquity in Egypt, Greece, or the Roman Empire. Baumard and Boyer claim that moralizing religions arose only 'at a much later stage', 'recently', and merely 'in some large-scale societies'. Their prime examples are Jainism, Orphism, Second-Temple Judaism, and Christianity.[6] In the article 'Explaining Moral Religions' (2013) they aim at elucidating why these large-scale religions incorporate moral prescriptions, and what accounts for the commonalities in the ethical rules. I discuss some recent answers to these questions in §4.2. The diagnosis that Egyptian, Greek, and Roman gods lacked any moral dimension is debatable, however. It may have resulted originally from the strategy of Christian or Muslim apologists to distinguish their religion positively from so-called paganisms.[7]

---

[4] Cf. Philipse (2011) for a refutation of Francis Collins (2006).
[5] For an overview, just read for example: McPherson and Plunkett (2017) and Shafer-Landau and Cuneo (2007).
[6] Baumard and Boyer (2013), p. 272. What they mean by 'recently' and 'at a much later stage' is somewhat unclear, given that they mention Jainism and Orphism as examples of moralizing religions.
[7] Cf. Norenzayan et al. (2016), pp. 8–9.

Although cognitive science models may help us to elucidate the moral aspects of religions, they will not account fully for the fact that particular moralizing religions became dominant in our world today, such as Christianity and Islam. Since each of these religions started historically as a small sectarian movement, we should wonder what caused their global expansion. Were their moral convictions crucial causes in this respect? In 2017, the Pew Research Center estimated that in 2015 nearly a third (31 per cent) of Earth's 7.3 billion people were Christians, that is, about 2.3 billion human beings. Muslims made up the second largest religious aggregation, consisting of about 1.8 billion people, 24 per cent of the world's population.[8] The expansion of these religious movements from their very beginning until our times has been a long historical process, which went through many different phases. In each of these phases, numerous causal factors may have played a role in their proliferation. For example, during the European colonial period from the fifteenth century onwards, Christian missionaries operated in nearly all of the colonies. Since by 1914 European colonial countries had gained control of about 84 per cent of the inhabited Earth, this territorial expansion has been a crucial cause of the Christian spread on our planet.

In §4.3, I focus merely on two much earlier amplifications of Christianity. A first question is concerned with the embryonic growth of the Jesus sect after Christ's crucifixion. I defend the view that both the belief that Jesus was resurrected and the initial propagations of this belief should be explained by cultural history combined with Leon Festinger's theory of cognitive dissonance. After Saul's conversion to Jesus, which I analysed in Chapter 1, he (Paul) started to propagate a Christian creed within the Roman Empire. In which sense should we qualify this creed as a moral religion, and how should we explain its dissemination within the Roman world until emperor Constantine converted to Christianity? This is the second question to be asked in §4.3, with regard to which I shall discuss briefly the hypothesis of group selection put forward by David Sloan Wilson.

In the final section (§4.4) of this chapter we move to the present and raise an ethical issue with regard to moralizing religions such as Christianity and Islam.[9] One cause of their predominance on Earth consists in their moral propagation of human procreation. Accordingly, Muslims and Christians have more children per woman on average than

---

[8] Hackett and McClendon (2017).
[9] I am using the adjectives 'moral' and 'ethical' as synonymous.

any other religious or secularized population.[10] Since the total fertility rate of Muslims in 2015–2020 is higher (2.9) than the Christian rate (2.6), and because both rates are higher than the replacement level of humans on Earth (2.1), followers of Muhammad will outcompete Christians during the coming decades. Both of these religions will be co-responsible for global population growth.[11] Will our Earth be able to accommodate these growing human populations during the present century, given the many catastrophic effects of human-induced global warming?

As the diversity of problems to be discussed in this chapter demonstrates, the overall theme of religion and ethics encompasses innumerable subtopics and areas of research. Readers who are looking for what unifies the chapter may conclude, correctly, that this general thesis is its main unifying bond.

4.1 RELIGIOUS JUSTIFICATIONS OF MORAL RULES

As has been argued in Part I, it is highly unlikely that any god or other supernatural being exists. It follows that we cannot justify legitimately the moral rules we endorse by claiming that they are divine commands. Let us assume for the sake of argument, however, that in fact there is a specific divinity, such as the Trinity-god of Christian monotheism called God, or the Muslim deity named Allah Almighty. If this were true, would it be possible to justify legitimately moral rules and values by claiming that they are God's, or Allah's, commandments? Such a justification is provided in biblical texts like Exodus 20, Deuteronomy 5, Matthew 19, and Paul's Letter to the Romans. It is also endorsed in Quran 6:151–154 and 17:22–37, for instance.

There are three main problems with regard to a religious justification of moral rules, each of which shows that it cannot be correct. First, there are many biblical texts in which moral imperatives are formulated which nowadays most of us would consider to be wicked. In §3.3, I quoted Deuteronomy 20:10–18, for example, according to which God has commanded that if his people besiege an inimical city, they should 'put all its males to the sword' but 'take as a booty for yourselves [...] the women

---

[10] Cf. Norenzayan et al. (2016), p. 16. Of course, other factors than religious belonging may be more important, since most countries with the highest fertility rates are in Africa, such as Niger, Somalia, and the Democratic Republic of Congo. Cf. http://worldpopulationreview.com/countries/total-fertility-rate/.

[11] Cf. Pew Research Center (2017), referred to in Hackett and McClendon (2017).

and the little ones, the cattle, and everything else in the city'. In towns 'that the LORD your God gives you for an inheritance', His followers should be even more radical, and 'save alive nothing that breathes' but 'utterly destroy them, the Hittites and the Amorites, the Canaanites and the Per'izzites, the Hivites and the Jeb'usites, as the LORD your God has commanded'. Christian believers might reply that these moral rules propagated in books of the Old Testament are overruled by those of the New, such as Paul's main commandment that 'You should love your neighbour as yourself', which applies to one's enemies as well (Romans 13:9).[12]

This reply raises a second problem for religious justifications of moral rules, however, which is even more serious than the first. If various so-called divine revelations contain moral norms that are mutually incompatible, how can we humans discover what are the real moral rules that God or Allah promulgates? Is there any reliable way of communicating with a god in this respect?[13] Paul's contention in Romans 2:15 that what the law requires is written on our hearts will not help us here, since in cases of conflict between mutually incompatible moral norms, what the heart of one individual seems to prescribe will contradict the heartfelt norms of someone else. Christians or Muslims may argue that of course God's or Allah's moral standards do not change but that He reveals these standards progressively to humans, so that later revelations are closer to the truth than earlier ones. This reply is not very convincing however: why would a morally perfect god reveal false moral standards to begin with? Furthermore, many moral imperatives that we now consider to be deeply wrong are endorsed in the New Testament as well, such as the command to slaves to 'be obedient to [...] your earthly masters, with fear and trembling, in singleness of heart, as to Christ' (Ephesians 6:5–6) or Christ's command to each of his followers that he should 'hate his own father and mother and wife and children and brothers and sisters, yes, and even his own life' (Luke 14:26).[14]

In his dialogue *Euthyphro*, Plato formulated the third challenge regarding religious justifications of moral rules, which is commonly called

---

[12] Whether Paul intended to apply this commandment to one's enemies as well is quite dubious, since the commandment also occurs in books of the Old Testament, such as Leviticus 19:18, which Paul was simply repeating.

[13] Interestingly, many religious authors who attempt to resolve the Euthyphro problem do not even discuss this issue. Cf., for example, Audi (2011), pp. 145ff.

[14] Cf. Elisabeth Anderson (2007) for many other instances.

the Euthyphro dilemma.[15] Whereas in this dialogue Socrates raises the dilemma with regard to the Greek pantheon, many Christian philosophers have adapted it to monotheism. Suppose for the sake of argument that God is the legislator of our moral norms, and that these norms are morally valid. Then it seems that there are only two possibilities, which are the horns of the dilemma. Either (1) God imposes these moral norms on us because they are morally valid or (2) the norms are morally valid because God imposes them on us. Both of these horns undermine decisively religious justifications of moral norms.

If horn (1) is true, the validity of moral rules and values does not depend on God's authority. Since it is rather easy to understand these rules, we humans are able to grasp them very well without any divine assistance and to appreciate their validity. That this is the case has been shown convincingly by cultures that endorse the same or similar moral rules despite the fact that any religious belief in God or Allah is lacking. As a consequence, both the validity of and our epistemic access to moral rules do not rely on the existence of a divinity such as Allah or God. On the other hand, if horn (2) of the Euthyphro dilemma is true, God cannot have had any *moral* reasons for imposing specific ethical norms on humans, since norms can become morally valid only if and because God imposes them. It follows that the God-commanded moral norms are ethically arbitrary, and that God cannot be 'good' in our moral sense. In principle, God might have decreed moral norms that are very different from the norms we humans happen to endorse. For religious believers who embrace horn (2), the only valid reason for behaving morally would be their conviction that God punishes humans for moral transgressions and rewards our moral rectitude. Most of us will object to this horn, however, that human actions cannot be morally decent if they are performed out of fear for divine revenge or because one longs for a religious remuneration.

Christian philosophers have discussed the Euthyphro dilemma intensively since the Middle Ages, but they could never agree which horn one should prefer.[16] Some of them, such as Gottfried Wilhelm von Leibniz or Richard Swinburne, largely embraced horn (1), because they held that God has to have moral reasons for acting that are objectively valid,

---

[15] Cf. Philipse (2016), pp. 156–157, and the Wikipedia page on the Euthyphro dilemma (https://en.wikipedia.org/wiki/Euthyphro_dilemma) for many details I cannot discuss here.
[16] Cf. Irwin (2006).

whereas many others, such as Ockham, Luther, Calvin, Descartes, and William Paley preferred the voluntarist horn (2), celebrating the sovereignty of God's will. Since the first horn shows that God is superfluous for validating our moral norms, whereas the second horn implies that God's decision to impose specific moral rules on humans cannot have been morally motivated, the Euthyphro dilemma effectively refutes any religious justification of moral rules. Recent attempts by Christian philosophers to rebut the dilemma, by going between its horns for example, are unconvincing, as I have argued elsewhere.[17]

Let us conclude from the three challenges discussed succinctly in this section, then, that even if a specific god were to exist, such as Allah or God, one cannot legitimately justify moral rules by claiming that they are Divine commandments. Hence, we have to reject the philosophical thesis (a) that only if God exists, moral norms can be valid. This refutation of (a) will enhance our interest in the empirical claim (b), according to which only religious believers tend to endorse ethical values and act morally well. If these believers cannot rely on valid arguments for their conviction that their moral norms and values are religiously justified, what explains the fact that they endorse this conviction? More generally, how should we account empirically for the origin and spread of so-called moralizing religions? During the last twenty years, this question has become a hot topic of discussion in the social sciences of religion.

4.2 MORALIZING RELIGIONS EXPLAINED

Readers who are not familiar with the technical terminology used by social scientists of religion will wonder what is meant, exactly, by the expressions 'moralizing gods' and 'moralizing religions'. Do not most divinities ever imagined in human cultures possess some moral properties, since they were conceived of 'as intelligent, voluntary agents, like ourselves; only somewhat superior in power and wisdom'?[18] Take, for example, the Greek deity Pallas Athena, who as a warrior goddess was thought to support fighters for a just cause only. However, when we study anthropological and historical overviews of the more than 4,000 religions worldwide, we discover that quite a few gods who are believed to cause specific natural or human phenomena may lack a manifestly moralizing

---

[17] Philipse (2016), p. 157, and, for example, Alston (1990). I discussed Swinburne's moral objectivism in Philipse (2012, 2014), §9.3.

[18] Apologies to readers for quoting David Hume again: Hume (1757), p. 48.

dimension. The explanatory function of stories about these gods may be more prominent than a moral one, although the latter rarely is absent altogether.

In the social sciences of religion, 'moralizing gods' are defined today as divinities that not only punish offences to themselves, such as when believers forget to sacrifice, but also penalize interhuman immoral actions and bad intentions. In other words, moralizing gods are conceived of as deities that monitor and enforce interpersonal human morality, often by punishing or rewarding persons hereafter. If a specific religion includes a belief in a very powerful moralizing god, technically called a 'Moralizing High God' or a 'Big God', it is classified as a moralizing religion. Usually, this label is applied as well to world-views such as versions of Buddhism that endorse a 'broad supernatural punishment' for bad human behaviour without postulating a god who enforces it. In order to make the definition of moralizing gods and moralizing religions somewhat more precise, one has to specify also what one means by 'morality', since our concept of morality is complex, and it is lacking in many cultures. The best way of doing so is to mention moral values that one considers as definitional for moralizing religions, such as reciprocity, fairness, and in-group loyalty.[19] God(s) of moralizing religions prescribe(s) these moral values to their believers, or to human beings in general, and impose supernatural sanctions for sins such as stealing, murder, lying, cheating, and adultery.[20]

Defined in this manner, moralizing religions are widespread today, like the various versions of Christianity and Islam. How should we explain this global fact from the perspectives of evolutionary anthropology and the cognitive sciences? Is there any causal connection between a community-shared human endorsement of a belief in a moralizing god on the one hand and specific non-religious properties of the society in which this belief is endorsed on the other hand?

In order to formulate this question properly, we have to distinguish between three different types of causal link. If one says that something (x) causes something else (y), one might mean either that x is a sufficient condition for y or a necessary condition, or that x contributes to y's genesis without being sufficient or necessary. If x is a sufficient cause of y, the existence of x implies that y will occur. If x is a necessary cause of y, the latter (y) cannot occur unless x is or was present. Finally, if x merely is a contributory cause of y, other causes are needed as well to produce y,

---

[19] Cf. Whitehouse et al. (2019), p. 226.   [20] Cf. Norenzayan (2013), p. 127.

whereas y can also occur without x. Social scientists don't always distinguish clearly between these different types of causality when they investigate causal connections between shared beliefs in a moralizing god on the one hand and properties of the relevant communities on the other hand. Let me now summarize briefly some prominent publications on the social function(s) of beliefs in Moralizing High Gods or Big Gods, mainly in order to raise the readers' interest and to formulate a new point of criticism.

A good start for readers on our topic is Ara Norenzayan's comprehensive book *Big Gods: How Religion Transformed Cooperation and Conflict* (2013). Studying religious beliefs from an evolutionary perspective, Norenzayan combines two explanatory accounts. One the one hand, the emergence of religious beliefs can be considered as a by-product of our evolved cognitive capacities. On the other hand, the cultural characteristic of sharing a specific type of religious belief may be fitness-enhancing for human groups – much more so than endorsing other religious creeds. Hence, we should incorporate cultural intergroup competition in our evolutionary model for studying religions and use a framework of multi-level selection. According to Norenzayan, there is a convincing cultural-evolutionary explanation that connects two striking aspects of many contemporary societies. On the one hand, (1) these societies consist of very large groups of humans most of whom are strangers for each other. On the other hand, (2) most religious believers today practise moralizing religions as defined, worshipping a Big God who punishes somehow human violations of moral rules.[21]

Having assembled manifold types of psychological, ethnographic, archaeological, and historical evidence, Norenzayan argues that these two aspects are causally connected in the following manner. When tribal societies grew larger gradually after the advent of agriculture about twelve millennia ago, it became ever more difficult to prevent free-riding, to install widespread trust, and to track criminals. In this situation, it was evolutionarily advantageous for human populations to share a demanding and ritualized religious belief in a moralizing Big God who is a well-informed supervisor of human life and who in this or a next world effectively penalizes our crimes and other immoral behaviours. Hence, communities that embraced such a moralizing religion and expelled or killed unbelievers often outcompeted communities that did

---

[21] Cf. also Norenzayan et al. (2016).

not, so that moralizing religions became widespread in human history. The causal connection in this context should be interpreted as a contributory one and not as a sufficient condition, since there have been many other factors that facilitated both large-scale cooperation within communities and outcompeting rival groups, such as economic productivity, military supremacy, routine rituals, and high sexual fertility. Moralizing religions are not a necessary condition for social cohesion in large communities either. This has been shown, for example, by their withering in well-organized Western societies after the Enlightenment. Strong secular institutions, the rule of law, social welfare systems, and other factors may make religions redundant in this respect.[22]

It has been objected that there is no reliable statistical evidence for this causal connection between moralizing religions and large-scale societies, since the data points are not mutually independent ('Galton's problem'), and nearly all historical evidence provided is linked to the expansion of so-called Abrahamic religions, mainly Christianity and Islam.[23] However, Norenzayan supports his hypothesis with multiple types of statistical evidence from experimental psychology and anthropology, using random assignment.[24] Furthermore, the causal hypothesis in this context is mainly a historical one. In historical investigations it is often difficult to support a causal hypothesis with statistical evidence that is both independent and historically relevant. Since the definition of the High or Big Gods variable has been inspired by the Abrahamic religions, it is not surprising that they are playing a central role in the historical evidence.

Even so, Abrahamic religions cannot have been a necessary condition for the transition from nomadic tribes to large agricultural societies. This transition started in the Middle East some 12,000 years ago, whereas Abrahamic religions originated much later.[25] Furthermore, many other aspects of these religions apart from the belief in a Big God may have been causally contributory to their evolutionary success, such as proselytization and stimulating procreation, whereas numerous Big God religions died out quickly. Readers who want to delve more deeply into these and many other empirical issues should read not only Norenzayan's book but also the captivating conversations with his critics.[26] For example, should

---

[22] Cf. Norenzayan (2013), chapter 10 and Norenzayan et al. (2016), p. 45: 'Therefore, we take the view that *prosocial religions are an important cause in a network of causes, but they are not a necessary, perhaps not even a sufficient cause, of large-scale cooperation*' (italics of the authors).
[23] Atkinson et al. (2015), pp. 267ff.   [24] Cf. Norenzayan (2015), p. 332.
[25] Atkinson et al. (2015), p. 271.   [26] Norenzayan (2015); Norenzayan et al. (2016).

Norenzayan have included meme theory in his framework of multilevel selection?[27] And how would he explain the cultural transition of polytheisms to Big God monotheisms, which I discussed in §3.3?

Let me stress again one crucial point that I did not discover in the conversations of Norenzayan and his critics. Nowhere in Norenzayan's book there is any epistemic evaluation of a religious belief. As a professional psychologist, he studies the mental and social functions of endorsing a Big God conviction without even asking whether this creed is true or false. However, it often depends on the epistemology which answers are correct with regard to the psychological problem why people hold a specific belief. If the belief is true, and subjects found out that it is true, this may explain fully why they are endorsing it. If the belief is false, however, or if it is impossible to detect reliably whether it is true or is false, the issue as to why people are endorsing this belief has to be resolved by studying the psychological and social functions of doing so. Hence, one cannot investigate reliably the causes of someone's holding a belief without first examining its epistemology and truth-value. Norenzayan might reply that he is mainly concerned with the social effects of believing in a Big God and not with its causes. Nonetheless, with regard to an illusionary belief the causes and effects of endorsing it often are intimately interrelated.

The evolutionary hypothesis that beliefs in moralizing Big Gods causally facilitated cooperation between strangers in large-scale societies has been tested further by Harvey Whitehouse et al., who published their results in 2019.[28] In order to overcome the limitations in the availability of global and longitudinal data, they coded records from 414 societies ('polities') that have existed during the last 10,000 years in 30 different geographical regions on Earth, from the beginning of the Neolithic period until the Western industrial and colonial expansion, using the Global History Databank Seshat. Employing fifty-one criteria for measuring social complexity and four measures of supernatural enforcement of moral norms, they discovered that on average the adoration of moralizing high gods followed rather than preceded the establishment of large-scale cooperation. Religions that postulated powerful moralizing Big Gods

---

[27] Cf. Susan Blackmore, 'Memes and the evolution of religion: We need memetics, too', in Norenzayan et al. (2016), pp. 22–23; reply on p. 51. As Peter Hacker argued in Bennett and Hacker (2003), pp. 431–435, the notion of memes is nonsensical.

[28] Whitehouse et al. (2019).

tended to originate after and not before the emergence of so-called megasocieties, the populations of which exceed one million.

These results refute the hypothesis that a shared belief in a moralizing high god is either a necessary or a sufficient causal condition for large-scale cooperation between humans. However, they may still confirm the claim that such a shared religious conviction was, and often still is, a contributory cause. Early instances of belief in moralizing high gods occurred in Egypt around 2800 BCE, when the Second Dynasty endorsed the doctrine that social order (*Maat*) is supernaturally enforced, and in China around 1000 BCE, for example. The evidence also suggests that rituals and institutionalized religious policing have been important preconditions for the rise of stable social complexity.

If a shared belief in a moralizing high god has been an important contributory cause that facilitated the evolution of complex societies, one would expect that in general social complexity increased more rapidly after the endorsement of beliefs in moralizing gods. When Whitehouse et al. tested this prediction by conducting time-series analyses, they found that the average increase rates of social complexity were 'over five times greater before – not after – the appearance of moralizing gods'.[29] Nevertheless, they still assume that endorsing a creed in a moralizing god 'may represent a cultural adaptation that is necessary to maintain cooperation' within comprehensive social clusters, in particular when large empires conquer smaller – but still complex – societies, so that they become multi-ethnic.[30] In order to make this conclusion consistent with the result that, in general, a shared religious belief in a moralizing high god is merely a contributory cause of social complexity and not a necessary one, one would have to redefine the notion of a necessary cause by connecting it to specific historical contexts.

However this may be, let me finish this section by stressing the main result of the nuanced empirical research done by Whitehouse et al.: throughout world history the emergence of complex societies preceded the endorsement of belief in moralizing high gods. In order to explain convincingly this endorsement, social scientists of religion should take into account the motives for doing so that I discussed in §3.3 and the solutions to many historical problems, two of which are proposed in the §4.3.

---

[29] Whitehouse et al. (2019), p. 227.   [30] Whitehouse et al. (2019), p. 228.

4.3 THE EARLIEST EXPANSIONS OF CHRISTIANITY

Christian believers may not be fascinated by the fact that their religion developed from the small Jewish Jesus sect into the largest religious community on Earth. Undoubtedly, they will assume, God steered humanity in this direction, revealing Himself to ever more human beings. Because God is the main power that caused Christian expansions, and since His ways are largely unfathomable, one should not attempt to understand the spread of Christianity by means of detailed historical research, they might contend. However, if there are no gods or other supernatural beings, as I argued in §2.4, the worldwide expansion of Christianity raises a huge number of fascinating historical problems. For example, how should we explain the conversion of Saul of Tarsus from a fanatic persecutor of Jesus' early disciples to the most prominent primordial preacher of the Christian creed, St Paul? It is quite likely that without Saul's conversion and propagation of Christianity in the Roman Empire, the Jesus sect would have died out quickly, as happened to innumerable other religious splinter groups. In §1.3, I argued that the most plausible (contributory) causal explanation of this crucial conversion was proposed only a few years ago, in 2015.

In the present section, two other historical issues will be discussed succinctly. The first one is concerned with the ways in which the followers of the first-century Palestinian preacher Jesus the Galilean reacted to his crucifixion and death. How should we explain their conviction that Jesus was resurrected and account for their proselytizing endeavours? Why didn't they give up their trust in Jesus after the crucifixion, which must have disappointed them deeply? As I argued at length in my book *God in the Age of Science*, a proper explanation of these facts will include the mechanisms of cognitive dissonance and collaborative storytelling combined with cultural features.[31] The second issue of this section is concerned with the spread of Christianity in the Roman Empire after Paul's death. How is one to explain the speed of this spread, which was so substantial that emperor Constantine converted to Christianity in about 312 CE (see §3.3)?

According to the four canonical gospels of the New Testament, Jesus was crucified during the reign of Pontius Pilate, the Roman governor of Judaea, which lasted from 26 until 36 or 37 CE. Most likely, the

---

[31] Philipse (2012, 2014), chapter 10.3–10.5.

crucifixion took place between 30 and 33 CE. Since scholars estimate that Saul's conversion occurred within the years 33–36 CE, it is plausible to assume that after Jesus' crucifixion Saul persecuted the early disciples of Jesus during many months or even several years before he converted. As is said in the Letter of Paul to the Galatians (Gal. 1:13), he 'persecuted the church of God violently and tried to destroy it'. This persecution would have been pointless if after Jesus' crucifixion many of the early followers had not started or continued to proselytize with great passion. How should we explain their motivations for doing so? And on which types of evidence can we rely in order to assess the plausibility of a specific explanation? Let me start by discussing the evidential problem.

Some Bible scholars argue that in order to explain why Jesus' early followers proselytized passionately after his crucifixion, the only evidential sources we should rely on are the oldest books of the New Testament, such as Paul's authentic letters to the Galatians, Corinthians, and Romans, interpreted within their historical context. Paul himself justified his preaching activities by the claim that Christ had been raised from the dead. If Christ had not been resurrected, he says, 'then our preaching is in vain' and 'your faith is futile' (1 Cor. 15:12–17). It is plausible to assume, then, that those followers of Jesus who were proselytizing before Paul wrote 1 Corinthians also believed that Jesus had been resurrected. But (1) why did they endorse such a belief? And (2) why did they proselytize so passionately?

The Bible scholars I am referring to affirm that the first fact (1) can be explained sufficiently by reference to Jewish cultural traditions. In these traditions, it was generally presumed that particularly meritorious persons were resurrected in heaven with a celestial body after their life on Earth had ceased. The followers of Jesus would have had good reasons to apply this resurrection creed to Christ as well, since they believed that Jesus met the criteria YHWH used for deciding which deceased human being He would resurrect, such as being a meritorious and suffering believer or being a Jewish martyr.[32] Accordingly, they interpreted their dreams and hallucinations of Jesus after his execution as reliable experiences of a resurrected Christ. In order to explain (2) why Jesus' disciples practised Christian preaching shortly after the crucifixion, it would be sufficient to assume that this was 'the continuation of the positive response which the historical Jesus had inspired among his followers

---

[32] Cf. De Jonge (1989), §4.

before his death'. 'In historical terms', that is, on the basis of the biblical sources, 'we know nothing of any disillusion and disillusionment among Jesus' disciples just before and after his crucifixion'.[33]

However, does the fact that biblical sources such as Paul's authentic letters do not mention any disillusionment among Jesus' disciples during the episode of his prosecution and crucifixion prove or make it probable that such disillusion did not occur? The oldest account available with regard to the belief that Jesus was resurrected and appeared to his followers is Paul's first epistle to the Corinthians (1 Cor. 15:3–8), which Paul wrote in Ephesus in about 55 CE. Does the fact that Paul did not mention any disenchantment among Jesus' disciples with regard to Christ's crucifixion show or make it probable that they were not deeply disappointed and horrified at the time of his execution, as is argued by the author I quoted?

For several reasons this argument is unconvincing. Paul was not among Jesus' disciples during the crucifixion process, so that he cannot have noticed their initial reactions. Since he wrote 1 Corinthians more than twenty years after the event, he could not rely on trustworthy testimony either. Furthermore, his letter was not meant as a report of historical and psychological research but rather as a preaching presentation of a gospel. Finally, the fact that Jesus' followers could rely on Jewish cultural traditions concerning the resurrection of meritorious deceased martyrs indicates a necessary condition of their conviction that Jesus was resurrected after his crucifixion but certainly not a sufficient condition. In order to explain their endorsement of the resurrection conviction, and their passion for proselytizing after Jesus' execution, we have to disclose other causal factors that are not discussed, and could not be mentioned, in the biblical sources, because they have been discovered only by recent psychological research. Let me briefly summarize the explanation I endorsed in my book *God in the Age of Science*.[34]

First, we have to wonder why quite some disciples of Jesus followed him when he went to Jerusalem. Is it plausible to assume that Jesus knew already that he would be crucified, and said so to his disciples, as is said in Matthew (21:17–19)? Clearly, this is not credible at all. In order to explain why the Jesus sect went to Jerusalem we should rather refer to another passage in Matthew (19:27–28), according to which his followers 'left everything' because Jesus promised them that they would 'sit on

---

[33] De Jonge (2002), pp. 52–53. [34] Philipse (2012, 2014), §§10.3–10.5.

twelve thrones, judging the twelve tribes of Israel'. Before Jesus was arrested, he and his followers will have believed this prediction in a secular sense, expecting for instance that they would liberate Jerusalem from its Roman occupation and establish an independent Jewish authority. This hypothesis is confirmed by a passage in Mark, which is commonly thought to be the oldest gospel included in the New Testament. According to this passage, the Roman soldiers who crucified Jesus affixed an ironical inscription of the charge against him, reading 'The King of the Jews' (Mark 15:18 and 15:26).

Given such expectations of Jesus and his followers during their arrival in Jerusalem, they would have become deeply bewildered when a team led by the chief priests arrested Jesus, condemned him to death, and delivered him to Pilate in order to be crucified. From a socio-psychological perspective we should assume that the disciples experienced an excruciating cognitive dissonance, since their hopeful expectations were refuted cruelly by the facts. As a large amount of recent empirical research on cognitive dissonance reveals, subjects who are suffering from it attempt to reduce the painful dissonance by trying to adapt their beliefs and actions to the facts they discovered. Some followers of Jesus will have managed to lessen their distress somewhat by applying to Jesus the traditional Jewish concept of a resurrection, imagining a divine Jesus in several ways, and interpreting their memories or dreams of Jesus as reliable experiences of a resurrected Christ. Other disciples may not have been able to overcome their cognitive dissonance and deserted the Jesus sect because the crucifixion showed that Jesus was not the effective Jewish liberator they intended to support.

As research on cognitive dissonance reveals as well, the mental suffering caused by this discord will often be reduced further by attempts to proselytize. The psychologist who created the concept of cognitive dissonance, Leon Festinger, once published a famous instance of such an investigation done by his team of collaborators.[35] The team carried out participating research on a small religious cult group, the members of which believed that they would be saved by a flying saucer when at a predicted time a cataclysmic flood would engulf the American continent. Before that crucial moment they barely proselytized, since they thought that the saucer would have space for their members only. However, when neither any flying saucer arrived nor a flood came, they adapted their

---

[35] Festinger et al. (1956). Cf. Festinger (1957), pp. 252ff.; Philipse (2012), p. 179.

theology during a period of intense deliberation and started to proselytize passionately, telling the press and the general public that God had saved the world because of their virtuous behaviour.

It is plausible to apply a similar explanation to the proselytizing passions of the Jesus sect after Christ's crucifixion.[36] Since its members had abandoned their homes and families when they followed Jesus to Jerusalem, expecting 'a hundredfold' reward (Matthew 19:29), Jesus' arrest and condemnation must have bewildered them completely because of the cognitive dissonance they experienced. As psychologists would predict, many members of the Jesus sect must have cooperated in order to invent a novel and apocalyptic story about Jesus that somewhat reduced their dissonance. They will have believed honestly that their dreams and fantasies of a living Jesus confirmed this story, because they interpreted these experiences as revelations of a resurrection. Proselytizing in order to spread the new narrative about Jesus will have further reduced their embarrassing cognitive dissonance. This explains why after the crucifixion many members of the Jesus sect started to preach and proselytize so passionately that Paul thought it necessary to persecute them. Let us now move to the second topic of this section.

In order to understand the formative history of Christianity from Paul's conversion until the reign of emperor Constantine, numerous fascinating problems have to be solved, about which there is a large amount of scholarly literature. For example, how should we explain that the so-called apocalyptic messianic Jewish sect formed by Jesus' earliest followers after his execution survived when no second coming of Jesus occurred? Why did Paul, a pious Jew, decide to proselytize also among Gentiles after his conversion to Jesus, so that the Jesus sect separated itself gradually from Judaism and could expand further within the Roman Empire? More generally, how should we account for the early proliferation of Jesus' followers, who had to compete with many antagonistic Jewish groups, such as Pharisees, Sadducees, Essenes, and Zealots? Here I shall focus on one of these problems only, which is quite general. What explains the seemingly miraculous transformation of the marginal Jesus sect of, say, about 1,000 participants within the Roman Empire around the year 40 into a religious community that became so large that emperor Constantine thought it wise to convert to Christianity before the Milvian Bridge battle in 312 CE (if indeed he did so)?

---

[36] Cf. Komarnitsky (2014) for a recent overview of research on cognitive dissonance applied to the Jesus sect. Cf. also Komarnitsky (2019).

In his celebrated sociological study *The Rise of Christianity* (1996), Rodney Stark argued on the one hand that the expansion of Christianity in the Roman Empire until Constantine's conversion was not miraculous at all, because its plausibly estimated early speed of about 40 per cent per decade can be explained completely with reference to mundane factors. On the other hand, he showed that this rise was in part an effect of chance or good luck, since some of these factors were accidental, such as the occurrence of devastating plague epidemics. Let me mention the main causes of the Christian expansion within an environment that was chaotic and even calamitous in many respects. The city of Antioch, the chief centre of early Christianity during Roman times, was often conquered by inimical forces, plundered and sacked, partly destroyed by hundreds of earthquakes, and once burned to the ground by Persian conquerors, whereas its population suffered from famines and killer epidemics. As many different ethnic groups inhabited the town, it was 'a city filled with misery, danger, fear, despair, and hatred', in which 'crime flourished and the streets were dangerous at night' (pp. 160–161).

Stark analyses many features of early Christianity that account for its gradual growth within the historical environment of Antioch and other Roman cities. For example (a), since Christians had abolished the strict laws of Judaism and separated theology from ethnicity, their religion was attractive both for Jews in the Roman Empire who wanted to integrate among non-Jews and for Gentiles who were longing for the strong cohesion of Jewish communities. Stark confirms this hypothesis through a quantitative analysis of twenty-two Roman cities, showing that Christianization correlated positively with Jewish influence. Second (b), since Christians prohibited birth control, abortion, and infanticide, their communities could evolve with a growth rate of about 40 per cent per decade, whereas on average the Roman population was declining. (c) While most male Roman citizens preferred to have only a few children, and often satisfied their sexual needs among men, Christians interdicted homosexuality and non-reproductive sexual behaviours. In addition (d), as Roman men often killed their female babies, preferring sons to daughters, the moral prohibition of infanticide yielded a more even sex ratio among Christians, resulting in a higher percentage of childbearing women. As a consequence (e), many Roman women converted to Christianity, convincing their husbands to follow them. Female conversions were also motivated by the facts (f) that in contradistinction to military Roman religions, Christianity allowed women to participate in worship, and (g) that it prescribed monogamy. Since (h) Christianity ordained charity primarily with regard to believers, their communities were miniature welfare states, causing (i) a higher life expectancy. Finally (j), whereas many Roman citizens fled from their cities when plagues occurred, most Christians stayed in town in order to care for diseased fellow believers. Their religious morality required this, promising redemption through sacrifice. As medical statistics have shown, the latter policy yielded a much higher survivor rate than the former during the serious epidemics of 165 and 251 CE for example, each of which killed about a third of the population. As a consequence, the percentage of Christian believers in the Roman Empire increased considerably during plagues.

Rodney Stark's historical account of the Christian rise in the Roman Empire shows convincingly that this expansion can be explained completely with reference to secular causes, such as growth through social networks and specific moral convictions. There is no need to invoke the Christian deity and His sacred string-pulling as a theoretical background assumption. Stark's own theoretical background is a very different one: the rational choice theory that is advocated by many economists. According to Stark's (1999) paper, 'all aspects of religion [...] can be understood on the basis of exchange relations between humans and supernatural beings' (p. 264). The imagined god(s) would provide goods that are either impossible in this world, such as surviving death, or unlikely to be obtained by humans, like rain during droughts. Believers would pay for these goods by engaging in many kinds of religious practices, such as prayer, sacrifices, and rituals. Their religious engagement would be rational since it is, or can be, justified by cost–benefit reasoning with regard to goods that we humans cannot produce.

In his book *Darwin's Cathedral* (2002), the evolutionary biologist David Sloan Wilson expresses great admiration for the research on religion of Rodney Stark and his colleagues, but he radically rejects their rational choice theory. His main objection to this theoretical framework is that it neglects the main empirical causes and effects of religious expansions, that is, why in a specific cultural context a particular shared religion enhances the spread of its communities compared to competing clusters. These causes and effects consist in the purely mundane advantages of belonging to a specific religious group, which can be analysed within the framework of multilevel evolutionary selection theory. With regard to each particular cultural trait (a–j), it may have been the case that from an evolutionary point of view it was merely a by-product, or that it was adaptive either at an individual level or at the level of a specific group. As the spread of each trait might require a different explanation, we should formulate competing hypotheses with regard to any particular feature (a–j) of early Christianity and derive predictions that can be tested empirically. This is what Wilson's research programme aims to do with regard to the evolution of Christianity and of religions worldwide. The main purpose of his book is 'to treat the organismic concept of religious groups as a serious scientific hypothesis' (p. 1). Since each feature of a religion may require a different explanation, 'evolutionary theory will turn the study of religion into quite a complex subject' (p. 10).

One should read Wilson's book in order to get an adequate impression of this complexity. Let me focus here on his explanation of one specific cultural trait of early Christianity only: (j) how Christian believers reacted to the plagues that occurred in the Roman Empire. Within the framework of evolutionary theory, we should distinguish sharply between the proximate and the ultimate explanations of their behaviour. If we wonder why during a plague epidemic Christians tended to stay in town in order to care for their diseased co-religionists at the risk of being infected and dying themselves, the proximate explanation will mention their moral and metaphysical motives for doing so, such as the belief that they would be remunerated in a next world for their self-sacrificial actions and the moral imperatives to imitate Christ's martyrdom and to love one's neighbour.

In order to provide an ultimate explanation, we should study empirically the survival rates of Christian communities compared to those rates of other populations when a plague occurred in the chaotic historical context of the Roman Empire. Whereas the so-called heathen tended to flee from plague-infected friends and families, most Christians stayed in town in order to care for their sick companions. Empirical research shows that in fact the 'death-embracing altruism' of Christians 'increased the survival of the group' compared to the survival rates of the heathen communities (Wilson 2002, p. 156). Since Christians transferred cultural traits (j) by education to each new generation, their religious groups functioned as adaptive units in the evolutionary sense. Furthermore, because the Christian communities did not merely consist of members of one and the same family tree, their evolutionary success with respect to trait (j) cannot be explained by a mechanism of kin selection. The hypothesis of group selection is indispensable in this respect, as D. S. Wilson has argued convincingly. I leave it to you, readers, to wonder what may be the best proximate and ultimate explanations of traits (a–i) of early Christianity and to what extent an evolutionary explanation of each trait will be appropriate. Most of the traits mentioned (b, c, d, g, h, j) consisted in the endorsement by early Christians of specific moral convictions, which unified their functional groups.

4.4 GLOBAL WARMING, POPULATION GROWTH, AND RELIGION

Let me finish this chapter on religion and ethics by discussing briefly what I consider to be the greatest moral challenge humanity is facing today: the problem of human-induced global warming. What role can religions, such as the many subdivisions of Christianity and Islam, play in order to mitigate the threatening and catastrophic effects of climate change? As the assessment reports of the Intergovernmental Panel on Climate Change show convincingly, the average surface temperature on Earth has risen already by more than one degree Celsius since pre-industrial times.[37] This recent rise of the global mean surface temperature has been caused mainly by anthropogenic greenhouse gas emissions, which increased substantially because of the growing human population and its economic endeavours, such as the still increasing use of fossil fuels. Today, the atmospheric concentrations of the greenhouse gases carbon dioxide, methane, and nitrous oxide have reached levels that are unprecedented during the last 800,000 years. If this proliferation persists, the increase of the global mean surface temperature on Earth in 2100 will range from 3.7°C to 4.8°C above the average for 1850–1900 according to baseline scenarios, that is, without any mitigation.[38]

Humanity will not be able to adapt successfully to such a situation. Let me just mention some of the most catastrophic consequences this increase of the global average temperature on Earth will already have caused by 2100. Since global warming results in the melting of land ice, one of its many effects is the rise of sea levels. As William Nordhaus argued in *The Climate Casino* (2013), '[s]ea-level rise is one of the most worrisome impacts of climate change' (p. 112). On average the level of the oceans will rise worldwide by about 66 metres if all the land ice on Greenland and Antarctica melts. Greenland's contribution (7.4 metres) is much smaller than Antarctica's. Recent research on ice melting on Greenland between 1992 and 2018 reveals that its ice sheet is losing about seven

---

[37] IPCC (2018), p. 6.
[38] IPCC (2014), pp. 44 and 20. During the last Ice Age, the mean surface temperature on Earth was only about 4°C lower than during post-glacial (pre-industrial) times.

times more mass per year than in the early 1990s.[39] Significant parts of Antarctica's ice sheets are also seriously out of balance. According to current calculations, the melting of land-based ice sheets and glaciers combined with the thermal expansion of the oceans will result in a sea-level rise of between 69 cm and 240 cm on average in 2100, depending on the amount of combusted fossil fuel and on population growth.[40] One expert estimated that, initially, for each centimetre of global sea-level rise about six million people on Earth will be exposed to coastal flooding.[41]

Another catastrophic effect of human-induced global warming is increasing desertification, defined in the broad sense of many types of land degradation because of water scarcity. Since land needs less heat to raise its temperature than water in the oceans, global warming has heated the land surface of the Earth more quickly than the global average, with about 1.6°C on average since the pre-industrial period (1850–1900). Increasing desertification is caused not only by human-induced global warming but also by the land management of the growing human population, such as deforestation, overgrazing, and overcultivation. Its impacts are plural and devastating for biodiversity, human food security, and the inhabitability of many areas on Earth, such as South Asia, the circum Sahara region, and the Middle East. Since the human population of drylands across the world is projected to increase to about four billion by 2050, there will be a multitude of climate refugees during the coming decennia. Clearly, humanity should prevent further desertification as soon as possible.[42]

Apart from these and many other gradual impacts of human-induced global warming, there are so-called 'tipping points', at which our climate system will change abruptly and irreversibly from one regime into another because of a self-reinforcing feedback. For example, the melting of the

---

[39] Shepherd et al. (2019).
[40] Cf. also: 'Global and Regional Sea Level Rise Scenarios for the United States' (NOAA Technical Report NOS CO-OPS 083), National Oceanic and Atmospheric Administration, January 2017, p. vi, https://tidesandcurrents.noaa.gov/publications/techrpt83_Global_and_Regional_SLR_Scenarios_for_the_US_final.pdf. 'The projections and results presented in several peer-reviewed publications provide evidence to support a physically plausible GMSL rise in the range of 2.0 meters (m) to 2.7 m, and recent results regarding Antarctic ice-sheet instability indicate that such outcomes may be more likely than previously thought.'
[41] This is estimated by Andrew Shepherd (University of Leeds). Cf. AWI (Alfred-Wegner-Institut; Helmholtz-Zentrum für Polar- und Meeresforschung), 'Out of Balance' (10 December 2019).
[42] Cf. IPCC, 2019.

permafrost soil in Siberia causes an increasing evaporation of methane into the atmosphere. Since methane is a powerful greenhouse gas, its release boosts global warming, which will speed up considerably and cause ever more methane release. Another tipping point is sea ice melting at the North Pole. Although the melting of sea ice will not raise the average level of the oceans, it will lower the so-called albedo, that is, the proportion of incident sunlight that is reflected. Since a darker Earth reflects less sunlight, it will heat up more quickly. There are many of these tipping points, so let me mention only one more. When the Greenland ice sheet melts increasingly, it will drop in elevation. Since temperatures are higher at lower altitudes, the shrinking of the sheet will further accelerate its melting. As it is not easy to predict when exactly such a tipping point will occur, it would be wise for humanity *to prevent any further global warming*.

According to the Paris Agreement, adopted on 12 December 2015 by consensus within the United Nations Framework Convention on Climate Change (UNFCCC), and until December 2020 ratified by 197 UNFCCC member countries, humanity should keep the increase of the global average temperature well below 2°C above pre-industrial levels and do its best to limit the increase to 1.5°C. It is an interesting question whether this target is sufficiently ambitious, since the very stable climate period of the last 7,000 years has been a necessary precondition for the development and spread of human civilizations on Earth. However this may be, the many international climate negotiations after the Paris Agreement, the overwhelming opposition from those who work in, or have interests in, CO_2-producing industries to proposals to reduce greenhouse gas emissions, and the fact that no country has met its pledged emission reduction target, show that humanity will not succeed in keeping global warming below the 2°C limit. Numerous new and radical efforts have to be made, and revolutionary measures should be taken everywhere on Earth, such as introducing a worldwide and severe carbon dioxide (CO_2) taxation or an effective global cap-and-trade regime for greenhouse gas emissions. Let me focus for a moment on one of these indispensable efforts only, to which religions can and should contribute.

Global population growth is one of the most important causes of the increasing emissions of carbon dioxide and other greenhouse gases. Since the world population is expanding by about eighty-one million people per year, this growth is a key driver of global warming. On 5 November 2019, a letter signed by more than 11,000 scientists has been published in *BioScience*. It called for a 'gradual reduction' in the world's population as one of six necessary conditions for preventing catastrophic global warming.[43] The authors do not point out, however, that such a reduction of the Earth's human population requires a religious revolution within Christianity and Islam. As I mentioned in the introduction to this chapter, Muslims and Christians contribute considerably to global population growth. Whereas the replacement level of humans on Earth requires a fertility rate of 2.1 children per woman during her lifetime, in 2015–2020 the Christian rate is 2.6, and the rate among Muslims amounts to 2.9. These high rates should be lowered immediately to the replacement level, because it is a moral obligation for all of us to do what is needed in order to prevent the catastrophic global warming on Earth that will result from our current behaviours.

Let me conclude this chapter, then, by recommending to all apostles, bishops, gurus, imams, pastors, patriarchs, priests, rabbis, and other religious leaders, to preach passionately a restraint in human procreation within their communities. In order to put this moral imperative into practice, it will help to foster other ethical targets as well, such as women's emancipation and better education. Since the future well-being of humanity is a legitimate moral aim for all of us, religious leaders should also urge their governments and their followers to take other measures that are necessary to save our climate, such as replacing fossil fuels with safe sources of energy; reducing emissions of other climate pollutants; protecting and restoring the ecosystems on Earth like coral reefs, wetlands, and primary forests; and restricting the production and eating of meat.

---

[43] Ripple et al. (2019).

PART III

APOLOGETIC STRATEGIES EVALUATED

5

The Decision Tree for Religious Believers

In Part I, I pointed out that none of the alleged primary epistemic sources of religious beliefs or methods of religious research could be validated. As a consequence, religious explanations have been eliminated from the sciences during the accelerating intellectual progress in Europe after the scientific revolution in the seventeenth century. However, the resulting separation of science and religion does not show that all scientific results are religiously neutral. On the contrary, there are many science-based arguments that undermine or falsify religious convictions. If we conclude, plausibly, that none of the religious beliefs to the effect that some supernatural being exists is true, it becomes a fascinating interdisciplinary problem how we should explain the worldwide human endorsement of such erroneous creeds.

This explanatory problem is complicated and wide-ranging. Part II focused on some of its most intriguing issues. Monotheist religions developed rather recently in human (pre)history, and were preceded by animisms and polytheistic faiths. How should we explain the origins and functions of polytheisms? Furthermore, what motivated the gradual transition of some polytheistic religions to versions of monotheism? Several hypotheses that account for these cultural developments were discussed in Chapter 3. Chapter 4 is devoted to the rise of the so-called moralizing religions. Various queries have been explored, such as whether a religious justification of moral rules can be valid and how the historical spread of moralizing religions should be explained. Furthermore, I compared two theoretical accounts concerning the impressive Christian proliferation within the Roman Empire and discussed one of the greatest moral challenges humanity is facing today.

As I argued in the introduction to Chapter 3, the explanatory Part II depends intrinsically on the philosophical results of Part I. If a belief is true, the explanation of why people or human groups endorse it may be very simple: that they discovered its truth. If the belief is false, such an explanation is excluded, and one has to investigate the mental and social impacts of sustaining this belief. Therefore, the empirical sciences of religion should not engage in explaining the many functions of holding specific religious beliefs without relying on the upshot of religious epistemology. As I stressed in the introduction to Chapter 3, these scientific disciplines cannot be 'neutral' concerning the question whether the investigated religious beliefs are true or false.

Consequently, those of you who are religious believers will not only tend to deny some conclusions of Part I but also criticize the explanatory accounts discussed in Part II. You may endorse these accounts fully with regard to religions you do not belong to but reject them at least to some extent concerning your own religious convictions. For example, Christian readers will not believe that the thirty-three *crore* deities of Tantra Hinduism do exist in fact. If informed about the many versions of Hinduism, these readers may be atheists with regard to the 330 million Hindu gods. Most of them will maintain, however, that the Christian god does exist, and assume or argue that adopting this belief is epistemically legitimate. Therefore, they might claim that the correct core explanation of the origin and proliferation of Christianity is that God exists and revealed himself somehow in Jesus, to apostle Paul, and to many other humans.

Such a reply raises crucial questions for present-day religious believers, questions to which Part III of this book is devoted. Can one still legitimize somehow the endorsement of a specific religious belief in our science-informed epoch in spite of the information and arguments provided in Parts I and II? Is there still any convincing apologetic strategy, that is, a reliable way of showing that a specific religious belief is true or otherwise acceptable for 'educated and intelligent people living in the twenty-first century'?[1] In this fifth chapter, contemporary apologetic strategies are classified, and I evaluate some non-argumentative ones, whereas Chapter 6 is devoted to an argumentative approach. Let me illustrate the various apologetic strategies with reference to some of the most prominent Christian philosophers in our times, such as Alvin Plantinga

---

[1] Plantinga (2000), p. viii. My apologies for quoting this text many times!

and Richard Swinburne, whose apologetics I assessed extensively in my 2012 book *God in the Age of Science? A Critique of Religious Reason*, and experts whose writings I did not discuss in that volume, like John Cottingham and Paul K. Moser.

Readers may wonder why so many of these different apologetic strategies have been developed. The short answer is that today scientifically well-informed religious believers are confronted with serious challenges if they intend to justify their religious belief in one or more god(s), as has been demonstrated in Parts I and II. Let me list three challenges in §5.1 in order to show that in our science-informed times apologetic strategies have to meet demanding criteria. §5.2 is devoted to a classification of these strategies, which I call the Decision Tree for Religious Believers.[2] If you consider yourself to be a religious believer, you should decide how you would legitimize your faith if you were confronted with someone who denies its truth and epistemic legitimacy. One possible reply is that your opponent misunderstands this faith if it is interpreted as a propositional belief that can be true or false independently of what the believers think, and can be evaluated separately from the relevant religious practices. Various versions of such a religious relativism, non-cognitivism, or non-factualism are discussed in §5.3. According to another prominent response, endorsed by Alvin Plantinga and examined in §5.4, the core of religious faith does consist of true beliefs about an independently existing divinity, but endorsing them does not need an epistemic justification in order to be legitimate. §5.5 is devoted to what I call Involvement Evidentialism, an apologetic strategy defended by John Cottingham as 'a More Humane Approach', whereas I discuss the 'personifying evidence of God' put forward by Paul Moser in the last section (§5.6) of this chapter. Since from an epistemological point of view none of these responses is very convincing, I raise the question in Chapter 6 whether there is an argumentative apologetic approach that is more credible.

5.1 CHALLENGES FOR RELIGIOUS APOLOGETICS

Those who aim at vindicating the endorsement of a specific religious creed, such as some version of Hinduism, Judaism, Christianity, or Islam, may focus on two very different kinds of justification, which

---

[2] Cf. Philipse (2012) and (2013b) for earlier versions of this 'decision tree'.

I distinguished in §1.1. From a functional point of view, they might argue that on average the good empirical effects of embracing a particular religious belief outweigh the blameworthy consequences. The belief may be 'salutary' even though it cannot be justified epistemically.[3] In order to show this, one will need credible criteria for distinguishing between good and bad effects and to engage in various types of empirical research concerning the causal connections between holding a specific religious belief and the beatitude or moral merits of believers. Our main perspective in Part III, however, is the epistemological one. We focus on the content of a religious conviction and wonder whether and how it can still be demonstrated, or reasonably believed, that its truth is more probable than its falsity, or at least not extremely unlikely, notwithstanding the results of Parts I and II.

If religious believers intend to legitimize epistemologically their belief that a specific divinity exists, they are faced today with demanding challenges. Let me start this chapter by listing three of these challenges, and by indicating briefly why they are exigent.

> a. The Semantic Challenge. In order to discuss whether a specific divinity exists, such as a deity named God, for instance, the topic of our conversation should be defined clearly. On various grounds, this semantic challenge with regard to the word 'God' is quite demanding. Since the term is written with a capital 'G', it may seem to be a proper name, whereas the same word without a capital 'G' is a common noun. Why would one elevate a common noun to the role of a proper name in this manner? We never name a child 'Human being', or a city just 'City', for example. Moreover, how can the noun 'God' function as a proper name, since different nouns or names (Dieu, Dio, Bóg, etc.) are used in other languages? Can we know that all these names refer to one and the same subject? One might conclude that the term 'God' should be used 'as a most exalted *title* rather than as a proper name'.[4] But then one would have to describe in detail the persons or entities to whom or to which we would attribute such a title.

In order to give meaning to a proper name, we have to indicate clearly who or what is its bearer. With regard to newborn children, for example,

---

[3] Cf. Long (2017).
[4] Moser (2010), p. 22 (Moser's italics). Cf. pp. 114, 144, 153–155, 162, 182, 192, 234, 236–237, 242, 258–259. Cf. also Moser (2013), pp. 11–13 and *passim*.

we may do so by pointing to them while pronouncing their name, but such a common method of naming is unavailable with regard to the proper name 'God' if believers claim that God is incorporeal. The only way available for giving meaning to this name is to define it explicitly, but religious believers who profess that 'God exists' have provided different definitions of the word 'God', many of which are mutually incompatible, too vague to be informative, or logically incoherent. Whom or what are they referring to when they say that God exists? If various experts provide divergent definitions of the word 'God' that are mutually incompatible, they cannot refer to one and the same being or entity by using this name.

Furthermore, the meaning of the words in terms of which the expression 'God' has been defined by Christian and other monotheist masterminds often is unclear. For example, what is meant by saying that God is omnipresent when one adds that God is immaterial, assuming that the meaning of 'omnipresent' should be distinguished from 'omniscient' and 'omnipotent'? Other defining epithets such as 'omnipotent' imply challenging paradoxes. If one wonders whether an omnipotent God can create a rock he cannot lift, for example, both the affirmative and the negative answer imply that He is not omnipotent. Recent attempts to show that theism can be defined coherently turn out to be quite demanding and require voluminous writings.[5] Christian philosophers have discussed these semantic conundrums during many centuries but still do not agree with each other. Some of them, such as Karl Barth and John Hick, even claimed that God is so drastically different from all mundane creatures that He is 'beyond characterization by the range of concepts available to human thought'.[6] This doctrine of 'divine ineffability' or 'transcategoriality' implies, however, that the word 'God' cannot be defined by using any human language, so that we cannot know what or whom these Christians are talking about when they say that God exists and should be glorified. Even worse, they cannot know it themselves.

    b. The Epistemic Challenge. If a clear and allegedly coherent definition of the word 'God' were provided, or an identifying description of the person or entity were given that deserves the title 'God', those who believe that God (as defined or specified) exists would have to tell us why they think that this belief is true. Suppose, for example,

---

[5] Cf. Swinburne (1993, 2016), for example. Swinburne discusses the 'Paradox of the Stone' in chapter 9 on God's omnipotence.

[6] Barth (1957), p. 76; the quote is from Hick (2000), p. 35. Cf. Plantinga (2000), pp. 43–63; Philipse (2012), p. 28.

that they define the term by saying that God is an all-knowing and all-powerful person, who is perfectly good, created the universe, and loves all human beings.[7] Are there any convincing grounds for endorsing the religious belief that such a divinity exists? As I argued in Part I, this epistemic (or epistemological) challenge for religious believers is demanding today for at least three reasons.

First, since none of the primary epistemic sources of religious beliefs has been calibrated, no religious credo can be justified by being based upon such a source. Scientific explanations of these sources have refuted the religious accounts, as I argued in §1.3 with regard to the conversion of Saul on a road to Damascus. Second, because there are no reliable epistemic sources of religious claims to truth, and many of these claims were falsified during the history of science, religious contentions have been excluded systematically from all domains within which reliable methods of investigation are applied, such as scientific disciplines or historical investigations. Finally, we saw that scientific progress has yielded many new empirical arguments against theism as defined, some of which were spelled out in §2.4. For these reasons, religious believers face an overwhelming epistemic challenge today if they are to succeed in defining clearly and consistently the content of their creed. How can it still be justified, reasonable, or warranted to endorse their specific religious belief?

c. The Explanatory Challenge. Historical and anthropological research with regard to the religious diversity on Earth has created a serious explanatory challenge for Jewish, Christian, Islamic, and other monotheists. As I set out in Chapter 3, polytheist religions preceded the cultural evolution of monotheisms. From a purely empirical and atheist perspective we can explain very well why during human (pre)history monotheisms developed gradually from polytheisms and became dominant in various regions on Earth. Suppose, however, that you are a believing monotheist and profess that there really is an omnipotent and omniscient deity who is perfectly good, created the universe, and loves all human beings. How can you explain, then, that your God, Elohim, Yahweh, or Allah was hiding from all humans during so many millennia and still does not reveal him/herself to each of us? Traditional religious

---

[7] Cf. Plantinga (2000), p. vii.

replies to this question of divine hiddenness, such as the claim that God hides himself from humans in order to punish them for their sins or to safeguard their moral autonomy, are unacceptable in the light of our present historical and anthropological knowledge. Were all humans sinful before monotheisms developed gradually in human (pre)history? If an omnipotent god would exist who loves all human beings like a good father, would this deity not have revealed himself clearly to each of us in every (pre)historical and cultural context?

Motivated by such challenges to religions, during the last decennia their apologetic experts have elaborated many different strategies in order to legitimize the endorsement of a specific religious belief. Let me classify these strategies in §5.2. Will any of them be promising from an epistemological point of view?

5.2 APOLOGETIC STRATEGIES CLASSIFIED

Religious believers who are impressed by the challenges outlined in §5.1 may decide to avoid them by reinterpreting radically the content of their beliefs. Instead of holding that in fact there is a specific divinity who exists independently of human convictions and practices, they might embrace a purely symbolical interpretation of religious existence claims, for example. By saying that the Christian God exists one would mean mainly that specific moral values are important and should be pursued. In his 1997 essay 'Nonoverlapping Magisteria', Stephen Jay Gould defended such an interpretation of religious beliefs in order to exclude any possible intellectual conflict between science and religion. If Christian convictions had merely a moral content, there could not be any epistemic incompatibility between this religion and evolutionary theory, for example.

Such a radical reinterpretation of religious beliefs may be called 'Religious Non-factualism'. It will be attractive to those of you who agree that the factual existence of any divinity is most unlikely in light of what scientific progress has taught us but nevertheless want to be a member of a religious community and endorse its moral commitments. However, most religious believers will hold that the god(s) of their religion do(es) exist in fact, independently of our beliefs, and that only someone who somehow acknowledges this fact really is religious. They embrace Religious Factualism. Non-factualism and Factualism may be considered as the two most fundamental options (a, b) in what I call a Decision Tree for

Religious Believers, the first node (I) of which is the choice between these two options.[8] If one prefers option (a) of non-factualism, one will have to face a second node (II) of the decision tree. With regard to the question whether any god or other supernatural being exists in fact, independently of our religious endeavours and conceptual schemes, one may either be (c) a universal atheist or prefer to be (d) agnostic, depending on the strictness of one's epistemic criteria and one's intellectual honesty. Non-factualism is an attractive position for scientifically well-informed religious adherents, because it covers up their agnosticism or universal atheism.

If you believe that the specific god(s) you adore do(es) exist in fact, independently of human religions, you are (b) a Religious Factualist. Such factualists may also be called Religious Realists. Many factualists will also be atheists or agnostics with regard to the divinities postulated by religions they do not belong to, so that they may be called selective atheists or agnostics. For example, most monotheists will deny that any divinity exists apart from their preferred deity, such as Yahweh, God, or Allah, who is often believed to exist necessarily in a sense. As a consequence, they will be confronted by a challenging dilemma, which is node III of the Decision Tree for Religious Believers. Either (e) they hold that their endorsement of a particular religious belief can be considered to be reasonable from an epistemological point of view, even though they reject all other religious beliefs that are incompatible with their own. Or (f) they agree with Søren Kierkegaard and his followers that such an endorsement cannot be epistemically reasonable, so that one should suspend epistemic reason if one wants to become or remain really religious and decide to make a leap of faith. Let me call option (e) Religious Reasonabilism and label (f) Religious Voluntarism or Fideism.

The next node (IV) of our Decision Tree for Religious Believers will be faced by those devotees who opt for (e) Religious Reasonabilism. They may hold either that (g) their religious beliefs have to be backed up by evidence or by good reasons in order to be epistemically legitimate, or that (h) such epistemic support is not needed since God, or another divinity they believe in, has implanted the relevant belief in their minds, so that this faith is infallible, if at least their god exists. Assuming that God (as defined) implanted a Christian belief in the minds of Reformed Protestants, for example, their confidence that this belief is true would be

---

[8] Monotheists who claim that God (as defined by them) exists 'necessarily' will be classified as factualists if they hold that God's necessary existence implies that this divinity exists in fact. If not, they are non-factualists.

perfectly reasonable or warranted, they might claim, as long as it has not been proven that the belief is false. Option (g) may be entitled Religious Evidentialism, whereas it would be appropriate to baptize end node (h) Religious Confidentialism. Both of these options are confronted by provocative challenges, as will be realized by those of you who read Part I of this book. Confidentialists (h) who believe that their religious convictions are true have to face the challenges of cultural contingency and religious pluralism, as explained in Chapter 1. Evidentialists (g) will have to convince us that a specific religious belief is supported by sufficient evidence or did result from investigations conducted by applying reliable methods of research, even though religious beliefs have been eliminated from the sciences because they could not be supported by trustworthy empirical evidence or result from the application of validated methods of research, as was shown briefly in Chapter 2.

In order to do justice to the great diversity of contemporary religious apologists, we have to elaborate the Decision Tree for Religious Believers by adding some further options. For example, there are three different types of Religious Evidentialism. According to node V of our decision tree, Evidentialists should tell us whether they hold that (i) the evidence supporting their religious belief is also publicly accessible in principle to unbelievers who are experts in the philosophy of religion, or that (j) the evidence is accessible only to those who have involved themselves into the relevant religious community. Those who defend the second option (j) will argue that the religious search for truth requires various motivational and emotional transformations, which will happen only to those who take part in the rituals and communal activities of a specific religion for quite some time in order to open themselves to the relevant religious evidence. Those who endorse option (i) may be named Unbiased Evidentialists, whereas supporters of (j) might be called Involvement Evidentialists, since they defend what has been called an 'epistemology of involvement' with regard to religious beliefs.[9] It is plausible to add a third option (k) to node V, because many apologetic experts will argue that options (i) and (j) have to be combined, given the diversity of the evidence that supports a specific religious belief. These religious apologists are (k) Amalgamated Evidentialists.

Both (i) Unbiased and (k) Amalgamated Evidentialists will have to face yet another node (VI) of the Decision Tree for Religious Believers.

---

[9] Cottingham (2014), p. 23. Cf. §1.4 and §5.5.

Evidentialists of both types hold that the endorsement of a religious belief can be epistemically legitimate only if it is supported by publicly accessible evidence and arguments, at least to some extent. Such evidence pro (and contra) specific religious claims to truth is assembled by experts in what is called 'natural' or 'rational' theology, which is the topic of Chapter 6. The dilemma confronting these experts is concerned with the methods and epistemic sources they do and should use in order to acquire and evaluate religiously relevant evidence for the existence of a well-defined divinity. Either (l) their methodology adopts the general methods scientists and scholars are applying when they investigate an existential (hypo)thesis, or (m) their epistemic sources and methods of investigation are unlike these calibrated ones. Both (l) Science-inspired Natural Theology and (m) Science-shunning Natural Theology are risky for religious believers. If they opt for (l), they will have to face many science-inspired empirical arguments against the contention that a specific god exists, as we saw in §2.4, and their religious belief may be refuted rather than supported by the aggregate of arguments *pro* and *contra*. Furthermore, they will have to explain why all religious claims and hypotheses have been eliminated from the sciences during the impressive scientific progress of the last two centuries. Option (m) is even more precarious, however, because one can have confidence in methods of research and primary sources of belief only if they have been calibrated. As I argued in §1.4, none of the primary sources of religious beliefs has been calibrated epistemically.

Readers who consider themselves to be religious believers should wonder which branch(s) of the Decision Tree they prefer, and what would be their optimal choice.[10] Is there any promising apologetic option available? Philosophers who want to justify their universal atheism will face an even more complex challenge. In principle, they would have to show that none of the branches of the decision tree will stand up to a critical evaluation. In §§5.3–5.4, the main non-argumentative apologetic strategies are assessed succinctly, and in §§5.5–5.6, I evaluate two prominent versions of Involvement Evidentialism. Chapter 6 is devoted to Unbiased Evidentialism, that is, to natural theology.

---

[10] Cf. Philipse (2012), pp. xiv–xv, (2013a), and (2013b) for earlier versions of this decision tree.

5.3 RELIGIOUS LANGUAGE GAMES

In order to evaluate convincingly each of the apologetic options for religious believers, we should focus on their most sophisticated advocates. With regard to option (a) of Religious Non-factualism, some of them seem to be Wittgenstein-inspired Christian philosophers of religion like Dewi Zephaniah Phillips or Fergus Kerr, who argue that we must take part in, and reflect on, religious practices and rituals if we want to understand properly what is meant when it is said that God is love or that one is longing for the grace of God, and so on. One should analyse the 'religious language game' from the point of view of its practitioners and not confuse it with other uses of language in different social contexts, such as scientific projects.

From his religion-internal linguistic analysis, D. Z. Phillips concluded that God cannot be conceived of as an individual superhuman being, a 'metaphysical subject', since '[n]o individual can be the element, the light, the spirit, in which we live, and move, and have our being'.[11] God's reality is not a matter of fact among other facts but (provides) an all-embracing perspective on reality that is radically different from all other perspectives, 'a whole mode of illumination, the illumination of grace'.[12] If we wonder whether this perspective presupposes the existence of God as a supernatural being, Phillips answers as follows: 'Coming to see that there is a divine reality is not like coming to see that an additional being exists. If it were, there would be an extension of one's knowledge of facts, but no extension of one's understanding"'.[13] In particular, we cannot conceive coherently of God as a 'pure consciousness' since this notion is incoherent, Phillips argues by raising four Wittgenstein-inspired logical objections, which show 'that the metaphysical realm in which God is said to dwell is an intellectual aberration'.[14]

How should we interpret, then, the traditional Christian profession that the 'illumination of grace' is a gift from God, for which we should be grateful to this divinity and express our gratitude in prayers? Do such confessions of faith not presuppose that God exists as an omniscient subject with whom we may communicate? Furthermore, if this deity exists 'necessarily' and 'eternally', being an absolute reality in some sense,

---

[11] Quoted by Brenner (2008), who confesses to have 'lost the exact reference for this quote' (note 13). Cf. Phillips (2005), p. 462.
[12] Phillips (2005), p. 463.   [13] Nielsen and Phillips (2005), pp. 370, 221.
[14] Phillips (2005), pp. 456–458.

doesn't it follow that God also exists in fact? If not, how could we receive God's love and grace? Do our notions of love and grace not imply that there can only be divine grace or love if in fact there is some subject who provides them to us?

Claiming to analyse 'the notion of divine reality' by 'endeavoring to elucidate its grammar' in his Wittgenstein-inspired manner, D. Z. Phillips rejects this common interpretation of Christian beliefs. As he wrote: 'It is a misunderstanding to try to get "behind" grace to God, since "grace" is a synonym for "God".' In other words: 'God's reality and God's divinity, that is, his grace and love, come to the same thing. God is not "real" in any other sense.'[15] These quotes suggest that according to Phillips the Christian God is 'real' in the sense of an all-embracing framework of grace or love, the spiritual reality of which is 'other than the world', and not in the sense of Someone who gives us this grace and love. Accordingly, one might classify Phillips as a Non-factualist, since he holds that facts can be stated only *within* some conceptual framework or perspective.[16]

Whereas Phillips is not a Non-factualist in sense (a) I defined in §5.2, these two types of non-factualism share an important feature. In both cases, it would be pointless to confront them with epistemic challenges as described in §5.1. With regard to religious beliefs, Phillips rejects the epistemological use of 'belief' according to which his Christian conviction would be a claim to truth that can be supported by arguments or evidence, and which is put forward within a specific logical space. According to his radical interpretation of what it means to acknowledge 'the reality of divine grace for the first time', this acknowledgement consists in acquiring a 'whole mode of illumination, the illumination of grace', an all-embracing light 'in which the believer sees all things'.[17]

In other words, if you 'come to acknowledge the reality of divine grace for the first time, no prior logical space awaited it', since you are acquiring a radically new and all-embracing logical space. As a consequence, it is 'an intellectual aberration' to assume that there is a 'metaphysical realm in which God is said to dwell'.[18] Phillips concludes that it would be a deep religious mistake for believers to engage in religious apologetics and to

---

[15] Phillips (2005), p. 461.
[16] Min (2008) defends a more realism-oriented interpretation of D. Z. Phillips' philosophy of religion, according to which 'God is indeed independent and transcendent but can be truly so acknowledged only on condition of faith' (p. 137). Nevertheless, Min criticises Phillips by arguing that 'a greater sense of the radical transcendence of God over a language game is necessary in order to avoid reductionism' (p. 131).
[17] Phillips (2005), p. 463.   [18] Phillips (2005), p. 458.

raise and resolve 'the problem of evil', for example.[19] Similarly, it would be erroneous for Christians to think that there is any epistemological space which does not presuppose the truth of Christianity, and within which they might attempt to justify their religious beliefs.

If this is what D. Z. Phillips has been arguing, we may confront his adherents with the following dilemma.[20] Either their aim is (1) to explicate what religious statements of Christian and other devotees mean by studying empirically the religious language games as they are played in fact, that is, to undertake a 'disinterested inquiry' as Phillips claimed to do,[21] or they intend (2) to suggest new rules for their own religious language game in order to safeguard the relevant religious convictions against any epistemic refutation. They might argue, as we saw, that God cannot be conceived of as a 'pure consciousness', and 'that the metaphysical realm in which God is said to dwell is an intellectual aberration'.[22] If they opt for (1) a purely descriptive endeavour, they will discover that most religious believers claim explicitly that in fact their god(s) exist(s) really and independently of their beliefs or pious practices. Most religious believers are (b) Factualists in this sense and not (a) Non-factualists, not even à la Phillips. Consequently, Religious Non-factualism will be refuted when its advocates claim to explicate religious language games as played in fact by most believers. When followers of Phillips opt for (2) a revisionary approach, however, they would be more honest if they said so clearly and admit that they prefer an (a) Non-factualist transformation of their religious creed, since they do not think that it can still be epistemically legitimate in our science-informed culture to endorse the conviction that in fact a specific well-defined deity exists.

Let me mention Don Cupitt of Emmanuel College, Cambridge, as one of the best-known defenders of such an explicitly revisionary approach, which he propagated in *Taking Leave of God* (1980), *After God* (1997), and many of his numerous later publications.[23] According to his non-factualism, religious beliefs about god(s) are not true in a realist sense. Christians should no longer construe their ritual sayings about God as referring to some being or entity but explicate them as expressing their commitment to specific values and ways of life.[24] Since Cupitt remained a practising priest in the Anglican Church until the 1990s, and left it only in

---

[19] Phillips (2005), p. 463.
[20] Cf. Hasker (2007), p. 158; Philipse (2012, 2014), pp. 28–29.
[21] Phillips (2005), p. 465.   [22] Phillips (2005), pp. 456, 458.   [23] Cupitt (1980, 1997).
[24] Cf. Cupitt (2000) for a popular summary of his views.

2008, one can understand that although he gradually lost his belief that in fact some god(s) exist(s), he went on reinterpreting and playing religious language games. A similar diagnosis holds for Dutch Protestant ministers such as Klaas Hendrikse, who also held that the word 'God' refers to human interrelations or interhuman happenings and not to a divinity that exists independently.[25] These Non-factualist reconstructions of religious language games may be appealing to those who lost their factual religious belief, but who are still longing to remain religious in an epistemically innocuous sense.

Since we focus on religious epistemology in this chapter, however, there is no need to discuss their views any further. If one conceives of 'divine reality' in the sense defended by D. Z. Phillips as an all-embracing perspective within which 'the believer sees all things', which is radically different from other global perspectives, including those of competing religions, it is denied that there is a logical space for arguing about God's existence from an epistemological point of view. Accordingly, we do not find any arguments for the existence of God in his writings, whereas Phillips' version of Christianity is confronted with the problem of religious pluralism raised in §1.1. The other Non-factualists, who redefine their religious beliefs purely in terms of commitments to specific moral values and forms of life, do not put forward an existence claim with regard to a divinity at all. Hence, their theological views will not raise any epistemological issue with regard to such a claim.

5.4 RELIGIOUS CONFIDENTIALISM

Those of you who believe that in fact some specific divinity exists, such as Yahweh, God, Hayyi Rabbi, or Allah, somehow defined, have opted for the Factualist (b) branch of the Decision Tree for Religious Believers. Another and more common designation of Factualism may be 'Religious Realism', so let me use these labels as equivalents. Religious factualists or realists are confronted by node III of the decision tree. They have to choose between what I called (e) Religious Reasonabilism, according to which the specific religious belief is reasonable from an epistemological point of view, and (f) Religious Voluntarism or Fideism, the alternative inspired by Kierkegaard et al., according to which one has to suspend epistemic reason in order to leap into a religious faith.

---

[25] Hendrikse (2007).

Paradoxically, religious voluntarists (f) may argue that their option is quite reasonable, both because all arguments in favour of a specific religious belief have been refuted many times, and since in view of the plurality of religions there are no convincing epistemic grounds for preferring one religious belief to the many competing ones which are incompatible with it. If voluntarists defend their view in this manner, however, one may confront them with a new dilemma. Either (n) their endorsement of a specific religious belief is nothing but an instance of wishful thinking embedded in a specific social and cultural context, or (o) they will discover that with or after their endorsement of this belief the grounds for endorsing it will become manifest to them, so that they move from Voluntarism to a specific version of Religious Reasonabilism (e), that is, either to a variety of (g) Religious Evidentialism or to (h) Religious Confidentialism.

If voluntarists admit that (n) is the case, they are in fact retreating into non-factualism (a) and we do not need to discuss their epistemic option any further. If they deny (n), however, they may hold, for example, that their endorsement of a specific religious belief is properly basic, so that one does not need to adduce any positive evidence in order to support it. This option (h) I categorized as Religious Confidentialism, and in §1.1 I discussed briefly the view of one of its most sophisticated protagonists, Alvin Plantinga. Let me explain somewhat more extensively why his Reformed approach is unconvincing from an epistemological point of view. Another apologetic option that I shall evaluate briefly in this chapter (§§5.5 and 5.6) is Non-evidentialist only in part, and I classified it as a subspecies of (g) Religious Evidentialism, to wit: (j) Involvement Evidentialism, as defended for example by John Cottingham and Paul Moser.

In his magnificent masterpiece *Warranted Christian Belief* (2000), recently summarized in *Knowledge and Christian Belief* (2015), Alvin Plantinga clearly confessed why he did not engage in Religious Evidentialism (option g). It would be pointless to propose any evidence or arguments to the effect that the Christian creed is true, since he does not 'know of an argument for Christian belief that seems very likely to convince one who doesn't already accept its conclusion'.[26] In the Decision

---

[26] Plantinga (2000), p. 201. Cf., however, p. 170: 'I believe there are a large number (at least a couple dozen) good arguments for the existence of God; none, however, can really be thought of as a *showing* or *demonstration*. As for classical Christianity, there is even less prospect of demonstrating its truth.'

Tree for Religious Believers we should classify Plantinga's apologetics of Christianity under branch (h) of Religious Confidentialism. Of course, a confidentialist approach will not convince unbelievers either, but this is no drawback for this strategy, since its aim is more modest. Plantinga intends to show merely that endorsing Christian belief is intellectually acceptable *for Christian believers*, even if they are 'educated and intelligent people living in the twenty-first century'.[27] One may wonder whether the faith of Christian believers might not be reinforced by providing arguments for God's existence, but let us analyse Plantinga's approach.[28] How does he develop his apologetic strategy? I summarize it in four steps.[29]

1. In contradistinction to authors such as D. Z. Phillips, Alvin Plantinga focuses on the epistemic acceptability of 'classical Christian belief', the content of which he describes as consisting of two components. According to its *theistic* component, there is only one divinity, called 'God', defined as an all-knowing and all-powerful person, who is 'perfectly good and wholly loving'. Like human persons, God not only has knowledge and beliefs, but 'also affections, loves, and hates'. He 'has created the universe and constantly upholds and providentially guides it'. According to the second component, which is 'uniquely Christian', 'we human beings are somehow mired in rebellion and sin', so that 'we consequently require deliverance and salvation'. This redemption has been arranged by God 'through the sacrificial suffering, death, and resurrection of Jesus Christ'.[30]

2. If we wonder whether it is intellectually acceptable to endorse the classical Christian belief as defined, or any other factual belief, we should distinguish between two different issues or problems, which Plantinga calls *de facto* and *de jure*. The *de facto* issue is whether the belief is true, whereas the *de jure* question asks whether endorsing this belief is somehow epistemically justified, rational, and/or warranted. Plantinga introduces this distinction between *de facto* and *de jure* with regard to objections to Christian belief; these objections may also be either *de facto* or *de jure*.[31] Many philosophers who criticized religious beliefs did assume that they could put

---

[27] Plantinga (2000), p. viii.
[28] Moser (2010), p. 134: 'Plantinga's reluctance to propose arguments for Christian belief is puzzling at best', etc.
[29] Cf. Philipse (2012, 2014), chapter 3, for a more detailed summary.
[30] Plantinga (2000), p. vii and *passim*.   [31] Plantinga (2000), pp. viiiff., 167, and *passim*.

forward conclusive *de jure* objections against the endorsement of such a belief without arguing convincingly that in fact the relevant divinity does not exist. Plantinga's central claim in *Warranted Christian Belief* is, however, that there can be no viable *de jure* objection against classical Christian belief independently from convincing *de facto* objections.[32] In other words, if one aims at showing that it is not epistemically legitimate to endorse the classical Christian belief, one cannot do so without first arguing convincingly that the belief is not true. This central claim, which Alvin Plantinga derives from his religious epistemology, is comforting for Christian believers, he contends, since according to him it is difficult, or even impossible, to show or demonstrate conclusively that God (as defined) does *not* exist.

3. Atheists and other unbelievers may object to Alvin Plantinga that it is not easy or possible either to show convincingly that God as defined by him *does* exist. Plantinga's answer to this challenge may be summarized briefly as follows. It is not the task of Christian believers to demonstrate God's existence by adducing any arguments or evidence. They do not need to do so, since God Himself is showing to them that He exists. Inspired by Thomas Aquinas and John Calvin, Plantinga holds that God created in us a natural, inborn sense of God, the so-called *sensus divinitatis*, that would be 'the origin and source of the world's religions'.[33] If this epistemic organ is functioning properly, Christian faith will originate spontaneously in us, so that it is 'properly basic' in the same sense as elementary perceptual beliefs: it does not need any epistemic justification. Furthermore, if this Christian faith is true, and God caused it in us via our *sensus divinitatis*, it may also have sufficient 'warrant' for knowledge, so that in fact many Christian believers *know* that God exists.

According to Plantinga's epistemology, a true belief amounts to knowledge if it has (enough) 'warrant', while a belief 'has warrant for a person S only if that belief is produced in S by cognitive faculties functioning properly [...] in a cognitive environment that is appropriate for S's kind of cognitive faculties, according to a design plan that is successfully aimed at truth'.[34] If God exists, and has implanted the Christian religious belief into Christian believers,

---

[32] Plantinga (2000), pp. 191, 242, 285, xii–xiii, and *passim*.
[33] Plantinga (2000), p. 148.   [34] Plantinga (2000), p. 156. Cf. pp. 178–179, 357.

and if they hold this belief quite firmly, they will have enough warrant for their Christian beliefs so that holding these beliefs amounts to religious *knowledge*, which can be 'sure and certain'.[35] Plantinga extends his Aquinas/Calvin (A/C) model of warranted Christian belief by stipulating that God is the 'single principal author' of the Bible, and that the Holy Spirit induces Christian faith in the hearts of Christian believers. In Plantinga's technical terminology, this faith is produced by an 'internal instigation of the Holy Spirit'. Christian beliefs 'are a supernatural gift', so that they have epistemic warrant without needing any (other) epistemological justification.[36]

4. Let me round off this short synopsis of Alvin Plantinga's apologetic strategy by summarizing his answer to a crucial question. If God as defined exists and loves all human beings like a good father, one would expect that He will bring forth Christian faith in each of us. Obviously, however, God did not and does not do so. As recent research on human evolution reveals, the biological species of *Homo sapiens* probably evolved between 350,000 and 260,000 years ago. Although we do not know when religious beliefs arose in human cultures for the first time, it is plausible to assume that all earliest religions were animist or polytheist, as I argued in §3.1. If the Christian god exists, it would follow that this divinity had been hiding from all humans during myriad millennia before revealing himself in and to Jesus Christ about 2,000 years ago. Furthermore, God would still hide Himself today to most human beings, even though in our times Christianity is the largest religion on Earth. How should we explain these facts of 'divine hiddenness'?

Plantinga provides a traditional Christian answer to this crucial question. All so-called unbelievers of past and present display(ed) an 'epistemic malfunction'. Their 'failing to believe in God is a result of some kind of dysfunction of the *sensus divinitatis*'.[37] This dysfunction is caused by our 'condition of being in sin, a state in which we human beings find ourselves from our very birth'.[38] Whereas according to Plantinga's Christian view the *sensus divinitatis* of all humans 'has been damaged and corrupted by sin', in decent Christian believers it is 'partly healed and restored to

---

[35] Plantinga (2000), p. 264.
[36] Plantinga (2000), chapter 8, quotes from pp. 243 and 245.
[37] Plantinga (2000), p. 184.   [38] Plantinga (2000), p. 207.

proper function by faith and the concomitant work of the Holy Spirit in one's heart'.[39] Although Plantinga does not advocate the traditional Christian doctrine that our 'condition of being in sin [...] from our very birth' results from 'the sinful actions of Adam and Eve', he stresses 'that in fact we are in the condition'.[40] He also argues that our sinfulness is 'both astonishingly deep and deeply elusive', and spends thirty-three pages describing its many cognitive and affective manifestations.[41] Furthermore, Plantinga claims that 'even in the state of sin' all humans 'typically have some grasp of God's presence and properties and demands', although most of us suppress this knowledge, since because of our sinfulness we 'are prone to hate God', even though we also are inclined to seek Him.[42]

What should we think of Plantinga's apologetic strategy, the full merits of which may be clear only to Christians reading his works repeatedly?[43] Let me mention some of the main objections in order to show that it should not convince any Christians who are 'educated and intelligent people living in the twenty-first century'. A crucial first objection I made in §1.1 is based on the baffling facts of religious pluralism and diversity. In chapter 13-II of *Warranted Christian Belief*, Plantinga formulates the problem of pluralism eloquently as follows: 'what about [...] the fact that the world displays a bewildering and kaleidoscopic variety of religious and antireligious ways of thinking, all pursued by people of great intelligence and seriousness?'[44] 'Given that I know of this enormous diversity, isn't it somehow arbitrary, or irrational, or unjustified, or unwarranted (or maybe even oppressive and imperialistic) to endorse one of them as opposed to all the others?'[45]

Having spent twenty pages on the question whether a Christian's awareness of the facts of religious pluralism would or should amount to a defeater for his or her Christian belief, conjoined with the conviction that there is no proof or argument for this belief that would convince non-Christians, Plantinga concludes that such an awareness can be, but does not need to be, a defeater of someone's Christian convictions. If

---

[39] Plantinga (2000), p. 186.   [40] Plantinga (2000), p. 207.
[41] Plantinga (2000), pp. 206–240.
[42] Plantinga (2000), p. 210. Cf. Plantinga (2015) for 'a shorter and (I hope) more user-friendly version' (p. vii) of (2000).
[43] Cf. Philipse (2012, 2014), chapters 3 and 4, for a more elaborate critical analysis of Plantinga's apologetic strategy.
[44] Plantinga (2000), p. 437. The same sentence occurs on p. 107 of Plantinga (2015).
[45] Plantinga (2000), p. 438; Plantinga (2015), p. 107.

Christians interpret the facts of religious pluralism as 'a manifestation of our miserable human condition' caused by Original Sin, their religious beliefs might maintain a degree of warrant sufficient for knowledge, so that these facts 'do not or need not constitute a defeater for Christian belief'.[46] For many Christians, a 'fresh or heightened awareness of the facts of religious pluralism' might even be 'an occasion for a renewed and more powerful working of the belief-forming processes' that induce Christian faith.[47]

Suppose, however, that some Christians were really interested in the question as to whether one of the many mutually incompatible religious convictions that are, or have been, adhered to in human cultures on Earth is true, and if so, which one. In order to find this out, they organize an open-minded debate with educated and intelligent representatives of many other religions whose creeds are incompatible both with Christianity and with each other, so that at most one of these doctrines can be true. Let us assume that when asked what justifies or warrants their religious creed, each non-Christian would contend like Plantinga that their god(s) implanted the relevant religious truths in the minds and hearts of all humans as properly basic beliefs, but that most human beings are mentally and/or morally deficient, so that they are not sufficiently aware of these religious truths. Each of them also claims that their divinity restored the human *sensus divinitatis* only in believers belonging to their own religion, such as Shia Islam, for example. More precisely, they hold that *if* their divinity exists, as they passionately believe, (S)He will have restored their own *sensus divinitatis*, so that their religious beliefs are true and have warrant, whereas the beliefs of all other religions are not and do not.

In terms of Plantinga's apologetics this would imply, however, that even if restored in some humans, nobody can trust legitimately the alleged results of one's stipulated *sensus divinitatis*. Whereas we can rely on our perceptual organs because they reveal the same features of one's environment to each of us, independently of our different cultural backgrounds, such an epistemic confidence would be unwarranted with regard to an alleged organ of religious information like a *sensus divinitatis*, since we know that it would divulge many mutually incompatible religious claims. Moreover, Plantinga's assumption that such an organ exists at all is completely incredible given the diversity of mutually incompatible

---

[46] Plantinga (2000), p. 457.　　[47] Plantinga (2015), p. 113; cf. (2000), p. 457.

religious beliefs on Earth. As Michael Tooley argued convincingly in his discussion with Plantinga, it is not 'reasonable to believe that there is in fact a reliable belief-forming mechanism that is specifically geared to religious beliefs'.[48] A purely secular explanation of why such beliefs arose and occur (as I sketched in Part II) clearly is more convincing than Plantinga's religious explanation.

A second objection against Plantinga's model of warranted Christian belief is that if all human beings had a *sensus divinitatis*, the malfunctioning of which can be restored by God, one would expect that (if He exists) God did so in many communities that were culturally independent of each other, since He loves all humans. As a consequence, the Christian religion would have arisen independently within many different cultures. Because this theological hypothesis has been refuted conclusively by empirical research on the worldwide spread of Christianity since its origin in Judea, a purely secular explanation of this spread is epistemically superior to a theological explanation. Such an Argument from Locality refutes any religious belief according to which a specific omnipotent divinity exists, is omnipresent, and loves all human beings.

Since Plantinga's model is meant not only to legitimize but also to explain the occurrence of Christian beliefs on the assumption that God (as defined by Plantinga) exists, his Calvinist model competes with purely secular explanations of this occurrence, as I just illustrated by my second objection. Each respect in which such secular explanations are superior to Plantinga's religious explanation yields an argument against his Christian theism, and there are many of such arguments, illustrated by Part II of this book. Another example, my third objection against Plantinga's model, may be called the Argument from Belated Manifestation. If God as defined by Plantinga existed eternally and created the universe, as he claims, one would expect that this divinity would have revealed Himself to humanity as soon as humans could conceive of any supernatural being. Since Christian monotheism originated myriad millennia later, and was preceded by polytheist religions, a secular explanation of its late occurrence (see Chapter 3) is much more plausible than Plantinga's religious account. Or should one really assume that all humans were too sinful for receiving God's revelation for at least 200,000 years?

A fourth objection focuses on Plantinga's claim that 'the Bible is a communication from God to humankind, a divine revelation'.[49] In other

---

[48] Plantinga and Tooley (2008), p. 243.   [49] Plantinga (2000), p. 383.

words, although the Bible is 'a collection of writings by human authors', it is 'specially inspired by God in such a way that he can be said to be its principal author'.[50] If this contention were true, one would expect that at least some biblical texts reveal God's omniscience by mentioning empirical facts that were still unknown to humanity when the Old and New Testament were composed. Since no such empirical facts are communicated in any biblical text, whereas many factual claims made in these scriptures have been refuted by the results of scientific progress, there is no reason whatsoever to assume that any of these texts has been inspired by a supernatural and omniscient mind. On the contrary, decent biblical exegesis rebuts such an assumption.

There are many more objections against Alvin Plantinga's model of warranted Christian belief, which show that his confidentialist apologetics is utterly unconvincing.[51] Let me finish this section by mentioning only two of these other objections. According to a fifth one, Plantinga's analogy between the postulated *sensus divinitatis* and our sense organs breaks down on many grounds. For example, with regard to our sense organs, it is clear which knowledge we can and do obtain by using them, and which beliefs cannot be based on their employment. We can neither hear sounds with our eyes nor see colours with our ears. With regard to the *sensus divinitatis*, such a criterion is lacking, since being omnipotent, God might implant anything in our minds, and other divinities or devils might do so as well. How can we know, then, that specific religious ideas we endorse were induced in us by God, whereas other religious convictions are illusionary? Even Christian authorities disagree among each other which beliefs were implanted into them by God or the Holy Spirit. On Plantinga's model, any religious conviction might be properly basic and warranted if the relevant divinity (or devil) existed.

Furthermore, we can study the workings of our sense organs scientifically and analyse the resulting brain activities. By doing empirical research, we can explain numerous features of these organs and of our perceptual capacities, such as the fact that your eyes function a bit better than mine or why specific perceptual illusions occur. If we really had a religious sense organ, a *sensus divinitatis*, it should be possible to localize this organ somewhere in our brain or heart and investigate its workings as well. Interestingly, Plantinga never attempts to inspire brain scientists in this respect. Suppose, however, it were discovered by neuroscientists that

---

[50] Plantinga (2015), p. 48.   [51] Cf. Philipse (2012, 2014), §3.4 and chapter 4.

when test subjects belonging to many different religions confess at specific moments that they are in-depth aware of their divinities, there always is some increase in activity in specific regions of their brains. Would this show that such a brain region can be compared to a 'sensus', a perceptual organ, that receives external information from above (or below)? And would it be possible to show that the *sensus* of Christians functions more properly than the same organ of adherents to other religions? Can brain scientists resolve the problem of religious pluralism? Let me take leave of Plantinga's confidentialist apologetic strategy, however, since readers may have become somewhat impatient by now.[52]

5.5 INVOLVEMENT EVIDENTIALISM

Religious devotees who agree with my criticisms concerning the apologetic options f (Religious Voluntarism or Fideism) and h (Religious Confidentialism à la Plantinga) of the Decision Tree for Religious Believers, and who remain Religious Factualists (b), have to situate themselves somewhere on branch g of Religious Evidentialism. As explained in §5.2, this branch confronts its adherents with a trilemma between (i) Unbiased Evidentialism, (j) Involvement Evidentialism, and (k) Amalgamated Evidentialism. Since both (i) unbiased and (k) amalgamated evidentialists focus primarily on types of evidence that are also accessible to unbelievers, mainly on philosophical arguments supporting the truth of their religious creed, these two options are explored in Chapter 6 on *Natural Theology*. In the two final sections of this chapter, I evaluate two versions of (j) Involvement Evidentialism, the ones expounded by John Cottingham (2014) in *Philosophy of Religion: Towards a More Humane Approach* and by Paul K. Moser in *The Evidence for God: Religious Knowledge Reexamined* (2010), works I discuss in the alphabetical order of the authors' surnames. Both of them stress 'the *primacy of the moral dimension* in understanding the religious outlook', and in both cases their own outlook is a Christian one.[53]

Cottingham's 'overall aim' in the philosophy of religion is 'to develop a more "humane" model' than the traditional enterprise of natural

---

[52] Elsewhere (Philipse 2013a) I argued that in his (2011) book *Where the Conflict Really Lies*, Plantinga overlooks the real conflict between science and religion, to wit, that scientific research uses reliable and validated methods of investigation, whereas Christian beliefs do not result from any validated epistemic methods or sources.

[53] Cottingham (2014) (Cottingham's italics); Moser (2010).

theology, which focuses only on arguments and counterarguments concerning the existence of a divinity.[54] When we wonder what '*kind of evidence*' we should consider with regard to the question whether God exists, Cottingham defends a '"Pascalian" approach', which is inspired by numerous philosophers of religion from Augustine to Paul Moser.[55] According to this approach, we should avoid both branches of a traditional epistemological dilemma with regard to religious evidence. One of these branches is the 'fideistic' stance à la Søren Kierkegaard, according to which religious beliefs would be beyond any rational evaluation since they are a gift of God. The other branch is embraced by natural theologians who hold that there is sufficient evidence for the existence of their divinity available to any expert in the philosophy of religion, whether a believer or not. Whereas the first branch would 'risk putting religious belief beyond rational evaluation', the second branch will not 'convince the detached sceptic', even though it might aim at doing so.[56] Going between these branches, Cottingham concludes that the appropriate method(s) to be employed in our search for religious truth may be called 'an *epistemology of involvement*', which should not be confused with 'an "epistemology of submission"'.[57] In the search for religious truth, we should realize that there is 'evidence of the grace of God', but that this evidence comes to light only when 'the prospective convert has made the decision to embark on a certain kind of spiritual journey'. In other words, religious 'evidence for God' requires 'certain personal transformations in order to be assessed'.[58] One should acknowledge that 'religion is a phenomenon that arises from deep longings of the human heart'.[59]

Since John Cottingham is not only a well-known ethicist and philosopher of religion but also an expert in the history of philosophy with a focus on the seventeenth century, his book *Philosophy of Religion: Towards a More Humane Approach* is 'intellectually brilliant' and 'historically well informed', as Charles Taliaferro says on the back cover. Many authors and topics are mentioned or discussed eloquently in order to provide an overview of the philosophy of religion for a wide readership. Here I try to focus on Cottingham's own view regarding 'the kind of evidence' one should rely on in 'the search for truth' within the domain of religion, that is, how we should construe 'the question of evidence for

---

[54] Cottingham (2014), p. 11.   [55] Cottingham (2014), p. 17.
[56] Cottingham (2014), pp. 17, 20.   [57] Cottingham (2014), p. 23.
[58] Cottingham (2014), p. 23, pp. 20–21.   [59] Cottingham (2014), p. 48.

God'.[60] In order to understand Cottingham's version of this question, we should first be clear about the conception of God he endorses. How does he define the word 'God'? The existence of What or Whom is the evidence meant to be for?

In order to answer this question, Cottingham expounds another traditional dilemma for religious believers, the semantic one. On the one hand, since God is assumed to be a supernatural being, whereas the descriptive terms of our language got their meaning by being applied to natural phenomena, it seems that we cannot use any words in order to characterize what kind of being God is supposed to be. When we use descriptive terms in order to give meaning to the word 'God', 'we no longer know what we are saying', as Anthony Kenny confessed in *What I Believe*.[61] On the other hand, if we decide to use the word 'God' as a proper name without attempting to describe what or whom this name is used to refer to, the name does not get any meaning either, since we cannot point to a supernatural being in order to define it.

A traditional solution to this semantic dilemma suggests that we can and should define the word 'God' by describing its referent merely in metaphors. Unfortunately, however, this solution implies another semantic dilemma, since we cannot interpret appropriately any metaphor without using some terms literally. Hence, if we merely use metaphors in order to define what we mean by the word 'God', this name will not get any sense or reference either, whereas using some words literally in order to characterize God will present us with the first semantic dilemma. Without really resolving these dilemmas, Cottingham concludes that 'if one wishes to retain the core content of traditional theism, one cannot dispense with at least some key properties [. . .] that are taken to be strictly and literally true of God'.[62]

Readers will be interested which key properties Cottingham mentions in this passage, and expect that he will list the traditional omni-properties ascribed to the Christian god, such as omnipotence and omniscience. How does he give meaning to the word 'God', which he uses continuously in his book as if it makes sense? I am afraid that the answer to this question is somewhat disappointing. As 'key properties' 'that are taken to be strictly and literally true of God' Cottingham mentions 'creativity, reason, justice, and love'. He adds that it 'is striking' 'that all four of these

---

[60] Cottingham (2014), p. 23.
[61] Kenny (2006), p. 11, quoted by Cottingham (2014), p. 50.
[62] Cottingham (2014), p. 51.

latter properties figure in the Bible as an ineliminable part of the Judaeo-Christian conception of God'.[63] Then he observes 'that our understanding of these terms stems from their use in the ordinary human world', so that we are landed again in the first semantic dilemma.[64] Having discussed the ways in which Thomas Aquinas and Anselm of Canterbury tried to elucidate their notion of God, he concludes again that the predicates by which the word 'God' is defined are merely 'applied by analogy to the ungraspable creative power that is the supreme pattern and source of whatever measure of those qualities may be found in created things'.[65] Although Cottingham claims that God is 'an objective being that exists independently of us', his description of God as 'the elusive and mysterious source of being' is so vague that we cannot know what or whom he is talking about.[66]

Critical readers of Cottingham's book will conclude that as long as the word 'God' has not been defined more clearly, one cannot even formulate a meaningful epistemic problem concerning the evidence for the truth of his version of theism. Let me explain briefly, nevertheless, Cottingham's account of religious epistemology. Its presentation starts from his conception of what an 'authentic theistic belief' consists in. The content of this belief does not need 'to be bolstered by a complicated panoply of metaphysical descriptions of the divine', since its 'core idea' is a purely moral one: the belief in 'the unsurpassable goodness of God', which is 'the prime mover and moral heart of the religious impulse'.[67] Even if one posits such 'a metaphysically pared down theism', however, which focuses 'simply on the moral demand placed on humans by a supremely perfect God', 'any philosophical defender of theism' has to face 'important epistemic problems'.[68] Apart from being 'satisfied of the philosophical coherence of the idea of God', such a philosopher will 'have to give some account of our supposed awareness of God – of the putative *modes of access* to the divine, and of their status and cognitive credentials'.[69] Why and in which sense should these 'modes of access to the transcendent reality we call God' 'taken to be, at least in part, veridical'?[70]

Based on biblical texts and the testimony of many authors, Cottingham claims that the kind of experience that supports belief in God concerns 'primarily a moral and spiritual call'. Since the god of Abrahamic

---

[63] Cottingham (2014), p. 51. [64] Cottingham (2014), p. 51.
[65] Cottingham (2014), p. 54. [66] Cottingham (2014), pp. 73 and 164.
[67] Cottingham (2014), p. 56. [68] Cottingham (2014), p. 56.
[69] Cottingham (2014), p. 56. [70] Cottingham (2014), p. 57.

monotheism is 'a universally loving and compassionate God', one should 'expect the call to be able to be heard without special training or expertise or intellectual prowess'.[71] Quoting Stephen Evans, Cottingham also holds that knowledge of God should be 'widely available, not difficult to gain' for all humans. However, God should not 'force' it on humans either, since this divinity respects human freedom. Hence, it would be 'necessary for God to make the evidence he provides for himself to be less than fully compelling. It might, for instance, be the kind of evidence that requires interpretation, and include enough ambiguity that it can be interpreted in more than one way.'[72]

Cottingham conceives of this religious evidence for theism 'as a kind of *bridge*' from our empirical experiences of, for example, 'the beauty and significance of the world we inhabit' to something superior, to 'our ultimate source and end'.[73] The most convincing evidence for God's existence Cottingham mentions, 'can be found in the exercise of our human moral faculties', which 'has often been thought of as a mode of access to the divine'.[74] But let me stress again that according to Cottingham religious evidence should not be compelling. The relevant empirical phenomena 'do not necessarily present as supernatural or miraculous interruptions into the natural world', although the theist might classify them 'under the category of *awareness of God by means of the natural light*', that is, 'glimpses of the sacred dimension'.[75] The human faculty that would enable us to have such 'transformative' religious experiences is our imagination in Plato's sense, a faculty having 'the power to lift the mind up to the highest realities'.[76]

Which philosophical credentials would Cottingham's picture of religious evidence possess? He admits that 'evidence' in this sense does not support any argument for God's existence, neither a coercive or a probabilistic one. Rather, he interprets the mentioned phenomena 'like a challenge, or appeal, to the integrity of the listener', which 'require a focused and sincere receptivity on the part of the subject' and even 'a moral change in the subject' if they are to be 'fully apprehended'.[77] Quoting a poem of A. E. Housmann, Cottingham suggests that when natural beauty is not interpreted as a 'glimpse of the transcendent', one

---

[71] Cottingham (2014), p. 57.
[72] Cottingham (2014), p. 58; Evans (2010), pp. 13 and 15.
[73] Cottingham (2014), pp. 60 and 70 (Cottingham's italics).
[74] Cottingham (2014), p. 62.   [75] Cottingham (2014), p. 63 (Cottingham's italics).
[76] Cottingham (2014), p. 64.   [77] Cottingham (2014), p. 66.

might experience 'a moral malaise', since the 'partly glimpsed' divine gift 'has been rejected'.[78] However, when we open ourselves to all aspects of our human experience, such as the moral and aesthetic ones, this will 'irradiate our lives with meaning and value that we cannot create for ourselves'.[79] When 'we open ourselves to something that is resistible', 'we ourselves are part of the evidence' for God, even though Cottingham conceives of God as 'an objective being that exists independently of us'.[80]

What should we think of John Cottingham's version of (j) Involvement Evidentialism? Although it may appease the intellectual conscience of some Christians, there are many reasons why it should not convince any reader whatsoever. Let me mention briefly some of these reasons. First, Cottingham has not resolved the semantic dilemmas with regard to the name 'God', as I have already explained, so that we don't know what he is talking about when using this name. It follows, second, that we cannot even formulate relevant epistemic problems concerning 'modes of access to the divine', since 'the divine' has not been defined properly. Third, many of my friends who were raised in Christian communities complained that they never experienced any 'glimpses of the transcendent', although they practised the prescribed rituals hopefully during many years and were longing passionately to receive some sign from the divine.[81] A good God would never disappoint people so cruelly, I suppose. Fourth, a related problem of divine hiddenness is concerned with the recent and local origin of Christianity. If there were a deity who 'cares about all humans', and who is 'an objective being that exists independently of us', one would expect that signs of His existence are and have always been 'widely available' for everyone.[82] This expectation has been refuted by empirical research on the (pre)history of religions, as I explained in Chapter 3. Christian monotheism has been a relatively late and local product of religious evolution, and, as I argued before, a secular explanation of this fact is vastly superior to a religious account. Finally, Cottingham's view on 'the evidence for the truth of religion', which would consist of a 'personal call to allegiance' addressed 'not to the analytic mind but to the heart', might be endorsed by adherents to many different religions, the truth-contentions of which are mutually incompatible.[83]

---

[78] Cottingham (2014), pp. 66–67. [79] Cottingham (2014), p. 69.
[80] Cottingham (2014), pp. 69 and 73. [81] Cf. Cottingham (2014), p. 68.
[82] Cottingham (2014), pp. 58 and 73; Evans (2010), pp. 13 and 15.
[83] Cottingham (2014), p. 170.

Given this problem of religious pluralism, we cannot trust the religious hearing-capacities of human hearts.

We should classify the Involvement Evidentialism propagated by John Cottingham as just one of the many strategies of immunization invented by religious believers after the Enlightenment. The objective of these strategies is to deprive religious outsiders of the epistemic capacity to evaluate religious truth-claims endorsed by insiders of a religious sect or community. In order to evaluate specific religious claims to truth, one must first understand them properly. The Involvement Evidentialist holds that such a proper understanding can be acquired only by religious insiders, who have participated in the relevant religious 'form of life' for quite some time, and who endorse passionately the relevant religious claims to truth. According to Cottingham, 'there can be no question of reaching a final verdict on the relevant truth-claims from outside the forms of practical and affective engagement through which alone genuine understanding flourishes'.[84] Only on the last page of his book does the author acknowledge that this strategy of immunization has its limits, since 'it remains possible' that someone who has participated in a religious form of life for a long time concludes that the relevant divinity does not exist. Numerous Christians did so during the last decennia.

5.6 PERSONIFYING EVIDENCE OF GOD

Let me round off this chapter by discussing the version of Involvement Evidentialism developed by Paul K. Moser in his wonderfully written (2010) book *The Evidence for God: Religious Knowledge Reexamined*. According to its preface, Moser 'approaches the question of whether God exists from a new perspective' on the 'evidence for God', resulting in 'a morally robust version of theism that is cognitively resilient, even against skepticism'.[85] Readers may be surprised by Moser's repeated insistence that his 'account of knowledge and evidence of divine reality' is 'new', and that the 'supernatural evidence' of God's reality described in his book is 'widely neglected'.[86] He aims at presenting 'adequate *evidence*' for the existence of the Christian God, the deity referred to by apostle Paul's

---

[84] Cottingham (2014), p. 171.   [85] Moser (2010), p. ix.
[86] Moser (2010), pp. 37 and 136; cf. pp. 44, 136, and *passim*.

letters in the New Testament, which Moser quotes continuously.[87] Wouldn't one expect that all possible types of (alleged) evidence for the existence of this god have been often identified and examined critically during the past two millennia? If so, Moser's contention that he develops 'a *new* perspective on the evidence for God' will be either exaggerated or very exciting.[88] What, exactly, is this new perspective? And what are its epistemological merits?

Moser claims to use our common concept of evidence in this religious context. If 'adequate *evidence* for God's reality' were available, it 'would indicate (perhaps fallibly) that it is true that God exists, or in other words, that God is real rather than fictional'.[89] Which type of evidence is needed for showing that an entity E exists depends on the nature of E. Accordingly, Moser starts his enquiry by creating 'some clarity regarding what (or whom) we are asking about', because the word 'God' has been defined in many different ways. He stresses first that he uses the term 'God' as 'a most exalted *title* rather than as a proper name'.[90] This has the advantage that we can use the word intelligibly even if there is no actual titleholder.[91] Then he defines the title 'God' as signifying 'a being worthy of worship', which requires 'inherent moral perfection' and a 'perfectly loving character', including 'perfect love toward one's enemies'.[92] Hence, the term 'God' is deserved only by a being that is '*perfectly loving* toward all humans'.[93] Would this title as defined apply to any or many of the divinities postulated in human cultures? According to Moser, 'we readily can exclude most claimants to the preeminent title "God" on the ground of moral deficiency'.[94] 'Moral defects bar a candidate from the status of being God, without an opportunity for appeal.'[95] He does not specify what the required moral perfection would consist in, however, apart from stressing that the 'required power of perfect love' includes 'the amazing

---

[87] Moser (2010), p. 37; cf. pp. 44, 103–112, 193–218, and *passim*. No author is quoted or referred to more often than apostle Paul by Paul Moser in his (2010) book. The same is the case in Moser (2013).
[88] Moser (2010), pp. ix, 1, and *passim*, my italics.
[89] Moser (2010), p. 21 (Moser's italics). Cf. pp. 38, 150, and *passim*.
[90] Moser (2010), p. 22 (Moser's italics). Cf. pp. 114, 144, 153–155, 162, 182, 192, 234, 237, 242, 258–259.
[91] Cf. Moser (2013), p. 12: 'A title can be meaningful but lack a titleholder'.
[92] Moser (2010), p. 23, with reference to Luke 6:27-36 and Matthew 5:38-48. Cf. pp. 113–114, 143–144, 182, and Moser (2013), pp. 11–18.
[93] Moser (2010), p. 182 (Moser's italics).   [94] Moser (2010), p. 24.
[95] Moser (2010), p. 234.

and rare phenomenon called *enemy-love*.[96] 'Failing to love even one enemy, including a particularly cruel and repulsive enemy, would entail moral imperfection and therefore disqualify one from being God'.[97] In other words, if we 'divorce the title "God" from the standard of enemy-love', 'that would be a move of ad hoc moral diminution of the category of being God'.[98]

Readers may wonder whether there is in fact any personal being that deserves the title 'God' as defined by Paul Moser and, if so, how one can know that this God or these Gods exist(s/ed). Some of us, who want to be certain about the existence of such (a) God(s), might argue that the honorific title 'God' as defined by Moser applies to morally supreme human beings, such as Mother Teresa of Calcutta, who received the Nobel Peace Prize in 1979. However, Mother Teresa would have refused to receive this verbal crown, while her critics argued that she was far from morally perfect. Professor Moser does not attribute the title 'God' to any human being either.[99] He holds that this appellation can be applied only to 'an invisible personal Spirit' whose character traits and purposes 'are perfectly authoritative and loving and thus morally superior to ours'.[100] How can we know that in fact one or more invisible personal spirits exist who deserve the title 'God' as defined by Moser, and how should one describe and identify them? If such an invisible spirit existed in reality, what evidence for its existence would be available to human beings? In other words, 'what *kind* of evidence and knowledge of God's reality would a perfectly loving God offer to humans'?[101]

As the last quote indicates, Moser assumes that if 'an invisible personal Spirit' really exists who merits the title 'God' as defined, and if there is any evidence available to us with regard to the existence of such a divinity, this evidence would be offered intentionally to humans by the God. In other words, the 'evidence of divine reality' would be 'available only in a manner suitable to *divine* purposes in self-revelation'.[102] This assumption implies that in order to find out which type of evidence would be provided, one cannot avoid embracing a hypothesis about the God's

---

[96] Moser (2010), pp. 24–25 (Moser's italics); cf. pp. 114, 234, and *passim*.
[97] Moser (2010), p. 144.   [98] Moser (2010), p. 114.
[99] Moser also mentions Mother Teresa: (2013), p. 69; cf. p. 16.
[100] Moser (2010), p. 13. Cf. p. 116: 'Obviously, we humans are imposters in playing god, in any domain, because we fail decisively to be worthy of worship'; p. 192: 'We humans, of course, cannot plausibly lay claim to our having satisfied such an exalted title.'
[101] Moser (2010), p. 14 (Moser's italics).
[102] Moser (2010), p. 40 (Moser's italics); cf. p. 116 and *passim*.

intentions concerning the way in which He would reveal His existence to human beings and about the set of humans who would receive the evidence. How can we know anything about such divine intentions? Having cited the biblical book Isaiah 45:15, Moser claims that God might retract any evidence of His existence 'given, for instance, willful human resistance to God', so that divine evidence allows 'for divine elusiveness and even hiddenness'.[103]

Paul Moser stresses repeatedly, however, that the evidence that the God would provide to humans should be 'a trustworthy truth indicator', which supplies 'a well-founded cognitive grounding for faith in God'.[104] Furthermore, Moser assumes plausibly that a perfectly loving God would provide 'morally transforming evidence' to *all* humans, which might produce 'a loving character in willing people, despite their obstruction at times'.[105] In order to specify more precisely which types of evidence are to be expected if a divinity exists who deserves the title 'God' as defined by Moser, we should know to which humanly stipulated god(s) Moser applies this title, if any. As readers may expect of a Christian author, he claims that, '[i]n the end, the perfectly loving God represented by Jesus is the only remaining serious candidate' who deserves the 'maximally honorific title "God"', 'once we acknowledge the crucial role of enemy-love'.[106] What would the 'distinctive kind of evidence appropriate for the reality of a God worthy of worship' consist in, according to Moser?[107] And what is the 'new perspective on the evidence for God' developed in his book *The Evidence for God*?[108]

In its first three chapters Moser expounds and criticizes three approaches to (religious) knowledge which he rejects: non-theistic naturalism, fideism, and natural theology as represented by the traditional arguments for God's existence. In chapter 1 he argues that the great explanatory success of the natural sciences does not justify ontological naturalism. On the contrary, an 'ontological monopoly for the objects of empirical science' would even exclude the intentional endeavours of human beings from our 'ontological picture', so that we would not be able to understand the successes of the natural sciences.[109] The second chapter, called 'Fideism and Faith', is devoted to authors such as

---

[103] Moser (2010), p. 151.   [104] Moser (2010), p. 125.
[105] Moser (2010), p. 136. Cf. p. 211 on 'all people'.
[106] Moser (2010), p. 114. Unfortunately, this claim is not justified by an impartial empirical analysis of all human conceptions of divinities. The moral merit of enemy-love may have been attributed to other divinities as well.
[107] Moser (2010), p. 20.   [108] Moser (2010), p. ix.   [109] Moser (2010), p. 86.

Kierkegaard and Alvin Plantinga. With regard to fideism à la Kierkegaard, Moser argues that each faith in God needs one or more 'trustworthy truth indicators' in order to be '*cognitively* commendable, because the faith in question commits one to the *reality* of God'.[110] By neglecting this need of 'trustworthy evidential indicators', fideism 'makes faith untrustworthy', so that 'fideist faith will be cognitively deficient'.[111] Having spent fifteen pages on Plantinga's 'reformed epistemology', he concludes again that such an '[a]rgument-indifferent fideism [...] robs theism of a needed cognitive basis for trustworthy commendation as true'.[112]

Having read Moser's refutations of non-theistic naturalism and non-argumentative fideism, one might expect that in his third chapter, devoted to natural theology, he would advocate or innovate arguments for theism developed by natural theologians during the last two millennia. However, this expectation is refuted by the first sentences of the chapter. Moser claims that '[t]he astonishing God acknowledged by Jews and Christians' is '*cognitively* elusive', because 'the available evidence for this God's reality typically escapes human control'.[113] Since the only reliable evidence for God's existence can be offered by God Himself, and would consist in 'an authoritative divine call' to 'receptive people' inviting them 'into divine–human fellowship and new life with God', whereas natural theology 'offers no evidence to accommodate such a call', this discipline 'is irrelevant at best and misleading at worst'.[114] Moser agrees with most evolutionary biologists, for instance, that Michael Behe's arguments for intelligent design presented in *Darwin's Black Box* (1996) are invalid.[115] The only plausible aim of natural theology that Moser accepts is to 'illuminate the *logical compatibility* between empirical science and theology', for instance by arguing that quantum physics does not exclude divine interventions in the universe.[116] Given Moser's evaluation of natural theology, one may now be quite impatient, and passionately interested, to learn what is the 'widely neglected' 'supernatural evidence' of God's reality that Moser promises to indicate, which he aims at doing eloquently in chapter 4.[117]

---

[110] Moser (2010), pp. 121, 120, cf. 125 (Moser's italics). [111] Moser (2010), p. 121.
[112] Moser (2010), p. 140. [113] Moser (2010), p. 142.
[114] Moser (2010), pp. 158–160. [115] Moser (2010), pp. 163–167.
[116] Moser (2010), p. 170, cf. p. 169.
[117] Moser (2010), pp. 37 and 136; cf. pp. 44, 136, and *passim*.

According to Paul K. Moser, the 'evidence of God's reality' is 'personifying', and his religious epistemology is 'incarnational', because it requires 'that human inquirers themselves become evidence of God's reality in virtue of volitional acquaintance with God'.[118] This happens to humans when they experience in their hearts a 'volitional transformation toward divine love', that is, to love 'unselfishly and with forgiveness toward enemies'.[119] Although we may manifest such a 'perfect unselfish love' without knowing '*that* we are acquainted with divine reality in this case', Moser argues that humans would not be able to manifest this kind of love without receiving a 'transformative gift' from God.[120] The main cause of our inability in this respect is that 'humans arguably are experts at a kind of selfishness that is antithetical to God's moral character of unselfish love'. Moser introduces the term 'sin' for this human 'selfishness and its accompanying pride', which includes 'one's preferring to exclude God from one's knowledge', and suggests that because of their sinfulness, many humans may not be 'well suited to receive or to appropriate evidence of God's reality'.[121]

In order to correct our 'sinful selfishness', we need a divinely inspired 'volitional transformation toward divine love'. Such a transformation of our will and hearts is 'salient evidence of God's reality', since it is 'elusive and humanly uncontrollable'.[122] In short, if we seek evidence of God's existence, God will challenge us 'to become the evidence of God we claim to seek' by 'willingly receiving and reflecting God's moral character for others'.[123] Furthermore, if we become 'willing humans' in this sense, God will offer us 'the opportunity to receive a life of divine love everlastingly, in lasting fellowship with God', as occurred to Jesus after his resurrection.[124]

According to Moser, we should not evaluate the resurrection story by way of a 'merely theoretical historical assessment regarding the resurrection of Jesus'.[125] I assume that he wants to avoid such a historical approach because it would stress the cultural parallelisms between Jewish or Ancient Greek resurrections stories and the early Christian tales regarding Jesus. As a historical-critical investigation of these resurrection stories will reveal, and David Hume already argued in 1748, there is never

---

[118] Moser (2010), p. 172.   [119] Moser (2010), pp. 200 and 196.
[120] Moser (2010), pp. 200–202 (Moser's italics).   [121] Moser (2010), pp. 192, 194.
[122] Moser (2010), pp. 197, 200, 264.   [123] Moser (2010), pp. 264, 262.
[124] Moser (2010), pp. 217, 219.
[125] Moser (2010), p. 227, with reference to Emil Brunner.

enough empirical evidence that would justify a belief in such a miracle.[126] Instead of engaging in historical biblical and philosophical scholarship, however, Moser passionately and uncritically confirms apostle Paul's account of '[t]he resurrection of Jesus from death' and argues that the 'cognitive basis for accepting the resurrection of Jesus' is 'God's evident authoritative intervention in the lives of willing people with a call to divine–human reconciliation'.[127] If we become 'willing humans' in this sense, we might 'have divine love *everlastingly*', like Jesus.[128]

How should we evaluate Moser's 'volitional theism' or 'kardiatheology' (a 'theology aimed primarily at one's motivational heart')[129] from an epistemological point of view? Can religious believers really 'become the evidence of God we claim to seek' by 'learning to love as God loves'?[130] Will such a religious engagement show or indicate 'that God is real rather than fictional', as Moser required of 'adequate evidence for God's reality' in the introduction to his book?[131] Let me discuss briefly some crucial problems Moser's volitional account of religious evidence is facing, which show that the 'evidence' Moser presents is not 'adequate' as required.

1. The first problem is semantic. As I indicated, Moser interprets the word 'God' as a 'maximally honorific title'.[132] In order to show or claim that there is a real holder of this title, one should not only define the title but also describe its alleged holder in some detail before presenting one's evidence that the holder exists. Whereas Moser defines the title 'God' in terms of being morally perfect and perfectly loving towards all humans, including all one's enemies, we do not find in his book any elaborate description of the title's alleged holder, apart from being 'an invisible personal Spirit' and being the divine father of Jesus. Christian philosophers used to describe the divinity called 'God' in terms of omni-properties such as omnipotence and omniscience, but Moser does not provide any such or other description, confining himself to apostle Paul's letters.

---

[126] Hume (1748), section X, part II, §98: 'Upon the whole, then, it appears, that no testimony for any kind of miracle has ever amounted to a probability, much less to a proof.' Cf. Philipse (2012, 2014), pp. 166–182. Moser does not mention David Hume even once in his (2010) book.
[127] Moser (2010), pp. 226–227. [128] Moser (2010), p. 216 (Moser's italics).
[129] Moser (2010), p. 235 and *passim*. [130] Moser (2010), pp. 264, 266.
[131] Moser (2010), p. 21.
[132] Moser (2010), pp. 22, 114, 144, 153–155, 162, 234ff., and *passim*.

It remains unclear, then, to which kind of (allegedly existing) invisible spirit Moser applies the title 'God'. As a consequence, his claim that God exists doesn't make much sense.

2. A second, epistemological problem is concerned with Moser's account of 'personifying evidence' for God's existence. The evidence that an X exists independently of us cannot consist in our believing that the X exists. This cannot be the case even if our believing that the X exists motivates us to change radically our behaviour. If Christians aim at becoming 'the evidence for God' or 'personifying evidence of divine reality' by practising specific virtues prescribed in biblical passages, their behaviour provides evidence for their *endorsement* of Christian beliefs but not for the *truth* of these beliefs. Readers should conclude that in the course of his book Moser risks radically reinterpreting the notion of evidence defined in its introduction, without confessing this to his readers. The morally inspired behaviour of Christians is no 'evidence that a morally perfect intentional agent worthy of worship actually exists'.[133] If Moser's *'new* perspective on the evidence for God' mainly consists in this conceptual confusion, it has no epistemological merits whatsoever.

3. Yet another conceptual problem with regard to Moser's account of religious evidence is related to the 'wilderness parable' with which he starts his book. If, 'during summertime hiking, we have become lost in the expansive wilderness area of Hells Canyon', we should try to contact a rescuer, relying on our 'direct telic discerning' of any evidence that there is one.[134] If we fail to find a rescuer, 'we will perish, given our breathtakingly austere wilderness surroundings'.[135] Similarly, Moser claims that during our earthly life we will be lost if we do not find a rescuer, entitled God, who might communicate with us via 'an authoritative call in conscience'.[136]

There are two aspects of Moser's wilderness parable that are deeply problematic, however. First, few atheists or agnostics will evaluate their life on Earth today as gloomily as the parable suggests. They might accuse Christians of devaluating our earthly life in order to arouse human longings for a divine rescuer and an eternal afterlife, and devaluating non-believers by claiming that they are characterized by 'sin'. Second, if there were a divinity

---

[133] Moser (2010), p. 38.   [134] Moser (2010), pp. 2, 8–9.   [135] Moser (2010), p. 4.
[136] Moser (2010), pp. 9, 205, and *passim*.

who deserves the title 'God' because He is *'perfectly* loving toward all humans', this divinity would not be hidden for us, I assume, like the rescuer in the wilderness parable.[137] On the contrary, one would expect that a divinity who really deserves the title 'God' as defined by Moser would reveal Himself somehow to all humans, because He loves each of them. Since the Christian religion emerged countless millennia after the evolution of humans began, and only very locally, the divinity Christians worship does not deserve the title 'God' as defined by Moser, if such a divinity were to exist.[138]

4. Paul Moser might reply that this objection presupposes that we humans are able to know something about God's intentions, whereas he assumes that we can acquire such knowledge only if God reveals His intentions to us by a *'self-revealing call'*.[139] However, Moser also claims that God's self-revealing call is often 'elusive and even hidden' to us 'for divine purposes of a moral challenge to humans'.[140] How can one legitimately attribute the intention to God to remain hidden or elusive for most humans while also maintaining that such an attribution to God can be epistemically legitimate only if God reveals this divine intention to us? Does God really reveal to religious believers such as Paul K. Moser that He intends to be hidden and elusive, that is, unrevealed, to most humans? If God intends to be hidden and succeeds in being concealed, how can one know that God has this intention? When we aim at explaining honestly 'the elusiveness of divine evidence', the hypothesis that this God (who allegedly loves all humans) does not exist is much more plausible than the hypothesis that God exists but intends to remain hidden to (most) humans.[141] We should classify Moser's claim that a divinity entitled 'God' exists but intends to remain hidden, so that the evidence for God's existence is 'elusive and humanly uncontrollable', as a traditional Christian strategy of immunization.[142]

5. The last chapter (chapter 5) of Moser's book is devoted to some traditional problems raised with regard to religions. Let me discuss

---

[137] The quote is from Moser (2010), p. 182 (Moser's italics).
[138] On the issue of 'Divine Hiddenness', cf. Philipse (2012, 2014), §§14.11–14.12 and Schellenberg (2006, 2015).
[139] Moser (2010), p. 182.   [140] Moser (2010), p. 182.
[141] The quote is from Moser (2010), p. 252. Cf. Philipse (2012, 2014), §§14.11–14.14 on Christian attempts to explain and justify divine hiddenness.
[142] The quote is from Moser (2010), p. 264.

only Moser's view concerning one of these problems, the issue of religious diversity, which I labelled the problem of religious pluralism (cf. Chapter 1). If we focus on the content of the religious beliefs endorsed by adherents of the '[f]amiliar candidates for religion' which Moser mentions, such as 'Judaism, Christianity, Islam, Buddhism, Hinduism, Confucianism, Sikhism, Taoism, Shinto, and Bahaism', we will agree with him that '[t]aken together, the claims of the various religions are logically inconsistent: they *cannot* all be true'.[143] In other words, '[l]ogical religious exclusivism [...] is compelling, given the actual logically contrary claims made by various religions'.[144] How should we find out whether one of these religious beliefs with regard to the existence of one or more gods is true, if any, so that all logically incompatible religious beliefs must be false?

Moser pretends that this problem of religious pluralism can be resolved by (a) arguing that the title 'God' as defined by him applies only to 'the God of Jesus' and (b) his 'kardiatheology', according to which the evidence for the truth of Christian theism is 'personifying', since it consists of human beings who 'themselves, are becoming personifying evidence for God' by 'willingly receiving and reflecting God's moral character for others', as defined.[145] Humans who behave lovingly towards their enemies, for example, moved by reasons in their hearts, will count as 'personifying evidence of divine reality' even if they do not believe at all 'that God exists'.[146] In other words, the 'elusive but profound God of perfect love and of kardiatheology', that is, the Christian God referred to in Paul's letters, 'can work *de re* in humans despite the absence of human belief that God exists'.[147] Moser concludes that 'the diversity of religious positions in circulation is no defeater of the evidence for this book's version of volitional theism'.[148] What should we think of his original 'solution' to the problem of religious pluralism?

The (dis)solution suffers from various fatal conceptual problems. First, as I noted under (2), types of human behaviour motivated by the belief that a specific divinity exists are no evidence for the truth of this belief but only for the endorsement of such a belief.

---

[143] Moser (2010), pp. 232, 234 (Moser's italics). [144] Moser (2010), p. 238.
[145] Moser (2010), pp. 237, 254. [146] Moser (2010), p. 253.
[147] Moser (2010), p. 253 (Moser's italics). [148] Moser (2010), pp. 253–254.

Second, this refutation of volitional theism is reinforced by the problem of religious diversity. If human behaviours that satisfy the moral norms of a religion were to count as evidence for the truth of the relevant belief that a specific god exists, there would be empirical evidence for the existence of many different gods, that is, evidence that confirms each of the 'logically contrary claims made by various religions'.[149] Clearly, this is a *reductio ad absurdum* of Moser's kardiatheology. If Islamic extremists risk their lives in order to kill unbelievers, do they become personifying evidence of Allah's existence by showing the supremacy of Islam over all other religions, as they think they do?

6. Moser would reply that such 'personifying' evidence for the existence of a god can count as evidence only with regard to the God of Jesus, since other divinities postulated by human cultures do not deserve the title 'God' as defined. 'Moral defects bar a candidate from the status of being God, without an opportunity for appeal'.[150] This holds even for the God of Psalms 5:5 and 11:5, for example, according to which 'God "hates" wicked *people*'.[151] Moser's reply triggers a third conceptual problem. One should not confuse the ordinary descriptive notion of divinities in the sense of 'invisible personal Spirits' who are superior to humans in various respects with Moser's normative conception of 'God' as a title that applies only to 'an intentional agent who is morally perfect and worthy of worship' and loves each enemy.[152] The question whether in fact a specific divinity exists is very different from the question whether such a divinity would deserve the honorific title 'God' as defined. Moser continuously confuses these two questions, for example when he argues that '[m]onotheism seems initially more credible than polytheism, because we are hard put to come up with even one case of an intentional agent who is morally perfect and worthy of worship'.[153] Our author does not attempt to refute the claims of polytheist religions that there are in fact many gods. He merely declares that such divinities do not deserve the honorific title 'God' as defined, as he also assumes with regard to the divinities of

---

[149] Moser (2010), p. 238.   [150] Moser (2010), p. 234.
[151] Moser (2010), p. 236 (Moser's italics).
[152] Moser (2010), p. 237. Cf. p. 144: 'Failing to love even one enemy, including a particularly cruel and repulsive enemy, would entail moral imperfection and therefore disqualify one from being God.'
[153] Moser (2010), p. 237.

non-Christian monotheisms. In short, Moser does not succeed in resolving the crucial problem of religious pluralism.

7. Furthermore, critics of Christianity will argue on many grounds that if the God of Jesus were to exist, this divinity would not deserve the honorific title 'God' as defined by Paul Moser. First, they will refer to New Testament texts such as Matthew 10:34, according to which Jesus said: 'Do not think that I have come to bring peace on earth; I have not come to bring peace, but a sword.' Second, they will stress the crucial role Christian missionaries have played in the colonial forces of European countries. Missionary ambitions often justified colonial conquests, and Christians interpreted these conquests as 'personifying revelatory evidence of God'.[154] Third, given what we now know about the evolutionary and cultural history of *Homo sapiens*, one would expect that a divinity who is 'perfectly loving toward all persons, including resolute enemies of God' would have revealed Himself to humans some 50,000 years ago, when symbolic culture and language developed.[155] If the Christian divinity were to exist, He would have been hiding himself completely from humans during countless millennia, so that He does not deserve the title 'God', as I said already.

8. Let me focus finally on the only *argument* that Moser offers in order to conclude on the basis of 'conclusive evidence' that 'God exists', that is, that there is a divinity who deserves the title 'God' as defined.[156] Moser seems to assume that humans will be able to practice the virtues prescribed by his version of Christianity, such as enemy-love, only if God offers them a 'transformative gift'. If a human being receives such a transformative gift, this must be 'the result of the authoritative power' of God (premise 1). Moser claims that 'I have been offered, and have willingly received, the transformative gift' (premise 2), and concludes (3) that 'God exists'.[157] How should we evaluate this argument? Since it is deductively valid, we have to wonder whether, and in which sense, each of the premises (1) and (2) is true, in order to assess its soundness. Let me discuss the second premise (2) first. What does it mean,

---

[154] The quote is from Moser (2010), p. 143.
[155] The quote is from Moser (2010), p. 144.   [156] Moser (2010), pp. 200, 208.
[157] Moser (2010), p. 200.

precisely, to claim that 'one has willingly received the transformative gift', and how can one decide whether this is true?

According to Moser's account of this premise, it is not a necessary condition for having been offered and willingly received 'the transformative gift' that one is or has become a believing Christian. He holds that we can be 'acquainted with perfect unselfish love', of which our 'conscience would be a focal place', even if we do not know '*that* we are acquainted with divine reality in this case or in any other case'.[158] What, then, are Moser's criteria for having 'willingly received the transformative gift'? One would expect that he specifies in detail empirical criteria for checking whether a human being received the transformative gift of enemy-love, for example, but the only empirical indications I discovered in his book are that people have willingly received this gift if they are good at 'conflict resolution, peace making, and community building', or manifesting '*default unselfish love and forgiveness toward all people*', at least to some extent.[159] Moser claims that manifesting such 'perfect unselfish love' cannot be 'just another *natural* human capacity', so that we need premise (1) to explain it.[160]

However, if 'God's reality' is presented as an explanation of empirical facts such as humans practising enemy-love, one should first specify these (alleged) facts much more precisely, establish them by presenting results of empirical research, and show that one's theistic explanation is epistemically superior to other, competing, explanations, such as cultural history since the Enlightenment, the impact of the Universal Declaration of Human Rights proclaimed after World War II in 1948, secular arguments for organizing developmental aid, and so on and on. Even if one important explaining factor would be the endorsement of religious beliefs by many communities, this would not show that the god(s) believed in exist(s) in fact. Unfortunately, I have not discovered any attempt in Moser's book to specify empirically the *explanandum* meant in premise (2).

As I argued in Chapter 2, religious explanations have been eliminated from the sciences since the scientific revolution because they contradict each other, cannot be verified, and have been replaced by superior scientific explanations, even in psychology

---

[158] Moser (2010), p. 201–202. [159] Moser (2010), pp. 203–204 (Moser's italics).
[160] Moser (2010), p. 203 (Moser's italics).

and the other social sciences. How a professorial colleague can still endorse the (hypo)thesis that God (as defined) exists in order to explain any empirical phenomena (even his own endorsement of the relevant religious belief and religiously motivated practices) is a mystery to me, unless convincing arguments for this explanation are offered. Moser's approach is sermonic rather than scientific.

9. With regard to the role of arguments for the existence of God as defined, Moser's book is deeply ambivalent. We saw that, on the one hand, he rejects Alvin Plantinga's reformed epistemology because merely relying on one's religious belief that God exists without providing any argument cannot justify this belief. As he stressed, such an '[a]rgument-indifferent fideism [. . .] robs theism of a needed cognitive basis for trustworthy commendation as true'.[161] On the other hand, we saw that Moser also rejects the argumentative enterprise of natural theology. This enterprise is 'cognitively beside the point', since it neglects 'the kind of evidence needed for conclusive belief in a personal God worthy of worship', which includes 'a divine call to receptive persons'.[162]

Readers will now wonder which argument(s) for his theism Moser considers to be legitimate. As we saw (point 8), the only argument Moser offers for his Christian belief is that he himself has received his religious conviction as 'a transformative gift' (premise 2) and that such a gift can only be provided by the Christian god (premise 1), so that this divinity exists.[163] Alvin Plantinga might observe, ironically and correctly, that this 'argument' or 'evidence' merely expresses the 'fideist' conviction which Moser criticized so conclusively.

However this may be, let us investigate in Chapter 6, on natural theology, whether there is an argumentative strategy in support of theism which is more convincing from an epistemological point of view. In terms of our Decision Tree for Religious Believers, such a strategy would belong either to the branch of (i) Unbiased Evidentialism or to (k) Amalgamated Evidentialism.

---

[161] Moser (2010), p. 140. [162] Moser (2010), p. 162. [163] Moser (2010), p. 200.

6

Natural Theology

Readers who believe in one or more gods should wonder which end node of the Decision Tree for Religious Believers (§5.2) they would prefer. Do you conclude from my evaluation of the apologetic strategies discussed in Chapter 5 that none of these will succeed in epistemologically justifying the endorsement of a specific religious belief? Then it follows that such a credence can be legitimate only if three conditions are fulfilled, assuming that the content of the belief is well defined: (1) the belief is sufficiently supported by arguments based on reason and empirical evidence; (2) the evidence is publicly accessible in principle, at least to a large extent; and (3) the evidence overrules the many arguments against the truth of such a belief indicated in §2.4. Specified in terms of the decision tree, a religious claim that a particular divinity exists would be legitimate from an epistemological point of view only if it is well defined and if, on balance, the arguments from reason and experience supporting its truth overrule the arguments against it, which is branch (i) or (k) of the decision tree. The endeavour to assemble the logical arguments and empirical evidence for and against a specific religious belief is called natural theology. In contrast to the many versions of revealed theology, natural theology aims at providing arguments and evidence that can be accepted in principle by both believers and non-believers.

Let me sum up very briefly the history of Western natural theology in §6.1. How can one still practise natural theology in order to justify epistemically one's religious conviction in spite of the elimination of religious beliefs from the scientific enterprise (defined broadly), which I outlined in Chapter 2? The next section (§6.2) is devoted to the definition of 'bare theism' provided by Richard Swinburne and to his Bayesian apologetic strategy, which I consider to be the most promising option for natural theologians today, at any rate if theism has a relatively high prior probability. In the remaining sections of this chapter, I explain why even this outstanding apologetic strategy is unconvincing. First, we inspect in §6.3 whether theism as defined by Swinburne really makes sense, as he claims. Does this version of theism meet the semantic challenge sketched in §5.1 (a)? Second, we should wonder whether theism as defined has any predictive power, which is required in order to apply Bayes' theorem. Furthermore, if some predictive power is attributed to theism, shouldn't we conclude that theism can be and has been falsified? Such questions are answered in §§6.4 and 6.5. To those of you who become interested in natural theology after having read the short summary in this chapter, I would recommend the study of the most recent editions of Swinburne's trilogy *The Coherence of Theism* (2016), *The Existence of God* (2004), and *Faith and Reason* (2005). Many experts in the philosophy of religion have evaluated Swinburne's evidential arguments for theism as 'the best on offer'.[1] This is why I examined his religious apologetics in my book *God in the Age of Science? A Critique of Religious Reason*. Having evaluated Swinburne's apology for theism, I argued that we should endorse either semantic or epistemic atheism.

One of the numerous issues we discussed is whether simplicity can be seen as a criterion of truth in science and metaphysics instead of being merely a pragmatic criterion for theory choice, as it normally is.[2] In a paper published in 2020, Swinburne stressed again, explicitly against my pragmatic interpretation, that simplicity is one of the criteria that render an explanatory hypothesis *true*: 'a hypothesis is probably true insofar as it is simple and leads us to expect the observable evidence which we would not otherwise expect'.[3] This interpretation of the simplicity criterion is crucial for Swinburne's natural theology. If 'the simple is more likely to exist than the complex', it follows that '[t]he intrinsic probability of theism is, relative to other hypotheses about what there is, very high', if at least 'the hypothesis of theism' has a 'great simplicity', as Swinburne contends.[4] Since Swinburne admits that there are 'innumerable other hypotheses [...] such that if they were true it is probable that we would find those same general features of the universe' which theism pretends to

---

[1] Plantinga (2001), p. 219. Cf. Philipse (2012, 2014), p. 29.
[2] Philipse (2012, 2014), §§11.7–11.9, §§12.8–9, and §13.2. Cf. §6.2 in this book for some details.
[3] Swinburne (2020), p. 134.   [4] Swinburne (2004), p. 109.

explain, his contentions that theism is the simplest of these hypotheses, and that simplicity is a crucial criterion of truth, are essential elements of his apologetic strategy.[5] I argued, however, that 'the topic of simplicity turns out to be of baffling complexity' if one studies in detail the various uses of this criterion for the selection of models and theories in scientific practices, and that Swinburne's use of the criterion is unconvincing.[6] My main reason for mentioning this controversy about the simplicity criterion is to provide an illustration of how complex are the numerous problems that have to be discussed thoroughly in order to evaluate the remaining evidentialist options (i, k) of the Decision Tree for Religious Believers.[7]

6.1 NATURAL THEOLOGY: DESCENT AND REVIVAL

Religious believers may wonder why natural theology is needed in order to justify their conviction that a specific divinity exists. Can't they merely trust the texts relied on by revealed theology, such as the Bible or the Koran?

There are at least six reasons why religious believers cannot interpret these texts as reliable divine revelations without any support by natural theology.[8] First, the texts contain many contradictions, and of two mutually contradictory statements at most one can be true. Second, numerous factual claims in such alleged revelations have been refuted by scientific progress and other empirical discoveries.[9] Third, as historical research has revealed, the content of these so-called sacred books has been influenced considerably by earlier sources and cultures which believers do not regard as divinely inspired. Fourth, none of the allegedly revealed texts contains reliable information that was not already available to the tribes or cultures that produced them. Consequently, we should not suppose that there has been any divine or other supernatural impact on their production. A fifth reason is that we rightly reject today some of the moral rules advocated in these texts, whereas the plurality of religions provides a sixth reason why we cannot rely only on an allegedly divine revelation in order to justify a belief that a specific god exists, since many of these so-called revelations contradict each other.[10]

---

[5] Swinburne (2020), p. 138.   [6] Philipse (2012, 2014), p. 214; cf. §§12.8–13.2.

[7] In the present chapter, many of these problems are merely mentioned, and I refer readers to my previous (2012, 2014) book if they are interested in more elaborate solutions.

[8] Philipse (2012, 2014), §§1.1–1.3 (pp. 4–14). Cf. also §5.4 in this book.

[9] Cf. Chapter 2.   [10] Cf. §5.4.

It follows from these six reasons that religious believers should not count (merely) on an alleged revelation in order to justify epistemically their religious conviction that a specific divinity exists. If they are Religious Realists and agree with my evaluation of the epistemic options discussed in Chapter 5, they should rely on results of natural theology, at any rate if these results are trustworthy. Atheists and other unbelievers may have good grounds to spend some time on studying natural theology as well. They will agree with religious believers that it may be of crucial importance to human life whether a specific divinity exists, such as Venus, Vishnu, God, or Allah. As Swinburne argues, for example, 'if there is a God of the kind that I have been analysing, we owe him obedience'.[11] Shouldn't all atheists investigate at least once in their lifetime whether the sum of arguments supporting the existence of a specific divinity overrules their reasons for denying the truth of any religious belief?[12]

In Western culture, the discipline of natural theology has had a long and fascinating history, which began in Greek and Judaic contexts many centuries before the origins of Christianity. For example, the Greek pantheon of anthropomorphic divinities was criticized severely by the poet-philosopher Xenophanes of Colophon (c. 570–c. 478 BCE), who seems to have argued that the (supreme) divinity should be identified with the universe as a whole, and that no human-like properties should be attributed to this god.[13] Although Aristotle (384–322 BCE) held that authors such as Xenophanes 'may be completely ignored, as being somewhat too crude in their views', he also argued that there is an immaterial 'primary essence' of the universe, which functions as the 'prime mover' and is 'one both in formula and in number'.[14] In book Lambda of his *Metaphysics*, Aristotle seems to equate the first final (teleological) cause of the assumed rotation of the stars around Earth with the divine whose life is 'most good and eternal', since it consists in 'the actuality of thought'. He defines this god as an immaterial 'living being, eternal, most good'.[15] However, Aristotle did not believe that the divinity created the universe. He argued extensively that the material world exists eternally, so that there neither is a temporal beginning nor an end to the cosmos.[16]

My main reason for mentioning Aristotle in this context is that his metaphysics inspired many monotheist philosophers in Jewish, Christian,

---

[11] Swinburne (2016), p. 288.   [12] Cf. Swinburne (2005), chapter 3.
[13] Cf. Aristotle, *Metaphysics* I. v, 12–13.
[14] Aristotle, *Metaphysics* I. v, 13, and XII. viii, 18.   [15] Aristotle, *Metaphysics* XII. vii, 9.
[16] Aristotle, *De Caelo* (*On the Heavens*) 279b–283b.

and Islamic traditions to develop arguments for their religious beliefs that did not rely on alleged revelations. In medieval Christianity, the Aristotle-inspired tradition of natural theology culminated in the writings of Thomas Aquinas (1225–1274 CE), who in his *Summa theologiae* developed such a theology on the basis of recent Latin translations of Aristotle's works.

After the Renaissance in Europe, however, the importance of natural theology declined quickly because of two opposite cultural trends. Whereas Reformed Christians like Luther and Calvin were convinced that Christianity should rely on biblical revelations alone, in order to avoid contamination of their creed by pagan authors such as Aristotle, science-inspired philosophers like David Hume and Immanuel Kant held that there are no sound arguments from premises about nature to the conclusion that God exists. Explanatory references to God were eliminated gradually from all scientific disciplines, as I illustrated in Chapter 2, since there did not seem to be any reliable method of discovery which humans might use in order to confirm a hypothesis postulating a specific god. The gradual decline of natural theology during the last two centuries motivated many Christians to develop one of the apologetic strategies I illustrated and evaluated in Chapter 5. Should religious adherents not conclude that there is no point any more in practising natural theology in order to justify their endorsement of a specific religious belief?

Although many Christian philosophers drew this conclusion, some devoted their intellectual life to a revolutionary resurrection of natural theology. They might argue, correctly, that the elimination of natural theology by philosophers such as David Hume and Immanuel Kant relied on outdated epistemologies. For example, Hume assumed that all laws of nature are concerned with relations between observable phenomena, whereas Kant considered some principles of Newton's mechanics as being 'synthetic a priori', the necessary truth of which he assumed, explaining it by his transcendental philosophy. Both of them concluded from their philosophy of science that there cannot be any sound empirical arguments for the existence of God, so that natural theology had to be abandoned.

However, the impressive progress of the natural sciences since the eighteenth century has refuted both Hume's and Kant's epistemology of scientific knowledge. According to the present Standard Model of particle physics, for example, there are subatomic elementary particles such as fundamental fermions and bosons. Without any doubt, these particles are unobservables in Hume's sense, whereas their behaviour is described by statistical laws of nature like Fermi–Dirac statistics (fermions) and

Bose–Einstein statistics (bosons). Since such proposed laws of nature are concerned with unobservables, while their theoretical framework supersedes Newton's mechanics, the endorsement of the Standard Model refutes the epistemologies of both Hume and Kant, as do many other instances of scientific progress. It follows that Hume- and Kant-inspired arguments against the epistemic possibility of natural theology are outdated as well.

This conclusion does not in itself imply that natural theology can be resurrected in an epistemically legitimate manner as an endeavour to argue for the existence of a specific divinity starting from natural phenomena. Admittedly, many religious believers may feel today an urgent need to resurrect natural theology. Let me quote a pregnant passage from the second edition of *Faith and Reason* which Richard Swinburne published in 2005:

> In an age of religious scepticism when there are good arguments against theism known to most people, and there are so often authorative atheists as well as authorative theists, most theists need arguments for the existence of God which start from rightly basic beliefs held very strongly by theist and atheist alike, and proceed thence by criteria shared between theist and atheist. To produce such arguments is the aim of natural theology. It starts from the most general natural phenomena – the existence of the world, its conformity to natural laws, the laws and initial conditions of the universe being such as to produce human organisms, and so on; and attempts to argue thence to the existence of God either by deductive arguments, or by criteria of inductive reasoning used in other areas of inquiry.[17]

That there is such an urgent need among religious believers does not show, however, that this resurrection of natural theology is legitimate from an epistemological point of view. On the contrary, the fact that religious contentions have been eliminated gradually from all scientific disciplines (in the broad sense of 'science' which includes historical research, for example), as I indicated in Chapter 2 seems to show that there are no reliable epistemic methods or arguments any more that can be used by natural theologians to show that their god exists. In other words, Swinburne's attempt to resurrect natural theology in order to justify his belief that a specific divinity exists is a heroic endeavour. How does Swinburne meet the challenges to religious believers specified in §5.1? Is his concept of God clearly defined in such a manner that it implies testable empirical predictions? And does his natural theology meet the numerous

---

[17] Swinburne (2005), pp. 91–92.

6.2 BARE THEISM AND BAYESIAN NATURAL THEOLOGY

Monotheist religious believers have endorsed many different varieties of theism, that is, of the contention that there is one god. Since many of these versions contradict each other, such as trinitarian and non-trinitarian theisms, they cannot all be true. This is one of the many reasons why it is profitable for a natural theologian to claim that there is a common core to all (mono)theisms, which one might call *'bare'* theism', to be distinguished from the diverse *ramified* theisms endorsed by divergent monotheists, and to argue that this basic doctrine of bare theism is probably true.[18]

In his extensively revised second edition of *The Coherence of Theism* (2016), Swinburne defines (bare) 'theism' initially as follows, and claims that 'Christians, Jews, and Muslims are all [...] theists' as defined, since they endorse 'the doctrine that there is a God in the sense of a being with most of the following properties: being a person without a body (that is, a spirit), present everywhere (that is, omnipresent), the creator of the universe, perfectly free, able to do anything (that is, omnipotent), knowing all things (that is, omniscient), perfectly good, a source of moral obligation, eternal, a necessary being, holy, and worthy of worship'.[19] It is the aim of that book to investigate 'which of the many forms of theism are coherent'.[20] Swinburne spends nearly 300 pages in developing a very nuanced concept of (t)his God. He then claims to have shown that the resulting theory of bare theism is coherent only if 'there are cogent arguments from the nature of the observable world that, if the concept of such a being is coherent, make it somewhat more probable than not that there is a God'.[21] In other words, Swinburne contends that his concept of God

---

[18] Swinburne sometimes uses the expression 'bare theism' in order to indicate a version of theism that allegedly is common to the established monotheistic creeds, e.g. Swinburne (2004), pp. 265–266.

[19] Swinburne (2016), p. 1. Cf. Swinburne (2020), pp. 137–138 and Swinburne (2004), pp. 7 and 93–96. Strictly speaking, this is a definition of 'theism' but not of 'monotheism', since according to Swinburne it does not exclude that there are other divinities as well. Cf. his (2004), p. 119: 'if God can make other divine beings, he must surely do so. A solitary God would be a bad state of affairs. God needs to share, to interact, to love, and he can do so most fully with equals.' Cf. also (2004), pp. 343–345.

[20] Swinburne (2016), p. 1.   [21] Swinburne (2016), p. 296.

can be coherent only if there are cogent empirical arguments for the existence of this divinity which overrule the arguments against.[22]

It is the purpose of *The Existence of God*, which Swinburne calls 'the central book of all that I have written on the philosophy of religion', to investigate whether theism as defined is true, by assessing 'the weight of arguments from experience for and against this claim'.[23] Since from a logical point of view such arguments are inductive, and many of them may affect each other's strength, Swinburne's 'crucial issue' is 'whether all the arguments taken together make it probable that God exists'. In other words, one should consider 'whether the balance of all the relevant evidence favours the claim of theism or not'.[24] We might wonder what is the set of 'all the relevant evidence' for and against theism, which Swinburne calls 'a hypothesis of enormous scope'. His reply is that 'theism purports to explain everything logically contingent (apart from itself)'. This would imply that 'there will be no background knowledge with which [theism] has to fit', so that it cannot be 'a disadvantage' to theism 'if it postulates a person in many ways rather unlike the embodied human persons so familiar to us'.[25]

In order to symbolize the way in which a specific piece of evidence (e) affects the probability (P) that a well-defined hypothesis (h) is true, Swinburne uses Bayes's theorem, originally invented by Reverend Thomas Bayes and Pierre-Simon Laplace:

$$\text{Bayes's theorem: } P(h|e\&k) = \frac{P(e|h\&k)\, P(h|k)}{P(e|k)}.$$

According to this basic theorem of confirmation theory, the occurrence of a specific piece of evidence (e) will raise the presupposed probability that a specific meaningful hypothesis (h) is true to the extent that, given our background knowledge k, it is more likely that e occurs if h is true than that e occurs anyway. In terms of the theorem, evidence e confirms hypothesis h given background knowledge k to the extent that $P(e|h\&k)$ is greater than $P(e|k)$, and it disconfirms the hypothesis to the extent that

---

[22] Swinburne (2016), p. 295: 'I have argued that, if we had good inductive evidence (on the assumption of its coherence) for the truth of this account of theism, we would thereby have evidence of its coherence. Only by such a route is there a hope of showing coherence.'

[23] Swinburne (2004), pp. v, 1.   [24] Swinburne (2004), p. 13.

[25] Swinburne (2004), p. 66. Cf. p. 71: 'The theist argues from all the phenomena of experience, not from a small range of them.' Cf. Philipse (2012, 2014), §11.6, for a critical analysis of this claim.

$P(e|h\&k)$ is smaller than $P(e|k)$. Clearly, however, by comparing these two likelihoods $P(e|h\&k)$ and $P(e|k)$, we cannot yet calculate the posterior probability $P(h|e\&k)$ that hypothesis h is true. In order to do so, we would also need to know how probable it is that h is true given merely our background knowledge k, so, what the value of the prior probability $P(h|k)$ is.

With regard to the prior probability $P(h|k)$ of a specific hypothesis h we should make two conceptual distinctions. First, the probability $P(h|k)$ may either be the probability that h is true prior to a particular piece of new evidence e_x, whereas the background knowledge k includes many other pieces of empirical evidence, or this probability $P(h|k)$ is meant to be the probability of h prior to all possible evidence. The prior probability of h in the latter sense may be called its *intrinsic* probability, that is, the probability that hypothesis h is true independently of its relation to any empirical evidence whatsoever.[26] In this case, the background knowledge k will be entirely a priori, consisting of what Swinburne calls 'mere "tautological evidence"'.[27]

The second distinction is concerned with the way in which this intrinsic probability of a hypothesis or theory h can and should be determined. Subjectivists will argue that there are no valid truth-criteria for comparing the intrinsic probabilities of various meaningful competing theories $h_1 - h_n$ that aim at explaining the same set of phenomena, so that they have the same explanatory scope. If each of them fits equally well with the relevant background knowledge, we should either attribute provisionally the same intrinsic probability to each of these competitors or just leave their intrinsic probability undetermined. As a consequence of the latter option, it would not be possible to calculate a specific value of the posterior probability $P(h|e\&k)$ of each hypothesis. We can only conclude that the available evidence confirms one hypothesis, h_1, better than another, h_2. Objectivists hold, however, that there is a reliable criterion for ranking the intrinsic probabilities of such competing theories which have the same explanatory scope.

It is easy to understand why a natural theologian such as Richard Swinburne should be an objectivist in this sense. He intends to argue that given all the empirical evidence *pro* and *contra*, the truth of his theory of theism is more probable than it being false. In terms of the Bayesian symbolism, his aim is to show that $P(h|e\&k) > P(\sim h|e\&k)$, that is, to

---

[26] Cf. Swinburne (2004), pp. 53, 67.   [27] Swinburne (2004), p. 67.

show that if all the relevant evidence *pro* and *contra* is included in *e*, the truth of the theistic hypothesis *h* is more probable than its falsity, so that, in technical terms, $P(h|e\&k) > 1/2$. Since such a conclusion can be argued for only if one is an objectivist with regard to the intrinsic probability of theism, this objectivism is obligatory for Swinburne.

However, such an objectivism with regard to the intrinsic probability of theism confronts the religious apologist with a demanding challenge. Can we, and if so how should we, determine the prior probability that theism or some other all-embracing theory is true? That this challenge for objectivists with regard to intrinsic probability of theism is demanding follows already from the facts of religious pluralism. Swinburne avows that 'clearly, innumerable other hypotheses are such that if they were true it is probable that we would find those same general features of the universe' which theism purports to explain.[28] For example, the countless versions of polytheism, competing varieties of monotheism, or various kinds of naturalism 'would lead us to expect' these 'most general features'.[29] If we were to attribute an equal intrinsic probability to theism and to each of these competing hypotheses, endorsing the Principle of Indifference, the prior probability of theism would approach zero, since the set of theories to which theism belongs has 'innumerable' many members, of which only one can be true.[30] However, if the intrinsic probability of theism were near to zero, it would be impossible to show that the posterior probability of theism given all the available evidence *pro* and *contra* exceeds 1/2, as Swinburne intends to demonstrate.[31] The only way to solve this apologetic problem would be to argue that the intrinsic probability of theism is much greater than that of its competitors. But why should this be so?

Swinburne's argument for this claim consists of two contentions with regard to 'simplicity'. The first contention is that the simplicity of a hypothesis is an important *criterion for its truth*, instead of being merely a pragmatic advantage. If two hypotheses h_1 and h_2 aim at explaining the same set of data, so that they have the same scope, and if there is no relevant background knowledge, the intrinsic probability of their truth would depend entirely on their simplicity. If h_1 is simpler than h_2, h_1 would be more likely to be true than h_2, Swinburne contends.[32]

---

[28] Swinburne (2020), p. 138. [29] Swinburne (2020), p. 139.
[30] Cf. Philipse (2012, 2014), §12.8.
[31] This is admitted by Swinburne (2004), p. 332, note 1.
[32] Swinburne (2004), p. 67; (2016), p. 271; (2020), pp. 133, 139.

Consequently, if we compare theism with its innumerable competing world-views, such as versions of physicalism or naturalism, '[t]he crucial determinant of the prior probability of theism must be simplicity'.[33] The claim that '*Simplex sigillum veri* ("The simple is the sign of the true") is a dominant theme' of Swinburne's theistic apologetics, as he stresses repeatedly.[34] He also holds that if there exists something at all, 'the simple is more likely to exist than the complex'.[35]

This first contention with regard to the prior probability of theism would not help its adherents, however, if they could not argue convincingly for a second thesis: that in fact the theory of (bare) theism is simpler than each of its competitors. Swinburne endorses this second claim as well. As he repeats many times, '[t]heism is rendered probable by the evidence, only because it is simpler than [...] any other explanation' of the same phenomena.[36] In other words, '[t]he intrinsic probability of theism is, relative to other hypotheses about what there is, very high, because of the great simplicity of the hypothesis of theism'.[37] Furthermore, the alleged great simplicity of theism is due to the fact that it 'postulates the simplest kind of person there could be'.[38]

This latter claim with regard to God (as defined by Swinburne) will not appear to be plausible to most of us, I assume, whether we are religious or not. We might agree, for example, that the mental life of a person X will be more complex than that of a person Y if X has more knowledge than Y. Would it not follow that at least in this respect theism postulates the most complex person there can be, since God is assumed to be *omniscient*? Furthermore, if God knows everything about all of the innumerable features of the existing universe, and also about the possibility that because of his omnipotence He might have created numerous other universes, does it not follow that his mind is much more complex than the existing universe and more complex than anything we might imagine? The same conclusion follows from Swinburne's contention that God

---

[33] Swinburne (2004), p. 72.
[34] Swinburne (2004), p. 59. Cf. pp. 70, 86, 93, 109, 150, 334f. and, for example, Swinburne (2020), p. 139: 'the simplest explanation of phenomena' is the explanation that is 'most probably true'.
[35] Swinburne (2004), p. 109.   [36] Swinburne (2020), p. 139.
[37] Swinburne (2004), p. 109.
[38] Swinburne (2004), p. 97. Of course, one should object to this claim that criteria of simplicity regarding theories should not be identified with criteria of simplicity concerning postulated entities!

(as defined) 'intentionally causes or permits all events that happen'.[39] How, then, does Swinburne defend his second contention, that the theory of theism is simpler than each of its competitors because God is 'the simplest kind of person there could be'?[40]

His first premise is that 'hypotheses attributing infinite values of properties to objects are simpler than ones attributing large finite values'.[41] Second, he argues that some of the properties attributed to God, such as omniscience and omnipotence, have infinite values. God is defined as 'infinitely powerful', and 'God's beliefs' would 'have a similar infinite quality'.[42] I suppose that in the latter quote Swinburne attributes infinitely many true beliefs to God. But why would it follow that God is 'the simplest kind of person there could be', and that the hypothesis of theism is simpler than each of its competitors? If God has infinitely many true beliefs, He is the most complex kind of person imaginable, at least with regard to His knowledge.[43] The same argument applies to other properties ascribed to God, such as omnipotence.[44]

It is neither legitimate to assume that an infinite value of a property is always somehow simpler than any large finite value, nor that this (alleged) kind of simplicity of a hypothesis is a valid criterion for determining the intrinsic probability of its truth instead of being merely a pragmatic criterion for choosing a theory or formula as a starting point for further research, for example.[45] Since these two assumptions with regard to simplicity and infinity are crucial for Swinburne's apologetics, we should conclude that his defence of theism is already shipwrecked before it sails out of its harbour.[46]

---

[39] Swinburne (2016), p. 143.   [40] Cf., again, Swinburne (2004), p. 97.

[41] Swinburne (2004), p. 55.

[42] Swinburne (2004), pp. 97–98. What Swinburne meant by the last quote is unclear in its context.

[43] Of course, Swinburne replied to this objection by arguing that we should not understand God's omniscience on the model of human propositional knowledge (Swinburne (2010), pp. 18–19). Cf. Philipse (2012, 2014), p. 254, for a critical evaluation of this reply.

[44] Cf. Swinburne (2016), chapter 9.

[45] I argued this extensively in §§11.7–11.10 and 12.8 of my (2012, 2014) book. In his book (2020), pp. 135–136, Swinburne discusses only two of my objections to his claim that the simplicity of a theory (always) is a criterion of its truth. But he does not even mention my main objections, that with regard to 'many measures of the simplicity of a theory, there is no intelligible connection between simplicity and truth, and many prominent philosophers of science hold that simplicity is not a truth-conducive criterion' at all (Philipse 2012, 2014, p. 214).

[46] Cf. Swinburne (2016), p. 271: 'If, however, we are forced to suppose that God is essentially a very un-simple being, that would be a very unwelcome result for theism,

6.3 THE SEMANTIC CHALLENGE FOR BARE THEISM

Religious apologists who practise Bayesian natural theology in order to argue for the truth of their theistic belief are confronted with three challenging intellectual tasks. The first is semantic: they should provide a coherent and meaningful account of the word 'God' so that we can know what or whom they are arguing about. What, exactly, is meant by the contention that God exists? To which kind of alleged entity does the word 'God' refer according to them? Second, their theistic hypothesis as defined should have predictive or explanatory power. This has to be specified by indicating the kinds of empirical evidence of which (all taken together) it would be more likely that they occur if God (as defined) exists than if there is no such divinity. Finally, the third task for the natural theologian is to show that given all the available empirical evidence *pro* and *contra* theism as defined, the truth of this theory is more probable than its falsity. There is a ranking between these three challenges, because it seems to be clear that the second challenge arises only if the first is met, and the third challenge presupposes that the other two are satisfied. Since the issue of simplicity discussed in §6.2 belongs to the third, epistemological challenge, readers may wonder whether Richard Swinburne's natural theology meets challenges one and two.

Unfortunately, his natural theology does not meet either of them, as I argued extensively in my book *God in the Age of Science? A Critique of Religious Reason*. With regard to the first, semantic challenge, I agree with Richard Swinburne that '[i]f theology uses too many words in analogical senses it will convey virtually nothing by what it says'.[47] According to my Wittgenstein-inspired account of language, however, any normal, non-analogical application of psychological expressions such as 'feels', 'believes', 'speaks', 'answers', 'intends', 'attempts', 'knows', 'is angry', or 'loves' relies largely on criteria concerning human behaviour, including uses of language. If these criteria were not crucial for the meaning of psychological terms, children would never be able to learn

---

because it would deprive us of any good probabilistic arguments from observable phenomena for his existence', since 'it is always the simplest hypothesis that leads us to expect some phenomenon that is the one that is most probably true.'

[47] Swinburne (1993), p. 72. In the second edition (2016), p. 74, this sentence is extended: 'If theology uses too many words in analogical senses, or loosens up the rules for their use too much, it will convey virtually nothing by what it says. The claim that he is using words in an analogical sense must be for the theist a last resort to save his system from a charge of incoherence that would otherwise stick.'

their usage.[48] Since the theist eliminates any use of behavioural criteria by defining God as a 'person without a body',[49] most applications of psychological expressions to such an alleged entity are analogical to various extents, if they have any meaning at all. It follows that the definition of 'God' by means of psychological predicates such as 'omniscient' (knowing all things) does not make sufficient sense, so theists cannot meet the semantic challenge.[50]

I also refuted Swinburne's arguments to the effect that the term 'person' is used without analogy when 'God' is defined as a 'non-embodied person'.[51] In the ordinary and non-analogical sense of the word 'person', persons are human beings, and humans are corporal beings. That our bodily nature is implied by the term 'person' follows from many of its uses. When I say that I cannot attend your birthday party in person, what I mean is that I cannot be physically present. If we add up this analogical use of 'person' to the many other analogical uses of words in theistic attempts to define the word 'God', we should conclude that theism as defined by Richard Swinburne is not a meaningful (well-defined) theory or hypothesis.[52]

If Swinburne and other sophisticated theists were to agree with my detailed arguments to this effect, we could conclude that a critical evaluation of their theism might have ended here. Since the hypothesis of theism is not defined with sufficient clarity, there would be no point in investigating whether it has any predictive or explanatory power (the second, *explanatory* challenge for theists) and whether arguments supporting the truth of theism if taken together overrule the arguments against (the third, epistemic or *epistemological* challenge). If theists do not adequately meet the first, *semantic*, challenge, the other two challenges will not arise. Should Swinburne not have agreed, given that in his book *The Coherence of Theism* (1993) he concluded that '[m]an does not have the concepts in terms of which to think about God adequately'? He

---

[48] Philipse (2012, 2014), §7.2 (Cf. Hacker (2007), chapter 10, and Hacker (2013), *passim*). In §7.3, I refuted Swinburne's criticisms of a Wittgensteinean conception of psychological concepts.
[49] Cf. Swinburne (2016), p. 104: 'That God is a person, yet one without a body, seems the most elementary claim of theism.'
[50] Philipse (2012, 2014), chapter 7.
[51] Swinburne (1993, 2016), chapter 7, the section on 'The Nature of Personal Identity', and Philipse (2012, 2014), §§7.5–7.6. Swinburne (2016), chapter 13, specifies other reasons why God as defined 'could be a "person" only in an analogical sense' (p. 255).
[52] Philipse (2012, 2014), §§7.5–7.6.

admits that a theist 'must stretch words in order to talk about God and does not fully understand what is being said when the words are stretched'.[53] I would conclude that there is no point whatsoever in examining whether theism has any explanatory power (the second challenge), or whether the empirical arguments in favour of theism overrule the arguments against (the third challenge), since the word 'God' has not been defined with sufficient clarity.

Clearly, however, this is not a conclusion Richard Swinburne endorses. Why not? In the second edition (2016) of *The Coherence of Theism*, Swinburne formulates his answer to this question as follows. He admits that he has been 'unable either to prove' his version of theism 'in its entirety to be coherent or to prove it to be incoherent by normal direct or semi-direct means', since 'some of the words in which the doctrine is expounded are words used in analogical senses'.[54] He argued, however, that 'if we had good inductive evidence (on the assumption of its coherence) for the truth of this account of theism, we would thereby have evidence of its coherence', adding that '[o]nly by such a route is there a hope of showing coherence'.[55] Is this a valid method for demonstrating that a doctrine is coherent or that a concept is coherently defined?

I do not think so, at least not in the case of theism. If it is unclear whether this hypothesis is coherently formulated in the sense Swinburne specified, we will not be able to determine its particular predictive or explanatory power.[56] If we cannot specify its specific explanatory power, we will not be able to discover whether there is any inductive evidence for or against the truth of the alleged hypothesis of theism. In other words, if one is to be able to spell out the predictive or explanatory power of theism, one should first show that it is a clearly defined meaningful theory. Moreover, such powers have to be specified convincingly before we can investigate whether there are any sound empirical arguments *pro* or *contra* this version of theism.[57]

In order to be charitable to Swinburne's apologetic strategy, however, in my book *God in the Age of Science? A Critique of Religious Reason* I employed what I called a 'strategy of subsidiary arguments'. First, I argued extensively in chapters 7 and 8 that Swinburne had not succeeded in showing that his version of theism is a well-defined and coherent

---

[53] Swinburne (1993), p. 307. This passage does not occur in the (2016) edition of *The Coherence of Theism*.
[54] Swinburne (2016), p. 295.   [55] Swinburne (2016), p. 295. Cf. (1993), p. 306.
[56] Cf. Philipse (2012, 2014), §8.6.   [57] Cf. Philipse (2012, 2014), chapters 7 and 8.

hypothesis or theory. Assuming counterfactually that he had succeeded in meeting this first, semantic challenge, however, I then investigated in chapter 9 how Swinburne attributes a specific predictive or explanatory power to his hypothesis of theism, which is required in order to support it by empirical evidence. Having argued that the grounds for these attributions are invalid, I concluded that Swinburne's theism does not meet the second, predictive challenge either. Finally, I applied my strategy of subsidiary arguments yet again, and presupposed counterfactually that theism as defined is a meaningful hypothesis that has specific predictive or explanatory powers, as Swinburne purports to have shown. I then investigated whether on balance the empirical arguments *pro* and *contra* this version of theism demonstrate that its truth is more probable than its falsity, and argued that they do not (chapters 10–15). Let me practise this strategy of subsidiary arguments here too, and assume for a moment, counterfactually, that it is meaningful to define 'God' as a bodiless person with both mental and many other personal properties who is an 'essentially ontologically necessary being'.[58] Would such a hypothesis of theism have any predictive or explanatory power?

6.4 THE PREDICTIVE OR EXPLANATORY POWER OF THEISM

Applying the strategy of subsidiary arguments for the first time, let us assume in this section that Swinburne's definition of 'theism' (the proposition 'God exists') makes adequate sense: 'there exists necessarily a person without a body (i.e. a spirit) who necessarily is eternal, perfectly free, omnipotent, omniscient, perfectly good, and the creator of all things'. Swinburne uses the word 'God' as the name of the bodiless 'person picked out by this description', and stresses that theism so defined 'is, of course, the core belief of the creeds of Christianity, Judaism, and Islam'.[59]

If this version of theism were a meaningful and coherent (hypo)thesis, natural theologians would have to face the second challenge. They should specify various types of possible empirical evidence that would confirm their theistic theory and other kinds of conceivable evidence that might disconfirm it. Which types of empirical evidence would be relevant to the truth or falsity of theism? What is the predictive or explanatory power of this theory, if any? Does theism possess such powers at least to some extent? Only if this second challenge is met do we face the third challenge

---

[58] Swinburne (2016), p. 275.
[59] Swinburne (2004), p. 7; cf. pp. 93–96 on 'The Nature of God'.

Natural Theology 181

and have to investigate whether, on balance, all available evidence *pro* and *contra* the claim that God exists makes it more probable that this version of theism is true than that it is false. How does Swinburne specify the predictive or explanatory power of theism? To do so, he has to face at least two dilemmas: (1) a dilemma of *explanatory emptiness* and (2) a dilemma of *predictive power*.

> (1) The first dilemma follows from Swinburne's claim that 'theism purports to explain everything logically contingent (apart from itself)', so that 'there will be no background knowledge with which it has to fit'.[60] This dilemma is concerned with the explanatory scope of theism. What is meant by saying that God is 'the creator of all things', and holding that therefore theism explains 'everything logically contingent'? Two options are available to theists in this regard, which we might baptize 'factualism' and 'possibilism'. Let us discuss the second option first. According to this possibilist approach, theists claim that their theory accounts for everything that is *or might be* the case, since God is both omnipotent and omniscient. God's omnipotence would imply that 'whatever happens happens because he makes it or permits it to happen'.[61] Imagine, for example, that a very large asteroid is moving on a path that might impact Earth. If the asteroid collides with our planet, all life will be wiped out, including humanity. If no collision occurs, life on Earth will continue. Possibilist theists would claim that whichever scenario is realized, their omnipotent God will have co-caused or permitted it on good grounds, although we humans are not always able to fathom divine motivations.

Clearly, however, this first, 'possibilist' option annuls all explanatory and predictive capacities of theism. If God might allow or support any empirical scenario whatsoever, the hypothesis of theism would lack explanatory and predictive powers, so that it is explanatorily empty. As a consequence, the very project of natural theology would not be viable. In order to attribute at least some explanatory or predictive power to theism, the claim that 'theism purports to explain everything logically contingent' should be interpreted in what I would call a 'factualist' sense. Since God is defined as both omnipotent and omniscient, He would co-cause or allow everything to happen that happens in fact, that is, 'the

---

[60] Swinburne (2004), p. 66.   [61] Swinburne (2004), p. 99.

universe and all its characteristics'.[62] The hypothesis of theism would have some explanatory or predictive power to the extent that given God's nature, it is more likely that He prefers what happens in fact than that He would opt for specific alternative scenarios. Swinburne holds that 'God is at each moment of the world's history responsible for its operation at that moment of its history'.[63] Natural theology would be possible if we humans were to have some epistemic access to these divine preferences. A piece of empirical evidence e would support theism only if, given God's preferences, it is more likely that e will occur if theism is true than if theism is false. But how can we humans know anything about such divine preferences? Since natural theology cannot rely on alleged religious revelations, our attribution of specific creative or caring intentions to God should be justified merely by the concept of God as defined.

Only one property attributed to God by the definition of theism is promising in this respect: the property that God is 'perfectly good'. Swinburne holds that 'given some idea of moral goodness, we have some idea of the kinds of world that God, if there is a God, would be likely to bring about'.[64] Let me call this contention concerning the predictive or explanatory power of theism the 'moral access claim'. Is it convincing? Do our human ideas of moral goodness provide any reliable access to the content of God's creative intentions? Swinburne's conclusion that this is the case relies on two views with regard to moral judgements. Concerning one of these views he admits that its correctness is 'a contentious philosophical issue'.[65] This is the thesis of moral realism or objectivism, according to which 'moral judgements to the effect that this action is morally good and that one is morally bad are propositions that are true or false'.[66] If 'moral judgements have truth values, an omniscient person will know them'. Since God is defined as 'perfectly free and omniscient', He 'can never do actions that are morally bad', and all His actions will be morally good, Swinburne argues.[67]

However, even if moral realism or objectivism were the correct account of moral judgements, our human ethical insights would give us some access to God's creative intentions only if the truth-criteria that hold for human morality would be identical with the truth-criteria of divine ethics. This assumption is the second claim regarding moral judgements

---

[62] Swinburne (2004), p. 108.   [63] Swinburne (2004), p. 94.
[64] Swinburne (2004), p. 114.   [65] Swinburne (2004), pp. 99–100.
[66] Swinburne (2004), p. 99; cf. Swinburne (2016), chapter 11.
[67] Swinburne (2004), p. 105.

Swinburne's conclusion relies on, although he does not even attempt to justify it. Why would it then be plausible to assume that we have epistemic access to the content of God's moral values from our human point of view? I argued that the normative contents of human morality depend on the kind of animals that we are.[68] As Darwin wrote in *The Descent of Man* (1871), if other species such as hive bees had developed moral norms, the content of these norms would differ drastically from the norms we humans endorse.[69] It follows that there is no good reason to assume that the content of God's ethics would match the true moral norms of human morality. One might even doubt whether a solitary person such as God has any need for ethics at all, since morality is a 'group-oriented phenomenon' whereas, according to monotheism, God is the only individual of His kind.[70] Hence, we should not assume that our human moral insights provide us with any access to God's aims and intentions. Even this attempt to attribute some explanatory or predictive power to theism fails dramatically. The hypothesis of theism suffers from explanatory emptiness, so that the very project of natural theology is pointless.

(2) If the hypothesis of theism were provided with some predictive or explanatory power on the grounds that our human moral convictions give us modest access to God's intentions, as Swinburne presumes, theists would be faced by a second challenge: a dilemma of predictive power. Assuming that our human criteria for moral goodness were also God's criteria, even though '[o]ur understanding of what is good and bad is very limited', we might predict God's actions, at least to some extent, since God is defined as being 'perfectly good'.[71] Let me quote again Swinburne's contention that 'given some idea of moral goodness, we have some idea of the kinds of world that God, if there is a God, would be likely to bring about'.[72]

This moral access claim is risky for theism, however, since scientific progress has refuted numerous religiously inspired explanations and

---

[68] Philipse (2012, 2014), pp. 154–156.   [69] Darwin (1871), p. 122.
[70] Cf. De Waal et al. (2006), pp. 161–162. One may wonder to what extent Swinburne's theism is strictly monotheistic, since he claims that 'if God can make other divine beings, he must surely do so. A solitary God would be a bad state of affairs' (Swinburne (2004), p. 119). Of course, Swinburne is a trinitarian Christian.
[71] Swinburne (2004), p. 113.
[72] Swinburne (2004), p. 114. Cf. p. 107: 'God's goodness [...] will lead us to expect to find a universe of one kind rather than another.'

predictions, as I illustrated in Chapter 2. For example, William Paley argued in his *Natural Theology* of 1802 that the functional complexity of biological species could be explained only by assuming that God created each of their first instances, since it would have been very good to do so. After Charles Darwin developed his theory of evolution, however, and research in evolutionary biology showed in detail how biological species evolved by genetic variation and natural selection, it became ever more obvious that an omnipotent divinity who shares our enlightened moral values would never have created biological species in this manner. As many experts have argued, there is so much 'natural evil' involved in evolutionary mechanisms that a morally good and omnipotent God would not have used these procedures in order to create the numerous kinds of animals and mankind on Earth.[73] In Chapter 2, I argued on many other grounds as well that such a divinity would never have created our universe.

It follows that if theists rely on our human moral values in order to provide theism with some predictive power, they will be confronted by the following dilemma. Its first horn is to rely on our moral intuitions in order to predict what God would do or would have done in the past. Such predictions might be derived from the theistic hypothesis (combined with our moral values) before we know whether they will be verified or falsified by empirical research, if at least we take seriously Swinburne's claim that '[t]he very same criteria which scientists use to reach their own theories lead us to move beyond those theories to a creator God who sustains everything in existence'.[74] As the rise of evolutionary theory illustrates, however, this first horn of the dilemma is very risky for theists, since many of their religious predictions and explanations have been falsified by scientific progress. It is not surprising, then, that Swinburne opts for the second horn of this dilemma of predictive power, according to which 'the hypothesis that there is a God [...] does not yield predictions such that we can know only tomorrow, and not today, whether they succeed'.[75] In other words, Swinburne denies that theism has any predictive power in the ordinary sense of 'prediction', so that his religious theory of theism does not run any risk of refutation by future scientific research.

---

[73] Cf., for example, Dupré (2003), chapter 4, in which he argues that 'Darwinism undermines the only remotely plausible reason for believing in the existence of God' (p. 56). Swinburne discusses the problem(s) of natural evil extensively in (2004), chapter 11, and in his (1998). Cf. Philipse (2012, 2014), §14.4 for a critical analysis of Swinburne's evaluation of evolutionary explanations.
[74] Swinburne (1996), p. 2.   [75] Swinburne (2004), p. 70.

Natural Theology

In order to exclude all possible conflicts between natural theology and results of scientific investigations, Swinburne restricts even more radically the explanatory power of theism, although he claimed initially that his theism 'is a hypothesis of enormous scope', because it 'purports to explain everything logically contingent (apart from itself)' or 'the universe and all its characteristics'.[76] Arguments to the existence of God should rely only on phenomena that are 'scientifically inexplicable', so that any epistemic competition between science and religion is excluded in principle. He distinguishes between two types of phenomena that are scientifically inexplicable in slightly different senses. There are 'phenomena that are too *big* to be fitted into any pattern of scientific explanation', such as the existing universe, or the fact that 'the most fundamental natural laws of all hold'. According to Swinburne, there are also 'phenomena that are too *odd* to be fitted into the established pattern of scientific explanation', that is, 'events that theists claim to be miracles'. Since these two types of 'scientifically inexplicable' phenomena 'form the normal starting point for arguments to the existence of God', the risk that theism can be refuted by empirical research is reduced quite radically although not entirely.[77] A purely secular and historical explanation of the alleged testimonies of Christ's resurrection is vastly superior to the 'miraculous' explanation that this resurrection occurred really.[78]

Does theism have any explanatory power with regard to phenomena that are 'too *big*' for the sciences, if we rely on our human moral values in order to specify theism's explanatory potentials? My moral intuition in this respect is that an omnipotent, perfectly good, and bodiless divinity, called God, *would never have created the existing universe*, which contains some hundred billion galaxies and is expanding at an increasing rate (cf. §2.2). If God were to exist, He would have created merely a number of other immortal bodiless spirits or gods, with whom He could communicate and share wholeheartedly his divine life. Swinburne seems to endorse this moral intuition to some extent, since he claims that 'if God can make other divine beings, he must surely do so. A solitary God would be a bad state of affairs', since 'God needs to share, to interact, to love,

---

[76] Swinburne (2004), pp. 66, 108. Cf. p. 71: 'The theist argues from all the phenomena of experience, not from a small range of them.'

[77] Swinburne (2004), pp. 74–75 (Swinburne's italics). Of course, there are serious risks that scientific progress refutes (and has refuted in fact) religious contentions that a specific miracle occurred. Cf. Philipse (2012, 2014), §§10.2–10.5.

[78] Philipse (2012, 2014), §§10.2–10.5.

and he can do so most fully with equals'.[79] Let me stress again, however, that according to my moral intuitions, an omnipotent and perfectly good god would never have created a material universe in which, very locally and during a relatively short period, there is a planet on which corporal life evolved by means of evolutionary mechanisms and on which all living beings are mortal and are subject to many kinds of suffering if they are conscious. It follows that it would be fatal for theism if its explanatory power were based upon our human moral intuitions.

Let us conclude, then, that the (hypo)thesis of theism (as defined by Swinburne) either has no explanatory power whatsoever or that its explanatory power is provided by our human moral intuitions. The first option implies that the project of natural theology is pointless in principle for theists, whereas the second option is ruinous for religious believers who engage in natural theology. As I indicated, according to my human moral insights the perfectly good and omnipotent God conceived of by Swinburne would never have created a material universe but only some other bodiless spirits in order to enjoy their immaterial company. Such a divinity would certainly not have designed our universe, in which life is extremely rare and the expansion of which will continue forever, resulting in a so-called Big Freeze that will last eternally and excludes the existence of any living beings. Those of you who study the recent progress of scientific cosmology will agree that an omnipotent and perfectly good God as defined by Swinburne would not have created our universe, if creating life is his main intention. In other words, there is a convincing cosmological argument against theism if this theism were a meaningful theory and if it had some explanatory power due to our moral intuitions.

6.5 THE FINAL, EPISTEMOLOGICAL CHALLENGE

Theists who practise natural theology in order to justify their belief that God exists are confronted by three demanding challenges, as I indicated. First, they must provide a meaningful definition of the term 'God', so that we will know what or whom they are talking about. If this first, semantic task is met successfully, the second challenge arises: to specify which kinds of empirical evidence would be relevant to theism as defined, either confirming or disconfirming its truth. In other words, theism should have some predictive or explanatory power. Only if such powers are specified

---

[79] Swinburne (2004), p. 119. Swinburne's point of this passage is related to the Christian doctrine of the Trinity. Cf. Swinburne (2004), additional note 1.

sufficiently are theists confronted by the third, epistemological challenge: to provide convincing empirical evidence which shows that God as defined exists and which overrules the evidence against their version of theism.

In order to do justice to Swinburne's admirable apologetic enterprise, in my book *God in the Age of Science? A Critique of Religious Reason* I practised 'a strategy of subsidiary arguments', which I am summing up briefly in the present chapter.[80] First, I argued that Swinburne does not succeed in defining the name 'God' with sufficient clarity, because key words of the definition are used analogically. By claiming that God is an incorporeal being, theists annul the conditions for applying meaningfully the many psychological predicates they use in order to specify what kind of entity the word 'God' names (cf. §6.3).[81] Let us call this conclusion *semantic atheism*. Assuming counterfactually that the word 'God' as defined makes sufficient sense, however, I then investigated whether this variety of theism would have any predictive or explanatory power. As we saw in §6.4, Swinburne's claim that we can rely on our human moral intuitions in order to attribute such powers to theism is both implausible and very risky for theists. If mental life were possible without relying on cortical activity, as is assumed by theists who conceive of their deity as a bodyless mind, my moral sense suggests that this divinity would never have created our material universe but only a number of other minds or bodiless spirits, at least if God were really a social being.

In order to take account of Swinburne's epistemic justification of his theism, one should practise the strategy of subsidiary arguments yet again. Assuming, counterfactually, that the elaborate definition of 'God' makes sufficient sense, and that the doctrine of theism as defined has at least some explanatory power, we should evaluate critically his impressive analysis of the (alleged) evidence *pro* and *contra* theism spelled out in the second edition of *The Existence of God* (2004) and in some of his more recent publications. Does Swinburne succeed in showing that, given all the (alleged) empirical evidence *pro* and *contra*, it would be more probable that theism is true than that it is false? He argues extensively that many matters of fact are more to be expected if God as defined were to exist than if God does not exist, such as the existence of a complex physical universe, its orderly nature, the existence of animals, the fact that humans exist and have moral awareness, and the human potential to

---

[80] Cf. Philipse (2012, 2014), p. 341. [81] Philipse (2012, 2014), chapters 7 and 8.

cooperate in acquiring knowledge and 'moulding the universe', for example. That there is 'some evidence of miracles', and that specific religious experiences often occur, would also confirm the hypothesis of theism.[82] Having evaluated some alleged counterevidence as well, such as the existence of various types of evil and the fact of 'divine hiddenness', Swinburne concluded that if we take into account all the evidence *pro* and *contra* theism, '[o]n our total evidence theism is more probable than not'.[83]

In part III of my book *God in the Age of Science? A Critique of Religious Reason*, I examined critically Swinburne's inductive arguments for theism and evaluated whether the sum total of arguments *pro* and *contra* theism shows that theism as defined is more likely to be true than to be false. Doing so, I assumed counterfactually that this version of theism is a meaningful theory with some explanatory powers. It took more than a hundred pages to evaluate Swinburne's inductive arguments and their cumulative strength.[84] Since in many cases the technical details of the arguments *pro* and *contra* theism are crucial for an evaluation of their validity, no short summary would do justice to Swinburne's cumulative case for theism or to my detailed refutation of his apologetics. Therefore, I finish at this point the final section of the present volume. Dear readers, have you been convinced by Parts I and II of this book that there are no gods or other supernatural beings? If you have not been persuaded yet, you might be interested to dive into natural theology, to study Swinburne's sophisticated arguments for theism and my *Critique* of his *Religious Reason*.

---

[82] The quoted passages are from Swinburne (2004), p. 328.
[83] Swinburne (2004), pp. 328, 342.   [84] Philipse (2012, 2014), pp. 221–337.

Conclusion

The Two Interrelated Core Questions

As I argued in the Introduction, the intricate topic of religion is of relevance to each of us, whether we are believers or not. One main reason for this relevance is that the fast-growing human population on our planet is becoming more religiously affiliated rather than less. On average, the fertility rate of religious people exceeds that of unbelievers, and most devotional parents educate their children accordingly. Furthermore, many religious organizations still proselytize, trying to inspire or urge unbelievers to convert to their creed. An investigation of *The Changing Global Religious Landscape* published in 2017 by the Pew Research Center predicted that by 2060 the proportion of religious people on Earth will be 87.5 per cent, which is larger than today. Since many human activities are motivated by the endorsement of specific religious beliefs, we need to have some knowledge of current religions in order to understand what is happening in our world.

Another reason for the relevance of religion is that we may wonder at least once during our lifetime whether any particular religious belief is true. Whereas the first relevance-reason may motivate us to read empirical studies of diverse religious cultures, the second one should prompt us to dive into the philosophy of religion and to study religious epistemology. The two core questions of this book are related to these two reasons. The second reason for the relevance of religion motivates us to raise the following, first core question: how likely is the existence of any particular divinity, god, angel, spirit, or devil? Shouldn't we conclude that the existence of such supernatural beings is very improbable, given the available evidence *pro* and *contra*? The second core question is related to the first reason. How should we explain the adherence to specific religious beliefs by individuals and human societies? What are and have been the mental and social functions of endorsing such beliefs? Whereas the first core question is central to the philosophy of religion, the second should be answered mainly by empirical research in psychology, sociology, anthropology, and the history of religions.

The answers to these two core questions are interdependent. If a specific religious belief were true, it would be plausible to explain the fact that many humans hold this belief by describing the ways in which such a truth has been discovered or revealed to believers by the relevant divinity. If, however, the belief is not true, the proper explanation of why people harbour it should be a purely secular one, provided by the empirical sciences of religion. Since the contents of the many different religious beliefs that are endorsed today by adherents of religions contradict each other, these beliefs cannot all be true. It follows from such simple philosophical reflections that empirical research regarding religious beliefs has to rely on the results of philosophical investigations. Consequently, the empirical sciences of religion cannot be philosophically neutral, although many scientists of religion pretend that this is so. The interdependence of the two core questions of this book explains and justifies its global set-up. The philosophical Parts I and III flank Part II, which is devoted to empirical research regarding religions. Each of these parts consists of two chapters, the main conclusions of which I shall now summarize very briefly.

PART I

Part I of the book is entitled 'The Reasonableness of Religious Beliefs'. Its first chapter has been devoted to 'Religious Epistemology'. Are there any reliable methods of religious research, or trustworthy epistemic sources, which will enable us to discover whether a specific belief that some supernatural being(s) exist(s) is true?

The urgency of this question should be clear to all of us, since we are aware of the religious diversity on Earth. As the contents of many religious convictions contradict each other, like monotheist and polytheist ones, or trinitarian and non-trinitarian monotheisms, these creeds cannot all be true. In §1.1 it was argued that holding a specific religious belief would not be legitimate from an epistemological point of view if the believer is aware of this incompatibility, and if all these mutually incompatible religious doctrines are epistemically on a par. The latter condition is met if no religious conviction relies on better accessible evidence or more trustworthy epistemic sources than other, incompatible ones. I argued, for example, that Calvinists such as Alvin Plantinga should not trust their alleged *sensus divinitatis*, since they do not really resolve this problem of religious pluralism.

§1.2 was devoted to epistemic sources of religious beliefs. Some important distinctions were made and elucidated, such as between primary and secondary sources and between the causal and the justificational grounding of beliefs. In order to investigate whether the extraordinary experiences that functioned as primary sources of major religious beliefs are reliable from an epistemological point of view, I examined in detail St Paul's conversion experience on the road to Damascus and the alleged communications between Apollo and the Pythia in the Oracle of Delphi (§1.3). Since secular explanations of these experiences are superior to religious ones, I concluded provisionally that the crucial epistemic credentials of religions that dominate the world today, such as Hinduism, Christianity, and Islam, are not any better than those of religious beliefs that all of us reject as false. Since none of the primary epistemic sources of religious beliefs have been validated or calibrated, all such beliefs should be rejected by well-informed people. This Epistemological Argument from Cultural Contingency also applies to the allegedly 'more humane' approaches of religious epistemology advocated by Paul Moser or John Cottingham, for example (§1.4).

In Chapter 2, 'Science and Religion', the scientific enterprise was defined in its broadest sense as the human search for truth by means of well-validated epistemic methods and resources. Since there are no such reliable methods or sources which can be used in order to legitimize religious claims to truth, the scientific attitude rules out the endorsement of any religious belief. After the scientific revolution in sixteenth–seventeenth-century Europe, the awareness that there is such a methodological conflict between science and religion grew gradually. As the methods of scientific research became ever more sophisticated, and scientific progress had refuted many religious claims, it became increasingly clear that there are no reliable epistemic sources of religious beliefs. As a consequence, the cultural domains of science and religion were separated ever more radically. Religious claims to truth were eliminated from all scientific disciplines, including the social sciences and the humanities.

This cultural development was illustrated in §2.1 by summing up the scientific progress concerning the place and relative importance of our human habitat in the universe, from Aristotle until the present. Whereas according to the biblical book Genesis the world was created by God mainly in order to house humanity, contemporary cosmology provides a radical refutation of this contention. Various phases in the history of cosmology are fascinating from a cultural point of view, such as the condemnation of Galileo to lifelong house arrest by the Roman Catholic Inquisition in 1633. Since we now know that the 'observable' universe contains at least 2 trillion galaxies, while there are between 100 and 400 billion stars in our galaxy alone, the Milky Way, the belief that there is a god who created the universe mainly in order to house mankind on Earth has lost its credibility completely.

This conclusion is supported further by results of cosmological research concerning the timescale of our universe, summarized in §2.2. For many centuries, Christian scholars relied on biblical chronologies of human generations from Adam to Abraham in order to calculate the age of the universe. Results of such calculations, like Archbishop Ussher's conclusion published in 1650 that God created the universe in October 4004 BC, were overruled by scientific research in the seventeenth century, such as the geological calculations of Benoît de Maillet. As recent radiometric datings of the oldest known terrestrial and lunar materials reveal, planet Earth originated from a process of accretion about 4.54 ± 0.05 billion years ago. Relying on many other timescale calculations, such as that of the evolutionary origin of life on Earth, of the human species, and of our universe since the postulated Big Bang, we should conclude that no omnipotent and omniscient god would have created such a universe, if at least one of her or his main intentions had been to create life and a biological species of humans. Recent cosmological predictions of a Big Freeze of the universe, which will result from cosmic expansion and last eternally, also refute the religious belief that there is an omnipotent and benevolent god who created the world.

§2.3 illustrated the gradual retreat of religious assumptions from the scientific enterprise by two other examples. Whereas Isaac Newton still resorted to a theological explanation of two prominent properties of our planetary system, Immanuel Kant and Pierre-Simon de Laplace developed purely physical accounts. Consequently, during the early nineteenth century scientifically informed Christian apologists focused on other aspects of our world in order to argue that these features could be explained only by reference to a divine creation. For example, William Paley contended in his *Natural Theology* of 1802 that God had produced the first instances of each biological species, and that there could not be a scientific explanation of complex parts of animals such as their eyes. Charles Darwin had studied Paley's works as a student in Cambridge when he still aimed to

Conclusion: The Two Interrelated Core Questions

become a clergyman. During the development of his evolutionary biology, Darwin became ever more sceptical with regard to religion. Would an omnipotent and perfectly good God have created animal species and mankind by the evolutionary processes which Darwin investigated? He realized ever more clearly that the mechanisms of natural selection caused so much suffering that the Christian God would never have created animals and mankind in this manner. As the elimination of religious assumptions from cosmology and biology illustrates, religious convictions cannot be supported by reliable methods of investigation, and many of them have been refuted by scientific progress.

Religious believers might object that it would be blasphemous to assume that we should discover the existence of a divinity by using our human methods of research. Many monotheists maintain that God decides autonomously to whom He reveals his presence. Consequently, the elimination of religious contentions from the sciences and humanities would be appropriate from a pious point of view. Science and religion should be strictly separated, they argue. Allegedly, no instances of scientific progress provide any reliable refutation of their religion, since the sciences are religiously neutral. §2.4 shows that there are numerous empirical arguments against theism and other religious creeds, arguments resulting from scientific progress. Consequently, the contention that the empirical sciences are essentially neutral with regard to religious beliefs is untenable.

PART II

If we conclude from the arguments of Part I that the existence of gods and other supernatural beings is very unlikely, we will wonder what explains the ubiquity of religious beliefs. How should we account for their occurrence, assuming that no religious conviction is true? Part II of this book, entitled 'The Evolution of Religion and Ethics' (Chapters 3 and 4), is devoted to empirical explanations of the origins and development of religious beliefs. As (pre)historical and anthropological research on religions has revealed, animist and polytheist creeds preceded monotheisms, and the latter evolved gradually from the former. Chapter 3, called 'Religions: Origins and Evolution', investigates how one should understand the origins of polytheistic faiths and what accounts for the gradual transitions from polytheist persuasions to monotheisms.

The first section (§3.1) of Chapter 3 starts by providing empirical evidence confirming the hypothesis that all the oldest religious cultures have been polytheistic. With regard to prehistoric periods, the evidence adduced may fail to convince some readers, since it does not contain any textual ingredients. However, since the hypothesis is supported by worldwide evidence regarding the earliest religious inscriptions and writings, it is plausible to assume that it holds for prehistory as well. Many examples of polytheistic inscriptions and documents are briefly discussed, such as those carved on the Saqqara pyramids in Egypt, the oldest tablets of the Epic of Gilgamesh, ancient Greek sources, and early Vedic texts. The second half of §3.1 is devoted to the gradual transitions from polytheisms to varieties of monotheism. When did the earliest instances of such transitions occur? Should we classify the Atenism advanced by the Egyptian pharaoh Amenhotep IV as a version of monotheism? Or should we glorify Zoroastrianism as the first monotheist religion? Be this as it may, many instances of historical evidence show that all monotheist religions grew gradually out of polytheisms.

§3.2 is devoted to the first core question of Chapter 3: how can we explain most plausibly the origins and endurance of polytheistic beliefs? The genesis of polytheisms has been investigated by experts of many different scientific disciplines, such as anthropology, evolutionary biology, psychology, and the cognitive sciences of religion. §3.2 evaluates some of their most prominent accounts and examines how much scientific progress there has been with regard to polytheistic (pre)history, for example since David Hume's book *The Natural History of Religion* (1757). According to Hume, polytheistic religious beliefs were triggered originally because early humans postulated supernatural anthropomorphic causes of circumstances that were crucial for their survival and which they could not yet explain scientifically. Various types of scientific progress since Hume are discussed and classified in terms of an evolutionary framework, such as the hypothesis that our brains contain a so-called hypersensitive agent detection device. It is stressed and illustrated how many different mental and social functions have been fulfilled by polytheistic beliefs and rituals.

The final section (§3.3) investigates what accounts for the gradual transitions of polytheistic religions to monotheisms. Inspired again by David Hume, this second core question of Chapter 3 is answered by arguing that there is an inner logic to such transitions which are triggered by various motives that inspire humans to attribute ever more impressive properties to their divinities. As soon as the properties of a particular god are conceived of as infinite in some sense, there does not seem to be any logical space left for other, superior or equivalent, divinities, and versions of monotheism gradually emerge. Whereas Hume focused on tribe-internal practices of praise or flattery with regard to the divinities believed in, it is argued in §3.3 that the motives for aggrandizing the properties of one's chief divinity were even stronger in situations of intertribal warfare. Several passages of the Hebrew Bible or Old Testament, and historical information about the Roman emperor Constantine, provide empirical evidence for this hypothesis.

Chapter 4, called 'Religion and Ethics', begins with the following famous quotation from Dostoevsky, who (allegedly) wrote in *The Brothers Karamazov*: 'If God does not exist, everything is permitted.' Since even today many authors argue that it is 'impossible for people to be moral without religion or God', we should evaluate this claim carefully. In order to do so, it is shown first that the contention is ambiguous. It expresses either (a) the philosophical thesis that only if God exists can moral norms be valid and legitimate, or (b) the factual thesis that religious believers tend to be more morally meritorious than atheists and other unbelievers. In §4.1, it is shown that even if God exists, one cannot correctly justify moral rules and ideals with reference to this (or any other) divinity. Religious justifications of moral norms are confronted by three main challenges, each of which refutes the legitimacy of such a justification. Fortunately, there are many good non-religious reasons that vindicate the validity of specific moral norms and values. Consequently, claim (a) is false. What should we think, then, of the factual contention (b)?

§4.2 is devoted to the genesis and prominence of so-called 'moralizing' religions, according to which a 'high' or 'big' god prescribes moral norms for interpersonal human behaviour and punishes or rewards us hereafter. Since such moralizing religions are widespread today, like many versions of Christianity and Islam, we might wonder how their prominence should be explained. In 2013, Ara Norenzayan proposed an evolutionary hypothesis according to which beliefs in a moralizing Big God enhance the fitness of large-scale societies, since such beliefs facilitate cooperation between strangers. Communities that endorsed a moralizing religion and expelled or killed unbelievers often outcompeted communities that did not, so that moralizing religions became widespread in human history. This hypothesis concerning cultural competition is examined with reference to the statistical research of 414 societies by Harvey Whitehouse et al. (2019). Although a shared belief in a moralizing high god turns out to be neither a necessary nor a sufficient causal condition for large-scale cooperation in human cultures, it is argued that it often has been a contributory cause.

In §4.3, the earliest expansions of Christianity are investigated. How should we explain, for example, that after Jesus' crucifixion and death on the cross many of his early followers started or continued to proselytize with great passion instead of losing their faith in him? On which types of evidence can we rely in order to assess the plausibility of the various proposed explanations? It is argued that the relevant evidence does not only consist of biblical sources and historical information but also results from recent research on cognitive dissonance. Plausibly, some disciples of Jesus 'left everything' and followed him to Jerusalem because they believed that they would 'sit on twelve thrones, judging the twelve tribes of Israel', as is mentioned in Matthew 19:27–28. Consequently, these disciples would have been deeply bewildered when a team led by the chief priests arrested Jesus, condemned him to death, and delivered Jesus to Pilate in order to be crucified. Today, we would diagnose their situation as an excruciating crisis of cognitive dissonance, which helps to explain why after the crucifixion some followers of Jesus started to proselytize fervently. As research on cognitive dissonance shows, the mental suffering caused by a refutation of one's convictions is often reduced by passionate attempts to proselytize.

The second issue regarding the rise of Christianity discussed in §4.3 is what caused the seemingly miraculous transformation of the Jesus sect, which was marginal around the year 40, into a religious community so large that emperor Constantine decided to convert to Christianity before the Milvian Bridge battle in 312 CE. Can this rise be explained from a purely secular point of view? In his fascinating sociological study *The Rise of Christianity* (1996), Rodney Stark investigated numerous mundane causes of the Christian expansion. These causal factors are summarized in §4.3, such as the Christian prohibition of birth control and homosexuality or the Christian policies during serious plagues that killed about a third of the population. When one adds up all these contributory causes of the spread of Christianity, one will agree with Stark that the rise of Christianity within and around the Roman Empire can be explained merely by reference to mundane factors. This does not imply, however, that we should endorse the theoretical framework of rational choice theory, which Stark uses in order to understand 'all aspects of religion'. As David Sloan Wilson argued in *Darwin's Cathedral* (2002), we should analyse the early rise of Christianity within the framework of multilevel evolutionary selection theory, since Christian communities had to compete with many other creeds and devotional clusters.

The final section (§4.4) of Chapter 4 is devoted to the greatest moral challenge humanity is facing today: the problem of human-induced global warming. What role can religions play in mitigating the threatening and catastrophic effects of climate change on Earth? The recent rise of the global mean surface temperature has been caused mainly by anthropogenic greenhouse gas emissions, which increased substantially because of the growing human population and its economic endeavours, such as the still amplifying use of fossil fuels. After an overview of some catastrophic effects of this climate change, like sea-level rise, increasing desertification, and so-called tipping points, it is argued that humanity should urgently prevent any additional global warming. Since impeding further population growth on Earth is one of the six necessary conditions for avoiding catastrophic global warming, whereas the average fertility rate of Muslims and Christians is much higher than the average global rate, it is argued that all relevant religious leaders should preach restraint in procreation within their communities.

PART III

Monotheists endorse faith in one particular divinity while being atheists or agnostics with regard to all other gods humans have worshipped or still revere. How do the most prominent present-day vindicators of monotheism justify such an exceptionalist position? Does any one of their justifications disprove or overrule the refutations of religious beliefs reported in §2.4?

Part III, 'Apologetic Strategies Evaluated', aims at assessing the most prominent instances of contemporary monotheist apologetics (Chapters 5 and 6). Can one still legitimize the endorsement of a particular religious belief in our science-informed times, in spite of the arguments and information provided in Parts I and II?

Chapter 5, 'The Decision Tree for Religious Believers', starts by explaining why monotheists developed so many different apologetic strategies. One might expect that if an omnipotent and perfectly good god existed, who loves all human beings, such a divinity would reveal her or his existence very clearly to all humans on Earth from the beginning of mankind. Since such a universal and incontestable divine revelation has not occurred, and the various monotheisms originated locally quite late in human (pre)history, we can understand that many types of religious apologetics have been tried out. The question whether any of these apologetic strategies is convincing from an epistemological point of view will be crucial for most monotheist believers.

In the first section (§5.1) of Chapter 5, it is argued that in order to be convincing, an apologetic strategy has to meet the following three challenges: (a) the Semantic Challenge to provide a clear and coherent description of the divinity believed in; (b) the Epistemic Challenge to show that there are good grounds for thinking that this divinity exists, although there do not seem to be any reliable methods of religious research; and (c) the Explanatory Challenge to account for the fact that if a specific god such as God or Allah existed, this divinity would be hidden to most humans. §5.2 classified all possible apologetic strategies of monotheists in terms of a Decision Tree for Religious Believers. In order to do justice to each end node of this decision tree, such as Religious Non-factualism, Voluntarism or Fideism, Confidentialism, and the many types of monotheist Evidentialism, one should evaluate the oeuvre of their most sophisticated advocates, which is the aim of Part III.

In this Conclusion, I shall mention only some of the main results, starting with the Non-factualist option, which is the topic of §5.3. According to a famous Non-factualist such as D. Z. Phillips, God's reality is not a matter of fact but rather an all-embracing framework of grace and love or an all-illuminating light, within which the believer perceives everything. In §5.3, such Non-factualists are confronted with an embarrassing dilemma. Do they aim at interpreting what most Christians mean when they claim that God exists by analysing the relevant religious language games, or do they intend to develop new rules for religious language in order to protect their religion against epistemic criticisms? Whereas the first option of non-factualism is refuted by an empirical analysis of most religious utterances, the second, revisionary alternative makes religion epistemically irrelevant. We should conclude that all real religious believers are Factualists or Religious Realists with regard to their God. They believe that this god really exists. On what grounds then does their faith rely?

§5.4 is devoted mainly to Religious Confidentialism as defended by Alvin Plantinga. If one rejects all versions of religious Voluntarism and Fideism because they are too irrational or arbitrary but also admits that there is no convincing public evidence showing that God exists, Confidentialism may seem to be the most attractive apologetic alternative for a theist. In his masterpiece *Warranted Christian Belief* (2000), recently summarized in *Knowledge and Christian Belief* (2015), Plantinga argued that holding classical Christian beliefs amounts to knowledge if these beliefs have enough warrant, and that they have enough warrant if God caused these properly basic beliefs in us as a supernatural gift. Human sinfulness would explain the disturbing fact that not all humans are aware of this divine endowment. Since according to Plantinga it is not possible to provide a sound proof that God does not exist, Christians can rely legitimately on their presumed *sensus divinitatis*, even if they are aware of the many mutually incompatible religious faiths. In order to evaluate Plantinga's Confidentialism, six objections were formulated, which show that his apologetic strategy is unconvincing.

In the last two sections of Chapter 5, two prominent versions of Involvement Evidentialism are evaluated. John Cottingham defends a 'Pascalian approach' to the kind of evidence available with regard to the existence of God. In his (2014) book *Philosophy of Religion: Towards a More Humane Approach*, he developed an 'epistemology of involvement', according to which evidence of the grace of God is provided to prospective converts only if they have 'made the decision to embark on a certain kind of spiritual journey'. In §5.5, I evaluate the sophisticated answers which Cottingham provides to core questions concerning the epistemic legitimacy of Christian belief, such as how the word 'God' can be defined and what kinds of experience or evidence supports belief in God's existence. It is argued that Cottingham's Involvement Evidentialism may be classified as a brilliant strategy of immunization, which deprives outsiders from the epistemic capacity to evaluate religious truth-claims of insiders.

Chapter 5 is rounded off in §5.6 by a critical analysis of the Involvement Evidentialism developed by Paul K. Moser in *The Evidence for God: Religious Knowledge Reexamined* (2010). Moser defines the word 'God' as a title which we should apply to a being that is morally perfect and loves each enemy. Since no human person would merit such a title, Moser holds that it can be deserved merely by an invisible personal Spirit whose character traits and purposes are morally superior to ours. He argues that only the divine father of Jesus can be legitimately called 'God', and that the evidence for the existence of this divinity is 'personifying', since it consists in humans having willingly received 'the transformative gift' of enemy-love. After a detailed summary of Moser's 'volitional theism' it was argued that this 'kardiatheology' is confronted by nine crucial problems.

Chapter 6 is devoted to 'Natural Theology', the discipline within which one provides and evaluates arguments and empirical evidence for and against a specific religious belief. If none of the apologetic strategies discussed in Chapter 5 succeed in vindicating a religious belief, such a conviction can be epistemically legitimate only if it is supported sufficiently by arguments and evidence accessible to both believers and unbelievers. The first section of this chapter (§6.1) provided a historical overview of natural theology in Western cultures from Aristotle onwards. Whereas the discipline was crucial for Christianity after the rediscovery of Aristotle during the High Middle Ages, its importance in Europe declined because of the Renaissance and the Protestant Reformation. Both David Hume and Immanuel Kant held that religious beliefs cannot be justified by empirical arguments, whereas references to God were eliminated progressively from all scientific disciplines, as illustrated in Chapter 2.

The remaining sections of Chapter 6 investigate whether the resurrection of natural theology in the works of Richard Swinburne is convincing. The focus is on the theory of 'bare' theism, according to which there is a bodiless divinity called God, defined by properties such as omnipresence, omnipotence, omniscience, and perfect goodness. Only if on balance the various arguments from experience show that there is such a god can it be epistemically legitimate for Jews, Christians, Muslims, or other (mono) theists to rely on the 'ramified' theism of their revealed theology. As a consequence, Swinburne's natural theology as elaborated in his book *The Existence of God* is relevant to all theistic religions. §6.2 explains how Swinburne applies Bayesian confirmation theory in order to structure his argumentative defence of theism, which aims to show that given all empirical evidence *pro* and *contra* it is more probable than not that there is a God as defined. Since similar empirical evidence might be adduced in favour of innumerable religious competitors of theism, it is a challenge for theists to show that the intrinsic probability of their theory (the probability independently of its relation to any evidence) is higher than that of its competitors. Swinburne claims to have shown this by arguing (a) that the simpler a hypothesis the more probable is its truth, and (b) that hypotheses attributing infinite values of properties to entities are simpler than ones attributing finite values, however large. Since he contends that God's (omni-)properties have infinite values, the intrinsic probability of theism would be higher than that of its numerous competitors. Both of Swinburne's contentions (a) and (b) are rebutted in §6.2.

Natural theologians who intend to argue that God exists by providing empirical evidence have to meet three challenges. The first, semantic one, is to show that their version of theism is a well-defined meaningful hypothesis. Second, it should be demonstrated that this theistic hypothesis has some predictive or explanatory power, in the sense that specific empirical phenomena would confirm their theory. Third, one has to establish that if taken together, the adduced empirical evidence supports theism sufficiently. In §6.3 it is argued that theists fail to satisfy the first, semantic challenge, because they define 'God' as a person without a body. Since behavioural criteria are crucial to the meaning of most psychological terms, the claim that God is a bodiless mind or spirit implies that these terms are deprived of their meaning when used to define the word 'God', so that it cannot be defined properly.

If we assume, counterfactually, that in *The Coherence of Theism* Swinburne provided a meaningful definition of 'theism' and 'God', even though he admitted that '[m]an does not have the concepts in terms of which to think about God adequately', we should wonder whether the second challenge is faced successfully: does theism as defined have any predictive or explanatory power?[1] As argued in §6.4, theists have to resolve two difficult dilemmas in order to show that their religious hypothesis might be confirmed by empirical evidence: (1) a dilemma of explanatory emptiness, and (2) a dilemma of predictive power. Since theists cannot resolve these dilemmas convincingly, as has been illustrated by Swinburne's sophisticated attempts to do so, the hypothesis of theism cannot be supported by any empirical evidence whatsoever, so the very project of natural theology is pointless for religious believers. If it were legitimate to attribute some predictive power to theism relying on our human moral intuitions, however, a convincing cosmological argument against theism could be formulated.

Finally (§6.5), we might suppose counterfactually not only that the word 'God' has been defined meaningfully but also that the defined version of theism has some explanatory power. If so, we can investigate whether the sum total of all empirical arguments *pro* and *contra* theism as defined demonstrate that the truth of this theory is more likely than its falsity, as Swinburne argued in *The Existence of God*. Since the soundness of such arguments depends on many technical details, I invite readers to study Swinburne's cumulative case for theism and the evaluation of his apologetics in my book *God in the Age of Science? A Critique of Religious Reason*.

---

[1] The quote is from the revised (1993) edition of *The Coherence of Theism*, p. 307.

Bibliography

Abbott, B. et al. (2016). 'Observation of Gravitational Waves from a Binary Black Hole Merger', *Physical Review Letters* (11 February 2016), https://doi.org/10.1103/PhysRevLett.116.061102.

Alston, William P. (1990). 'Some Suggestions for Divine Command Theorists', in: Michael D. Beaty (ed.), *Christian Theism and the Problems of Philosophy*. Notre Dame, IN: University of Notre Dame Press, pp. 303–326.

American Psychiatric Association (2000). *Diagnostic and Statistical Manual of Mental Disorders*, 4th edition, text revision. Washington, DC: American Psychiatric Association.

Anderson, Elizabeth (2007). 'If God Is Dead, Is Everything Permitted?', in: Hitchens (2007), chapter 39.

Aristotle (1933). *The Metaphysics*, books I–IX, with an English translation by Hugh Tredennick. The Loeb Classical Library, Vol. 271. Cambridge, MA: Harvard University Press.

  (1935). *Metaphysics*, books X–XIV, with an English translation by Hugh Tredennick. The Loeb Classical Library, Vol. 287. Cambridge, MA: Harvard University Press.

  (1939). *On the Heavens*, with an English translation by W. K. C. Guthrie. The Loeb Classical Library. Cambridge, MA: Harvard University Press.

Armstrong, Karen (1994). *A History of God: The 4,000-Year Quest of Judaism, Christianity and Islam*. New York: Ballantine Books.

Atkinson, Quentin D., Andrew J. Latham, and Joseph Watts (2015). 'Are Big Gods a Big Deal in the Emergence of Big Groups?', in: Ara Norenzayan (ed.), *Book Symposium: Big Gods, Religion, Brain & Behavior*, Vol. 5., No. 4, 266–274.

Atran, Scott (2002). *In Gods We Trust: The Evolutionary Landscape of Religion*. New York: Oxford University Press.

Audi, Robert (1998). *Epistemology: A Contemporary Introduction to the Theory of Knowledge*. London and New York: Routledge.

(2011). *Rationality and Religious Commitment*. Oxford and New York: Oxford University Press.

Baker-Hytch, Max (2014). 'Religious Diversity and Epistemic Luck', *International Journal for Philosophy of Religion*, Vol. 76, pp. 171–191.

Barbour, Ian G. (1998). *Religion and Science: Historical and Contemporary Issues*. London: SCM Press Ltd.

Barrett, J. L. (2004). *Why Would Anyone Believe in God?* Walnut Creek, CA: AltaMira Press.

(2009). 'Cognitive Science, Religion, and Theology', in: J. Schloss and M. Murrary (eds), *The Believing Primate: Scientific, Philosophical, and Theological Reflections on the Origin of Religion*. Oxford: Oxford University Press, pp. 76–99.

(2012). *Born Believers: The Science of Children's Religious Beliefs*. New York: The Free Press.

Barth, Karl (1957). *Church Dogmatics II*. Edited by G. W. Bromley and T. F. Torrance. Edinburgh: T. & T. Clark.

Baumard, Nicolas, and Pascal Boyer (2013). 'Explaining Moral Religions', *Trends in Cognitive Sciences*, Vol. 17, No. 6, pp. 272–280.

Behe, Michael J. (1996, 2006). *Darwin's Black Box: The Biochemical Challenge to Evolution*. New York: The Free Press.

(2007). *The Edge of Evolution: The Search for the Limits of Darwinism*. New York: The Free Press.

Bennett, M. R., and P. M. S. Hacker (2003). *Philosophical Foundations of Neuroscience*. Malden, MA and Oxford: Blackwell.

Bergmann, Michael, and Patrick Kain, eds (2014). *Challenges to Moral and Religious Belief: Disagreement and Evolution*. Oxford: Oxford University Press.

Bermejo-Rubio, Fernando (2017). 'The Process of Jesus' Deification and Cognitive Dissonance Theory', *Numen*, Vol. 64, Nos 2–3, pp. 119–152.

Blatner, David (2014). *Spectrums: Our Mind-boggling Universe from Infinitesimal to Infinity*. New York: Bloomsbury USA.

Boyd, James W., et al. (1979). 'Is Zoroastrianism Dualistic or Monotheistic?', *Journal of the American Academy of Religion*, Vol. 47, No. 4, pp. 557–588.

Boyer, Pascal (2001). *Religion Explained: The Evolutionary Origins of Religious Thought*. New York: Basic Books.

Boyer, Pascal, and H. C. Barrett (2005). 'Domain-specificity and Intuitive Ontology', in: D. Buss (ed.), *The Handbook of Evolutionary Psychology*. Hoboken, NJ: John Wiley, pp. 96–118.

Brenner, William H., (2008). 'D. Z. Phillips and Classical Theism'. *New Blackfriars*, Vol. 90, No. 1025, pp. 17–37.

Brooke, John Hedley (1991). *Science and Religion: Some Historical Perspectives*. Cambridge: Cambridge University Press.

(2006). 'Contributions from the History of Science and Religion', in: Clayton and Simpson (2006), pp. 293–310.

Brown, Peter (2003). *The Rise of Christendom*, 2nd edition. Oxford: Blackwell Publishing.

Clayton, Philp, and Zachary Simpson (2006). *The Oxford Handbook of Religion and Science*. Oxford: Oxford University Press.

Clement of Alexandria (around 200 CE). *Stromata* (Miscellanies), Complete translation by Alexander Roberts and James Donaldson. Available via ellopos.net.

Cohen, H. Floris (2012). *How Modern Science Came into the World: Four Civilisations, One 17th-century Breakthrough*, 2nd edition. Amsterdam: Amsterdam University Press.

Collins, Francis S. (2006). *The Language of God: A Scientist Presents Evidence for Belief*. New York: Free Press.

Copernicus (1543). *De Revolutionibus Orbium Caelestium*. English translation: *On the Revolutions of the Heavenly Spheres*. Translated with an introduction and notes by A. M. Duncan. Newton Abbot: David & Charles; New York: Barnes and Noble, 1976.

Cottingham, John (2014). *Philosophy of Religion: Towards a More Humane Approach*. New York: Cambridge University Press.

Cupitt, Don (1980). *Taking Leave of God*. London: SCM Press.

(1997). *After God: The Future of Religion*. New York: Basic Books.

(2000). 'The Radical Christian Worldview'. *CrossCurrents*, Vol. 50, Nos 1–2, *The Wisdom of the Heart and the Life of the Mind: Fiftieth Anniversary Issue*, pp. 56–67.

(2006) *Radical Theology*. Salem, OR: Polebridge Press, Westar Institute.

Dalrymple, G. Brent (1994). *The Age of the Earth*. Redwood City, CA: Stanford University Press.

Darwin, Charles (1859). *The Origin of Species*. Edited with an introduction and notes by Gillian Beer. Oxford: Oxford University Press, 1996.

(1868). *The Variation of Animals and Plants under Domestication*. New York: Appleton.

(1871). *The Descent of Man, and Selection in Relation to Sex*. With an introduction by James Moore and Adrian Desmond. London: Penguin Books, 2004.

(1958). *The Autobiography of Charles Darwin 1809–1882*. With the original omissions restored. Edited and with appendix and notes by his granddaughter Nora Barlow. London: Collins.

(2002). *Autobiographies*. Edited by Michael Neve and Sharon Messenger. London: Penguin Books.

Dawkins, Richard (1989). *The Selfish Gene*, 2nd edition. Oxford: Oxford University Press.

(2006). *The God Delusion*. London: Bantam Press.

De Boer, J. Z., J. R. Hale, and J. Chanton (2001). 'New Evidence for the Geological Origins of the Ancient Delphic Oracle (Greece)', *Geology*, Vol. 29, No, 8, pp. 707–711.

De Jonge, H. J. (1989). 'Ontstaan en ontwikkeling van het geloof in Jezus' opstanding'. *Té-èf. Blad van de Faculteit der Godgeleerdheid van de Rijksuniversiteit te Leiden*, Vol. 18, No. 3, pp. 33–45.

(2002). 'Visionary Experience and the Historical Origins of Christianity', in: R. Bieringer, V. Koperski, and B. Lataire (eds), *Resurrection in the New*

Testament. Festschrift J. Lambrecht. Leuven, Leuven University Press, pp. 35–53.
Dennett, Daniel C. (1987). *The Intentional Stance*. Cambridge, MA: MIT Press.
   (2006). *Breaking the Spell: Religion as a Natural Phenomenon*. London: Allen Lane.
Desmond, Adrian, and James Moore (1992). *Darwin*. London: Penguin Books.
Devièse, Thibaut, et al. (2017). 'Direct Dating of Neanderthal Remains from the Site of Vindija Cave and Implications for the Middle to Upper Paleolithic Transition'. *Proceedings of the National Academy of Sciences of the United States of America*, Vol. 114, No. 40, pp. 10606–10611.
De Waal, Frans (2019). *Mama's Last Hug: Animal Emotions and What They Tell Us about Ourselves*. New York: W. W. Norton.
   et al. (2006). *Primates and Philosophers: How Morality Evolved*. Princeton: Princeton University Press.
Dostoevsky, Fyodor (1990). *The Brothers Karamazov*. Translated by Richard Pevear and Larissa Volokhonsky. San Francisco: North Point Press.
Drummond, Henry (1896). *The Lowell Lectures on the Ascent of Man*. London: Hodder and Stoughton.
Dupré, John (2003). *Darwin's Legacy: What Evolution Means Today*. Oxford: Oxford University Press.
Edis, T., and Maarten Boudry (2014). 'Beyond Physics? On the Prospects of Finding a Meaningful Oracle'. *Foundations of Science*, Vol. 19, pp. 403–422.
Eno, Robert (2008). 'Shang State Religion and the Pantheon of the Oracle Texts', in: John Lagerwey and Marc Kalinowski (eds), *Early Chinese Religion, Part One: Shang through Han (1250 BC – 220 AD)*. Leiden: Brill Academic Publishers, pp. 39–102.
Evans, C. Stephen (2010). *Natural Signs and Knowledge of God*. Oxford: Oxford University Press.
Eyghen, Hans van, Rik Peels, and Gijsbert van den Brink, eds (2018). *New Developments in the Cognitive Science of Religion: The Rationality of Religious Belief*. Cham: Springer.
Festinger, Leon (1957). *A Theory of Cognitive Dissonance*. Stanford: Stanford University Press (renewed 1985 by author).
Festinger, Leon, H. Riecken, and S. Schachter (1956). *When Prophesy Fails*. Minneapolis: University of Minnesota Press.
Finocchiaro, Maurice A. (2005). *Retrying Galileo 1633–1992*. Berkeley, Los Angeles, and London: University of California Press.
Fisher, Ronald A. (1918). 'The Correlation between Relatives on the Supposition of Mendelian Inheritance'. *Transactions of the Royal Society of Edinburgh*, Vol. 52, pp. 399–433.
Freud, Sigmund (1939). *Der Mann Moses und die monotheistische Religion*. Translated by Katherine Jones, Moses and Monotheism. New York: Vintage books, 1967.
Frieman, Joshua A., Michael S. Turner, and Dragan Huterer (2008). 'Dark Energy and the Accelerating Universe'. *Annual Review of Astronomy and Astrophysics*, Vol. 46, No. 1, pp. 385–432.

Gillespie, Charles Coulston (1997). *Pierre-Simon Laplace 1749–1827: A Life in Exact Science*. Princeton: Princeton University Press.

Gingerich, Owen (2006). *God's Universe*. Cambridge, MA: The Belknap Press of Harvard University Press.

Glass, David H. (2017). 'Science, God and Ockham's Razor'. *Philosophical Studies*, Vol. 174, pp. 1145–1161.

Gnuse, Robert Karl (1997). *No Other Gods: Emergent Monotheism in Israel. Journal for the Study of the Old Testament*, Supplement Series 241. Sheffield: Sheffield Academic Press Ltd.

Godfrey-Smith, Peter (2009). *Darwinian Populations and Natural Selection*. Oxford: Oxford University Press.

Gould, Stephen Jay (1997). 'Nonoverlapping Magisteria'. *Natural History*, Vol. 106, pp. 16–22.

  (1999). *Rocks of Ages*. New York: Norton.

  (2002). *Rocks of Ages: Science and Religion in the Fullness of Life*. New York: Ballantine Books.

Hacker, P. M. S. (2007). *Human Nature: The Categorial Framework*. Oxford: Blackwell Publishing.

  (2013). *The Intellectual Powers: A Study of Human Nature*. Chichester: John Wiley and Sons, Ltd.

Hackett, Conrad, and David McClendon (2017). 'Christians Remain World's Largest Religious Group, but They Are Declining in Europe'. *Factank*, Pew Research Center, 5 April.

Hacking, Ian (1983). *Representing and Intervening: Introductory Topics in the Philosophy of Science*. Cambridge: Cambridge University Press.

Hahn, Roger (2005). *Pierre Simon Laplace 1749–1827: A Determined Scientist*. Cambridge, MA: Harvard University Press.

Hale, John R., Jelle Zeilinga de Boer, Jeffrey P. Chanton and Henry A. Spiller (2003). 'Questioning the Delphic Oracle'. *Scientific American*, Vol. 289, No. 2, pp. 66–73.

Hartmann, William K. (2015). 'Chelyabinsk, Zond IV, and a Possible First-century Fireball of Historical Importance'. *Meteoritics & Planetary Science*, Vol. 50, pp. 368–381.

Hasker, William (2007). 'D. Z. Phillips' Problems with Evil and with God'. *International Journal for Philosophy of Religion*, Vol 61, No. 63, pp. 151–160.

Heiser, Michael S. (2008). 'Monotheism, Polytheism, Monolatry, or Henotheism? Toward an Assessment of Divine Plurality in the Hebrew Bible'. *Bulletin for Biblical Research*, Vol. 18, No. 1, pp. 1–30.

Hendrikse, Klaas (2007). *Geloven in een God die niet bestaat: Manifest van een atheïstische dominee*. Amsterdam: Nieuw Amsterdam.

Henrich, Joseph (2015). *The Secret of Our Success: How Culture Is Driving Human Evolution, Domesticating Our Species, and Making Us Smarter*. Princeton: Princeton University Press.

Hick, John (2000). 'Ineffability'. *Religious Studies*, Vol. 36, pp. 35–46.

Hitchens, Christopher (2007). *The Portable Atheist: Essential Readings for the Nonbeliever*. Philadelphia: Da Capo Press.

Hood, Bruce M. (2010). *The Science of Superstition: How the Developing Brain Creates Supernatural Beliefs.* London: HarperCollins.

Howson, Colin (2011). *Objecting to God.* Cambridge and New York: Cambridge University Press.

Hume, David (1748). *An Enquiry Concerning Human Understanding.* In *Enquiries* etc., reprinted from the posthumous edition of 1777, 3rd edition by P. H. Nidditch. Oxford: Clarendon Press, 1975. References are to the marginal sections of this edition.

— (1757, 1779). *The Natural History of Religion* (1757) and *Dialogues concerning Natural Religion* (1779). Edited by A. Wayne Colver and John Valdimir Price. Oxford: Clarendon Press, 1976.

Hussayn Haykal, Muhammad (2008). *The Life of Huhammad.* Selangor: Islamic Book Trust.

Huxley, Julian (1942). *Evolution: The Modern Synthesis.* With a new foreword by Massimo Pigliucci and Gerd B. Müller. Cambridge, MA: MIT Press, 2010.

IPCC (2014). *Climate Change 2014: Synthesis Report – A Report of the Intergovernmental Panel on Climate Change.* Geneva: IPCC.

— (2018). *Global Warming of 1.5°C: An IPCC Special Report on the Impacts of Global Warming of 1.5°C above Pre-industrial Levels (&c).* Geneva: IPCC.

— (2019). *Climate Change and Land: An IPCC Special Report on Climate Change, Desertification, Land Degradation, Sustainable Land Management, Food Security, and Greenhouse Gas Fluxes in Terrestrial Ecosystems.* Geneva: IPCC.

Irwin, T. (2006). 'Socrates and Euthyphro: The Argument and Its Revival', in: L. Judson and V. Karasmanis (eds), *Remembering Socrates: Philosophical Essays.* Oxford: Oxford University Press, pp. 58–71.

Jackson, Patrick Wyse (2006). *The Chronologer's Quest: Episodes in the Search for the Age of the Earth.* Cambridge: Cambridge University Press.

James, William (1902). *The Varieties of Religious Experience.* The Gifford Lectures delivered at Edinburgh, 1901–1902. Glasgow: Collins, Fount Paperbacks, 1977.

Kant, Immanuel (1755). *Allgemeine Naturgeschichte und Theorie des Himmels, oder Versuch von der Verfassung und dem mechanischen Ursprunge des ganzen Weltgebäudes nach Newtonischen Grundsätzen abgehandelt.* Königsberg and Leipzig: Johann Friedrich Petersen. Also in: Immanuel Kant, *Werke in zehn Bänden,* Herausgegeben von Wilhelm Weischedel, Band 1, pp. 221–400. Darmstadt: Wissenschaftliche Buchgesellschaft, 1968.

Kelemen, D., and E. Rosset (2009). 'The Human Function Compunction: Teleological Explanation in Adults'. *Cognition,* Vol. 111, pp. 138–143.

Kelemen, D., J. Rottman, and R. Seston (2013). 'Professional Physical Scientists Display Tenacious Teleological Tendencies: Purpose-based Reasoning as a Cognitive Default'. *Journal of Experimental Psychology: General,* Vol. 142, pp. 1074–1083.

Kenny, Anthony (2006). *What I Believe.* London: Continuum.

Kerr, Fergus Gordon Thomson (1986). *Theology after Wittgenstein.* Oxford: Blackwell.

Kirsch, Jonathan (2004). *God against the Gods: The History of the War between Monotheism and Polytheism*. New York: Viking Compass.
Komarnitsky, Kris D. (2014). *Doubting Jesus' Resurrection: What Happened in the Black Box? An Inquiry into an Alternative Explanation of Christian Origins*, 2nd edition. Draper, UT: Stone Arrow Books.
  (2019). 'The Rationalization Hypothesis: Is a Vision of Jesus Necessary for the Rise of the Resurrection Belief?' Posted on *Kelsos*, 4 January 2019, http://celsus.blog/2019/01/04.
Kragh, Helge (1999). *Cosmology and Controversy: The Historical Development of Two Theories of the Universe*. Princeton: Princeton University Press.
Kuhn, Thomas S. (1957). *The Copernican Revolution: Planetary Astronomy in the Development of Western Thought*. Cambridge, MA: Harvard University Press.
Landsborough, D. (1987). 'St Paul and Temporal Lobe Epilepsy'. *Journal of Neurology, Neurosurgery and Psychiatry*, Vol. 50, pp. 659–664.
Laplace, Pierre-Simon (1824, 1835). *Exposition du système du monde*, 5th edition. Paris: Fayard, 1984.
Lendering, Jona, and Vincent Hunink (2018). *Het visioen van Constantijn: Een gebeurtenis die de wereld veranderde*. Utrecht: Uitgeverij Omniboek.
Lieberman, Philip (1991). *Uniquely Human: The Evolution of Speech, Thought, and Selfless Behavior*. Cambridge, MA: Harvard University Press.
Long, Joseph W. (2017). 'When to Believe upon Insufficient Evidence: Three Criteria'. *Contemporary Pragmatism*, Vol. 14, pp. 176–184.
Longman III, Tremper, and Daniel G. Reid (1995). *God Is a Warrior: Studies in Old Testament Biblical Theology*. Michigan: Zondervan Publishing House.
Maitzen, S. (2006). 'Divine Hiddenness and the Demographics of Theism'. *Religious Studies*, Vol. 42, No. 2, pp. 177–191.
May, Herbert G. and Bruce M. Metzger, eds (1973). *The New Oxford Annotated Bible: Revised Standard Version*. New York: Oxford University Press.
McKay, Ryan, and Harvey Whitehouse (2015). 'Religion and Morality'. *Psychological Bulletin*, Vol. 141, No. 2, pp. 447–473.
McPherson, Tristram, and David Plunkett, eds (2017). *The Routledge Handbook of Metaethics*. New York: Routledge.
Min, Anselm K. (2008). 'D. Z. Phillips on the Grammar of "God"', in: E. T. Long and P. Horn (eds), *Ethics of Belief: Essays in Tribute to D. Z. Phillips. International Journal for Philosophy of Religion*, Vol. 63, Nos 1–3, pp. 131–146, Dordrecht: Springer.
Morris, Brian (2006). *Religion and Anthropology: A Critical Introduction*. Cambridge: Cambridge University Press.
Moser, Paul K. (2010). *The Evidence for God: Religious Knowledge Reexamined*. New York: Cambridge University Press.
  (2013). *The Severity of God: Religion and Philosophy Reconceived*. New York: Cambridge University Press.
Murray, Evan D., Miles G. Cunningham, and Bruce H. Price (2012). 'The Role of Psychotic Disorders in Religious History Considered'. *The Journal of Neuropsychiatry and Clinical Neurosciences*, Vol. 24, pp. 410–426.

Nagasawa, Yujin (2011). *The Existence of God: A Philosophical Introduction*. New York: Routledge.
Newton, Sir Isaac (1730). *Opticks or a Treatise of the Reflections, Refractions, Inflections and Colours of Light*, based on the fourth edition, London, 1730. New York: Dover Publications, 1979.
Nielsen, Kai, and D. Z. Phillips (2005). *Wittgensteinian Fideism?* London: SCM Press.
Nietzsche, Friedrich (1881). *Morgenröte: Gedanken über die moralischen Vorurteile*. Stuttgart: Alfred Kröner Verlag, 1964.
Nola, Robert (2018). 'Demystifying Religious Belief', in Eyghen et al. (2018), pp. 71–92.
Nordhaus, William (2013). *The Climate Casino: Risk, Uncertainty, and Economics for a Warming World*. New Haven and London: Yale University Press.
Norenzayan, Ara (2013). *Big Gods: How Religion Transformed Cooperation and Conflict*. Princeton: Princeton University Press.
—— et al. (2015). 'Big Questions about Big Gods: Response and Discussion'. *Religion, Brain & Behavior*, Vol. 5, No. 4, pp. 327–342.
—— et al. (2016). 'The Cultural Evolution of Prosocial Religions'. *Behavioral and Brain Sciences*, Vol. 39, pp. 1–65.
Norris, Pippa, and Ronald Inglehart (2004). *Sacred and Secular: Religion and Politics Worldwide*. Cambridge: Cambridge University Press.
Oppé, Adolphe Paul (1904). 'The Chasm at Delphi'. *Journal of Hellenic Studies*, Vol. 24, pp. 214–240.
Paley, William (1802). *Natural Theology or Evidence of the Existence and Attributes of the Deity, Collected from the Appearances of Nature*. Edited with an introduction and notes by Matthew D. Eddy and David Knight. Oxford: Oxford University Press, 2006.
Pew Research Center (2012). *The Global Religious Landscape: A Report on the Size and Distribution of the World's Major Religious Groups as of 2010*. Pew Forum on Religion and Public Life. www.pewforum.org/global-religious-landscape.aspx.
—— (2017). *The Changing Global Religious Landscape*. Pew Research Center Religion and Public Life. www.pewforum.org/2017/04/05/the-changing-global-religious-landscape/.
Philipse, Herman (2004). *Atheïstisch manifest en De onredelijkheid van religie*. With a preface by Ayaan Hirsi Ali. Amsterdam: Uitgeverij Bert Bakker.
—— (2011). 'God, Ethics and Evolution', in: Harriet A. Harris (ed.), *God, Goodness and Philosophy*. Farnham and Burlington: Ashgate, pp. 131–161.
—— (2012). *God in the Age of Science? A Critique of Religious Reason*. Oxford: Oxford University Press.
—— (2013a). 'The Real Conflict between Science and Religion: Alvin Plantinga's Ignoratio Elenchi'. *European Journal for Philosophy of Religion*, Vol. 5, No. 2, pp. 87–110.
—— (2013b). 'A Decision Tree for Religious Believers'. *Philo*, Vol. 16, No. 1, pp. 9–23.
—— (2014). *God in the Age of Science? A Critique of Religious Reason*. Oxford: Oxford University Press.

(2016). 'Ethics and Religion Disconnected', in: Stephan Herzberg and Heinrich Watzka (eds), *Transzendenzlos glücklich? Zur Entkoppelung von Ethik und Religion in der postchristlichen Gesellschaft.* Münster: Aschendorf Verlag, pp. 153–166.

(2018). 'Das Problem des religiösen Pluralismus', in: Romy Jaster and Peter Schulte (eds), *Glaube und Rationalität: Gibt es gute Gründe für den (A) theismus?* Paderborn: Mentis Verlag, pp. 103–128.

(2019). 'Evidential Objections to Theism', in: Graham Oppy (ed.), *A Companion to Atheism and Philosophy*, Hoboken, NJ, and Chichester: Blackwell, pp. 191–203.

Phillips, D. Z. (2005). 'Wittgensteinianism: Logic, Reality, and God', in: William J. Wainwright (ed.), *The Oxford Handbook of Philosophy of Religion.* Oxford: Oxford University Press, pp. 447–471.

Plantinga, Alvin (2000). *Warranted Christian Belief.* Oxford: Oxford University Press.

(2001). 'Rationality and Public Evidence: A Reply to Richard Swinburne'. *Religious Studies*, Vol. 37, pp. 215–222.

(2011). *Where the Conflict Really Lies: Science, Religion, and Naturalism.* Oxford: Oxford University Press.

(2015). *Knowledge and Christian Belief.* Grand Rapids, MI: William B. Eerdmans Publishing Company.

Plantinga, Alvin, and Michael Tooley (2008). *Knowledge of God.* Malden, MA: Blackwell Publishing.

Purzycki, Benjamin Grant, et al. (2018). 'The Cognitive and Cultural Foundations of Moral Behavior'. *Evolution and Human*, Vol. 39, No. 5, pp. 490–501.

Qadi 'Iyad ibn Musa (1149). *Kitab Ash-Shifa bi ta'rif huquq al-Mustafa (The Book of Healing).* Translated as *Muhammad, Messenger of Allah* by Aisha Abdurrahman Bewley. Revised behavior edition 2011. Norwich: Diwan Press.

Riekki, T., M. Lindeman, and T. T. Raij (2014). 'Supernatural Believers Attribute More Intentions to Random Movement than Skeptics: An FMRI Study'. *Social Neuroscience*, Vol. 9, pp. 400–411.

Ripple, William J. et al. (2019). 'World Scientists' Warning of a Climate Emergency'. *BioScience*, Vol. 70, No. 1, pp. 8–12.

Ritter, Joachim, Karlfried Gründer, and Gottfried Gabriel, eds (1971–2004). *Historisches Wörterbuch der Philosophie*, 12 Vols. Basel: Schwabe and Co. AG.Verlag.

Saler, Benson, and Charles A. Ziegler (2006). 'Atheism and the Apotheosis of Agency'. *Temenos*, Vol. 42, No. 2, pp. 7–41.

Schellenberg, J. L. (2006). *Divine Hiddenness and Human Reason.* Ithaca, NY: Cornell University Press.

(2015). *The Hiddenness Argument: Philosophy's New Challenge to Belief in God.* Oxford: Oxford University Press.

Schredl, Michael (2010). 'Dream Content Analysis: Basic Principles'. *International Journal of Dream Research*, Vol. 3, No. 1, pp. 65–73.

Shafer-Landau, Russ, and Terence Cuneo (2007). *Foundations of Ethics: An Anthology.* Malden, MA and Oxford: Blackwell.

Shaver, John H. (2013). Review of Norenzayan (2013). *Journal for the Cognitive Science of Religion*, Vol. 1, No. 2, pp. 246–249.
Shepherd, A. et al. (2019). 'Mass Balance of the Greenland Ice Sheet from 1992 to 2018'. *Nature*, https://doi.org/10.1038/s41586-019-1855-1852.
Singh, Simon (2010). *Big Bang: The Most Important Scientific Discovery of All Time and Why You Need to Know about It*. Glasgow: HarperCollins.
Smart, Ninian (1998). *The World's Religions*, 2nd edition. Cambridge: Cambridge University Press.
Smith, Mark S. (2001). *The Origins of Biblical Monotheism: Israel's Polytheistic Background and the Ugaritic Texts*. Oxford: Oxford University Press.
Sober, Elliott (2008). *Evidence and Evolution: The Logic behind the Scene*. Cambridge: Cambridge University Press.
Sosis, Richard, and Jordan Kiper (2014). 'Religion Is More than Belief: What Evolutionary Theories of Religion Tell Us about Religious Commitments', in: Bergmann and Kain (2014), pp. 256–276.
Spiller, Henry A., John R. Hale, and Jelle Z. de Boer (2002). 'The Delphic Oracle: A Multidisciplinary Defense of the Gaseous Vent Theory'. *Journal of Clinical Toxicology*, Vol. 40, No. 2, pp. 189–196.
Stark, Rodney (1996). *The Rise of Christianity: A Sociologist Reconsiders History*. Princeton: Princeton University Press.
  (1999). 'Micro Foundations of Religion: A Revised Theory'. *Sociological Theory*, Vol. 17, pp. 264–289.
Swinburne, Richard (1993). *The Coherence of Theism*, revised edition. Oxford: Oxford University Press.
  (1996). *Is There a God?* Oxford: Oxford University Press.
  (1998). *Providence and the Problem of Evil*. Oxford: Clarendon Press.
  (2004). *The Existence of God*, 2nd edition. Oxford: Oxford University Press.
  (2005). *Faith and Reason*, 2nd edition. Oxford: Oxford University Press.
  (2010). 'God as the Simplest Explanation of the Universe'. *European Journal for Philosophy of Religion*, Vol. 2, pp. 1–24.
  (2016). *The Coherence of Theism*, 2nd edition. Oxford: Oxford University Press.
  (2020). 'The Criterion of Simplicity in Metaphysics and Ethics', in: Julia Hermann, Jeroen Hopster, Wouter Kalf, and Michael Klenk (eds), *Philosophy in the Age of Science? Inquiries into Philosophical Progress, Method, and Societal Relevance*. London and New York: Rowman and Littlefield, pp. 131–145.
Tinbergen N. (1963). 'On Aims and Methods of Ethology'. *Zeitschrift für Tierpsychologie*, Vol. 20, pp. 410–433.
Van der Tempel, Jan, and James E. Alcock (2015). 'Relationships between Conspiracy Mentality, Hyperactive Agency Detection, and Schizotypy: Supernatural Forces at Work?', *Personality and Individual Differences*, Vol. 82, pp. 136–141.
Van Inwagen, P. (2005). 'Is God an Unnecessary Hypothesis?', in: A. Dole and A. Chignell (eds), *God and the Ethics of Belief*. Cambridge: Cambridge University Press, pp. 131–149.
Wade, Lizzie (2015). 'Birth of the Moralizing Gods'. *Science*, Vol. 349, No. 6251, pp. 918–922.

Watts, Fraser, and Léon Turner (2014). *Evolution, Religion, and Cognitive Science: Critical and Constructive Essays*. Oxford: Oxford University Press.
Weedman, Mark (2010). 'The Polemical Context of Gregory of Nyssa's Doctrine of Divine Infinity'. *Journal of Early Christian Studies*, Vol. 18, No. 1, pp. 81–104.
Weinberg, Steven (2015). *To Explain the World: The Discovery of Modern Science*. New York: HarperCollins.
Westfall, Richard S. (1981). *Never at Rest: A Biography of Isaac Newton*. Cambridge: Cambridge University Press.
White, Andrew D. (1896). *A History of the Warfare of Science with Theology in Christendom*. Great Minds Series. Buffalo: Prometheus Books, 1993.
Whitehouse, Harvey, et al. (2019). 'Complex Societies Precede Moralizing Gods throughout World History'. *Nature*, Vol. 568, pp. 226–229.
Wilson, David Sloan (2002). *Darwin's Cathedral: Evolution, Religion, and the Nature of Society*. Chicago and London: University of Chicago Press.
Zuckerman, P. (2008). *Society without God*. New York: NYU Press.

Index

Aboriginal communities, 72
Abraham, 22
Acts, 23–27
adyton, 27, 29
Ahura Mazda, 75
Alexander III of Macedon, 93
Allah, 5, 62, 100–103, 128, 130, 161
Amalgamated Evidentialism, 131, 145
Amenhotep IV, 63, 74, 194
Amesha Spentas, 75
Andrasta, 90
Annales veteris testamenti, 51
Anselm of Canterbury, 148
Antarctica, 117
Apollo, 23, 27, 29–32, 61, 71, 94, 191
apologetic strategies, 4–5, 44, 124, 129, 165, 197–198
    classified, 129
Aquinas, Thomas, 46, 76, 139–140, 148, 169
Argument from Cultural Contingency, 12–17, 32, 61
Argument from Divine Hiddenness, 57
Argument from Locality, 64
Aristarchus of Samos, 14
Aristotle, 46, 76, 168
astronomy, 47, 57
Atenism, 74
atheism, 62, 83, 130, 132, 166
authentic theistic belief, 148

bare theism, 171–176
    defining, 171
    explanatory power, 171–176
    hypothesis, 178
    semantic challenge for, 171–176
Barth, Karl, 127
Baumard, Nicolas, 4, 98
Bayes, Thomas, 172
Bayes's theorem, 172
Behe, Michael, 155
Bessel, Friedrich, 48
Big Bang, 2, 53–54
Big Freeze, 54, 57, 186, 192
BioLogos, 57
BioScience, 119
Boer, Jelle Zeilinga de, 28
Book of Healing, The, 39
Boyer, Pascal, 4, 98
Boyle, 41
Brahe, Tycho, 48

calibration argument, 31–40, 42, 60
Calvinism, 15
causal condition, 108, 195
causal grounding, 19
causal links, 104
Celestial Mechanics, 57
Changing Global Religious Landscape, The, 6
Christian Calvinism, 32
Christianity, 2, 4, 11, 15, 23, 38, 43, 46–47, 55, 64, 72, 94–95, 98–99, 124–125, 150, 160, 168–169, 195
    early expansion of, 109–117
chronology, 55–63
Clement of Alexandria, 94

215

cognitive dissonance, 99, 109, 112–113, 196
Cognitive Sciences of Religion, 3
Coherence of Theism, The, 166, 171, 178
Collins, Francis, 60
Constantine, 94–95, 99, 109, 113
Constantinus, Flavius, 94
contra theism, 177, 187–188, 201
Copernicus, 14, 41, 47
cosmic inflation theory, 49
cosmology, 53–55
Cottingham, John, 145–149, 199
Croesus of Lydia, 28
crucifixion, 109–111
cultural contingency, argument from, 12–14, 16, 32, 38, 61, 191
Cupitt, Don, 135

darshan, 38
Darwin, Charles, 43, 52, 55–61, 79, 183–184
Dawkins, Richard, 81
Decision Tree for Religious Believers, 4, 123–125, 130–132, 136, 138, 164–165, 198
deities, war represented by, 89
Der Mann Moses und die monotheistische Religion, 74
Descartes, 41
Descent of Man, The, 58–59
desertification, 118
Deuteronomy, 91, 100
Diagnostic and Statistical Manual of Mental Disorders, 24
Dialogue Concerning the Two Chief World Systems, 48
divine hiddenness, 5, 38, 59, 129, 140, 150, 188
Drummond, Henry, 60
dual inheritance, 79

Earth, 43
  place in universe, 44–50
  time of Man on, 44–50
Eiffel Tower, 17
Einstein, Albert, 37, 53
End of Times, 42
endorsements, 123–125
enemy-love, 153
enthusiasmos, 27
Epic of Gilgamesh, 73

Epistemic Challenge, 127
epistemic grounding, 19
epistemic peers, 16
epistemic sources, 17–23, 69, 190
epistemological challenge, 177, 186–188
epistemology, 11–12, 69, 139
epistemology of involvement, 146
error theory, 4
ethics, 97, 100, 117
  expansion of Christianity, 97
  global warming, 97
  justifying moral rules, 97
  moralizing religions, 97
Euthyphro, 101
Euthyphro dilemm, 102
evidence, 34, 37–38
evolutionary framework, 79–81
Existence of God, The, 166, 172
Exodus, 91, 100
expert consensus, 55–61
Explanatory Challenge, 128
explanatory emptiness, 181
Exposition du système du monde, 56

factualism, 4–5, 16, 43–44, 97, 129, 136, 181
Faith and Reason, 166
Festinger, Leon, 112
Fideism, 130, 136, 145, 154–155
fitness, 79–81
Flaubert, Gustave, 23
Freud, Sigmund, 74

Galatians, 26
Galilei, Galileo, 14, 41, 48
Genesis, 45–47, 50
geocentrism, 48
Giant Void, 50, 62
global warming, 117–120, 197
God
  concept of, 170–171
  conception of, 103–108, 147–148, 161
  defining, 89, 178
  evidence for, 37, 125, 156–157, 162, 164, 198–199
  'god', 103–108
  legislator of moral norms, 102–108
  maximally honorific title, 157
  moralizing, 103–108
  name, 103–108, 147
  non-embodied person, 178

Index

perfectly good, 182
personifying evidence of, 103–108
title, 103–108, 126–127, 152–154, 157, 159–161, 199
God in the Age of Science, 109, 111
God-of-the-gaps fallacy, 60
gods, 33, 64, 73–79
goods, 115
Gould, Stephen Jay, 44, 129
Greece, 76
Greenland, 117

Hartmann, William, 25
Hebrew Bible, 75, 91–92
heliocentrism, 48
Hendrikse, Klaas, 136
henotheism, 74, 92
Hick, John, 127
Hinduism, 13, 73, 76, 86, 124–125, 160, 191
Housmann, A. E., 149
Hume, David, 3–4, 6, 70, 73, 76, 83, 86–89, 93–94, 169, 194–195
hyper-active intentional stance (HIS), 85
Hypersensitive Agent Detection Device (HADD), 3, 81–83

iconography, 73
illumination of grace, 134
infinity, 88, 93, 175–176
intentional stance, 84, 93
Intergovernmental Panel on Climate Change (IPCC), 117
intrinsic probability, 166, 173–176, 200
Involvement Evidentialism, 132, 145–151
Involvement Evidentialists, 131
Isaiah, 154
Ishta devata, 38

James, William, 20–22
Jesus, 22, 24, 31, 42, 89, 99, 109–112, 140, 154, 156, 160
Josiah, 87
Judaism, 75, 125
Jupiter, 48, 56, 73
justificational grounding, 19, 27, 30, *See also* Pythia

Kant, Immanuel, 43, 56, 169–170, 192, 200
Kant-Laplace nebular hypothesis, 56
kardiatheology, 157, 199
Kelvin, Baron, 52

Kenny, Anthony, 147
Kepler, 14, 41, 47
Kerr, Fergus, 133
Kierkegaard, Søren, 130, 146
knowledge
 primary source, 18
 secondary source, 18
 secondary source of, 20
Krapina site, 71

language games, 132–136
Laplace, Pierre-Simon, 56–57, 172, 192
Lemaître, Georges, 53
Letter to the Romans, 100
lex parsimoniae, 30
Liber de Mortibus Persecutorum, 94
light years, 37, 50

Maillet, Benoît de, 51
Manasseh, 87
mankind, time of, 50–55
Matthew, 100, 111
meganumerophobia, 2
memes, 93
Mendel, Gregor, 59
Menhit, 90
methodological conflict, 42
Middle Palaeolithic Age, 71
Middle Stone Age, 71
miracles, 21
model of things below, 93
modern evolutionary synthesis, 59
modern synthesis, 79
modus ponendo ponens, 32
monolatry, 74–75, 86–87, 91–93
monotheism
 human conception, 89
 infinite properties, 93
 inter-tribal warfare, 89
 transitions to to, 86–96
 varieties, 171
 varieties of, 74, 174, 194
Moon, sphere of, 47
moral realism, 182
moral rules, justifying, 100–103
morality, 97, 103–104, 182
Moser, Paul, 151–155, 160–162, 199
Moses, 22
Mother Teresa of Calcutta, 153
multiplied beyond necessity (*Non sunt multipicanda entia sine necessitate*), 32

Musa, Qadi 'Iyad ibn, 39
Muslims, fertility rate of, 100

Natural History of Religion, 74, 76, 78, 87
natural theology, 36, 165, 168–169
    Bayesian form of, 165–167
    descent and revival of, 165–167
    history of, 165
    resurrection of, 165
Natural Theology, 145, 155
    final epistemological challenge of, 165–167
Nebuchadnezzar, 87
New Testament, 23, 35, 93, 101, 109–110, 112, 144, 152, 162
Newton, Isaac, 55–56, 169–170, 192
NOMA-principle, 44
Non-Factualism, 125, 130, 133–135, 137, 198
Nordhaus, William, 117
Norenzayan, Ara, 105–107, 195

observable universe, 49
Ockham's Razor, 30, 33
Old Testament, 101
omphalos, 27
On the Heavens, 46
Oppé, Adolphe Paul, 28
Oracle of Delphi, 27, 29, 85
ouranos, 46

paganisms, 98
pagans, 85
Paley, William, 43, 57, 184, 192
paradoxes, 65
Paris Agreement, 119
Pew Research Center, 6, 69, 97, 99, 189
Phillips, Dewi Zephaniah, 133–136, 138, 198
philosophers, job of, 23
place
    of Earth in Universe, 44–50
planets, 56
Plantinga, Alvin, 15, 137–140, 191, 198
Plutarch, 27, 29
pneuma, 27
polytheism
    evolutionary perspective, 76–86
    historical priority of, 73
    origins, 76–86
    transitions to monotheism, 76–86

prayers, 85
predictive power, 42, 166, 181–182
primary source, 2, 11, 18–23, 27, 30–34
Principle of Credulity, 35
prior probability, 173–176
Proxima Centauri, 48
Psalm, 73
Ptolemy, Caludius, 46
Pythia, 23–32, 191

Qualifiers, 48
Quran, 100

Ranganathaswamy Temple, 12
Reasonableness of Religious Beliefs, The, 2, 11
religion
    apologetic strategies, 69–71
    core questions, 69–71
    epistemic sources of, 17–23
    ethics and, 97
    evolution of religion and ethics, 69–71
    faith, 20
    family resemblance, 20
    moralizing, 4, 69–71, 98–99, 103
    origins and evolution of, 69–71
    prehistory, 69–71
    primary sources of, 21
    reasonableness of religious beliefs, 69–71
    religious epistemology, 11, 13, 38, 41–65, 156, 189
    science and, 41, 69–71
    term, 20
religious believers, 167–168
Religious Confidentialism, 131, 136–145
religious diversity, 2, 7, 11–12, 16, 39, 58–59, 128, 160–161, 190
religious epistemology
    Argument from Cultural Contingency, 12–32
    calibrating sources of, 12–32
    sources, 12–32
    St. Paul and the Pythia, 12–32
religious evidence, 131, 146, 149, 157–158
Religious Evidentialism, 131, 137, 145–151
Religious Non-Factualism, 129
religious pluralism, 11, 145, 160, 162, 174, 191
Religious Realism, 136
Religious Reasonabilism, 130, 136
Religious Voluntarism, 130, 136, 145, 198

Index

resurrection, 42, 110–112, 156
Revealed Theology, 165, 167
revelations, 167
Rise of Christianity, The, 114
Romans, 101

sacred books, 167
Saturn, 56
Saul. *See* St. Paul
science, 41
   Biblical chronology, 41, 50, 52, 192
   empirical evidence, 41
   expert consensus evolution, 41
   mankind, 41
   place of Earth in Universe, 41
Science-Inspired Natural Theology, 132
Science-Shunning Natural Theology, 132
scientific enterprise, 41
self-revealing call, 159
semantic atheism, 187
Semantic Challenge, 126
sensus divinitatis, 12, 14–15, 17, 41, 139–140, 142, 144, 191, 199
Shamanism, 15, 32
Shinto, 86
Siderius Nuncius, 48
Simplex sigillum veri, 175
simplicity, 1, 165–166
sources, calibrating, 31–40
St. Paul, 22–32, 96, 101, 109, 157, 191
Standard Model of particle physics, 169
Stark, Rodney, 114–115
Strabo, 27
strategies of immunisation, 151, 159
supernatural, 20
supernatural beings, 3–5, 21–23, 32–33, 42, 69–70, 76–77, 115, 123
Swinburne, Richard, vii, 35, 102, 125, 165–166, 168, 170–174, 200–201

Taliaferro, Charles, 146
Tantra Hinduism, deites in, 1
teleological bias, 85
testimony, 17–18
theism, 5
   bare theism, 57–65
   defined, 180
   empirical evidence against, 41–65
   evidence pro and contra, 173–174, 177, 181, 187–189, 200
   explanatory power of, 57–65
   predictive power of, 57–65
   religious evidence for, 41–65
   truth, 2, 41, 55, 60, 69, 101, 158
Theophilus of Antioch, 51
theory of mind (ToM), 84
Thomson, William, 52
time
   of Man and Universe, 50–55
tipping points, 118–119
Tooley, Michael, 143
transcategoriality, 127
truth, 2, 41, 55, 60, 69, 101, 158

unbelievers, 140
Unbiased Evidentialism, 131–132, 145
undercutting defeater, 16–17
United Nations Framework Convention on Climate Change, 119
United States
   science in, 22
universe, age of, 2, 49, 51, 192
universe, place of Earth in, 44–50
Ussher, James, 51, 53

validation, 34
Varuna, 61

warranted, 15, 61, 128, 131, 138, 140, 143–144
Whitehouse, Harvey, 107–108, 195
Wikipedia, 18
wilderness parable, 158
Wilson, David Sloan, 6, 53, 99, 115–116, 196
Woden, 61
Wyrd, 61

Xenophanes, 76
Xenophanes of Colophon, 168

Yahweh (YHWH), 62, 73, 87, 91–93, 128, 130, 136

Zarathustra, 74
Zoroastrianism, 74–75, 86, 194